COMPUTER GRAPHICS IN ENGINEERING EDUCATION

Dr DAVID F. ROGERS is Professor of Aerospace Engineering and Director of Computer Aided Design Interactive Graphics at the U.S. Naval Academy. He is the co-editor of *Computers & Education.* In 1959 he earned a B.A.E. degree from Rensselaer Polytechnic Institute and subsequently was awarded the M.S.A.E. and Ph.D. degrees. Dr Rogers has both experimental and theoretical research background. He has published papers in the areas of hypersonic viscous flow, boundary layer theory, computer aided education and computer aided design and interactive graphics. He is the co-author of two textbooks: *Mathematical Elements for Computer Graphics,* McGraw-Hill (1976) and *Computer Aided Heat Transfer Analysis,* McGraw-Hill (1972). He is a member of AIAA, APS, ACM and SNAME. His consulting experience includes work in aerodynamics, hydrodynamics, vehicle dynamics, computer aided design and interactive graphics. Professor Rogers was an Honorary Research Fellow and studied Naval Architecture at University College in England during 1977-1978. He was one of the original faculty who established the Aerospace Engineering Department at the U.S. Naval Academy in 1964.

COMPUTER GRAPHICS
IN
ENGINEERING EDUCATION

Edited by

DAVID F. ROGERS

PERGAMON PRESS

OXFORD · NEW YORK · TORONTO · SYDNEY · PARIS · FRANKFURT

U.K.	Pergamon Press Ltd., Headington Hill Hall, Oxford OX3 0BW, England
U.S.A.	Pergamon Press Inc., Maxwell House, Fairview Park, Elmsford, New York 10523, U.S.A.
CANADA	Pergamon Press Canada Ltd., Suite 104, 150 Consumers Rd., Willowdale, Ontario M2J 1P9, Canada
AUSTRALIA	Pergamon Press (Aust.) Pty. Ltd., P.O. Box 544, Potts Point, N.S.W. 2011, Australia
FRANCE	Pergamon Press SARL, 24 rue des Ecoles, 75240 Paris, Cedex 05, France
FEDERAL REPUBLIC OF GERMANY	Pergamon Press GmbH, 6242 Kronberg-Taunus, Hammerweg 6, Federal Republic of Germany

First edition 1982

ISBN 0 08 028949 5

Published as Volume 5, Number 4, of the journal *Computers & Education* and supplied to subscribers as part of their subscription. Also available to non-subscribers.

Printed in Great Britain by A. Wheaton & Co. Ltd. Exeter

CONTENTS

LIST OF CONTRIBUTORS

J. ALAN ADAMS
Department of Mechanical Engineering
U.S. Naval Academy
Annapolis
MD 21402
U.S.A.

JOHN A. CHARLES
Department of Mechanical Engineering
The Ohio State Univeristy
206 West 18th Avenue
Columbus
OH 43210
U.S.A.

JAMES E. A. JOHN
Department of Mechanical Engineering
The Ohio State University
206 West 18th Avenue
Columbus
OH 43210
U.S.A.

RICHARD L. PHILLIPS
Computer, Information & Control Engineering
The University of Michigan
Ann Arbor
MI 48109
U.S.A.

DONALD R. RILEY
Department of Mechanical Engineering
Univeristy of Minnesota
Minneapolis
MN 55455
U.S.A.

MARK S. SHEPHARD
Center for Interactive Computer Graphics
Rensselaer Polytechnic Institute
Troy
NY 12181
U.S.A.

DAVID CHALMERS
RCNC Office
Mechanical Engineering Department
University College London
Torrington Place
London WC1 E7JE
U.K.

ARTHUR G. ERDMAN
Department of Mechanical Engineering
University of Minnesota
Minneapolis
MN 55455
U.S.A.

GARY L. KINZEL
Department of Mechanical Engineering
The Ohio State University
206 West 18th Avenue
Columbus
OH 43210
U.S.A.

J. D. RICHARDSON
Computer Aided Design/Interactive Graphics Group
Division of Engineering and Weapons
U.S. Naval Academy
Annapolis
MD 21402
U.S.A.

DAVID F. ROGERS
Aerospace Engineering Department
U.S. Naval Academy
Annapolis
MD 21402
U.S.A.

P. R. SMITH
Department of Nuclear Engineering
Queen Mary College
Mile End Road
London E1 4NS
U.K.

MICHAEL J. WOZNY
Center for Interactive Computer Graphics
Rensselaer Polytechnic Institute
Troy
NY 12181
U.S.A.

PREFACE

Computer graphics, Computer Aided Design (CAD) and Computer Aided Manufacturing (CAM) have become of increasingly greater interest since I first started putting this special issue together well over two and one half years ago. Computer graphics and CADCAM are now looked upon as tools for solving a number of pressing problems in industry. With this also came the realization that the engineering schools, with some exceptions, were not producing graduates that had an understanding of or even an exposure to Computer Graphics and CADCAM. The principle reason for this has been lack of funds for equipment. Fortunately, the surge of interest in computer graphics and CADCAM is making funds from both government and private industry more available.

The emphasis in this issue is two fold. First, to illustrate how computer graphics can be and is being used in engineering education. The examples are deliberately concentrated in what I choose to call the "mechanical" engineering topics in contrast to the "electrical" engineering topics, i.e. in fluids, statics, strength of materials, structures, etc. The use of computer graphics in the electrical engineering topics, i.e. circuit design and analysis, printed circuit board layout, integrated circuit layout, etc., is sufficiently rich that it could easily be the subject of a special issue itself. Any volunteers for guest editor?

Secondly, to illustrate how several of the pioneer institutions, in the use of computer graphics in engineering education, developed facilities and integrated them into the curriculum. No attempt has been made to provide a survey of the use of computer graphics in engineering education. Rather, an attempt has been made to provide selected examples of noteworthy work based on the editor's personal knowledge. Neither has any attempt to present a unified viewpoint with respect to how to use computer graphics been made. All the papers in this issue were actively solicited by the editor. My thanks to the authors for their efforts.

David F. Rogers

Aerospace Engineering Department
United States Naval Academy
Annapolis, MD 21402, U.S.A.

Comput. & Educ. Vol. 5, pp. 165 to 182, 1981
Printed in Great Britain

0360-1315/81/040165-18$02.00/0
Pergamon Press Ltd

COMPUTER GRAPHICS AT THE U.S. NAVAL ACADEMY

DAVID F. ROGERS

Aerospace Engineering Department, U.S. Naval Academy, Annapolis, MD 21402, U.S.A.

INTRODUCTION

The Unites Stated Naval Academy has been involved with the uses of computers and computer graphics in engineering education for well over a decade. During the late 60s and early 70s a number of pilot studies[1,2] were undertaken. This allowed the determination of techniques for optimum use of computers and computer graphics in university level engineering education. At the same time, the design and construction of a new Engineering Studies Complex was progressing. This allowed the full integration of computer and computer graphics use into the design of the building. The underlying philosophy developed during the pilot studies significantly influenced the selection of equipment and the building design.

Within the Engineering and Weapons Division at the U.S. Naval Academy the underlying philosophy for computer and computer graphics use at the university level in engineering curricula does not, in general, support the traditional CAI and CMI concepts. The traditional concepts of CAI and CMI do not provide adequate return on investment. They are too labor intensive and, hence, too costly; too structured and, hence, too inflexible. An alternate philosophy called computer aided analysis (CAA) has evolved. Basically, this philosophy considers computers and computer graphics as just another engineering tool. As such, it should be available and reasonably easy to use after initial familiarization. It should be usable to provide answers, to reduce work load in providing answers or insites into problems. It should be capable of use to answer the perennial iterative engineering question "what if?". The above requires that computer graphics be usable in the classroom or lecture hall, in the laboratory, in the design office and in the production shop. It also requires that computer facilities be available at the normal teaching location.

In engineering education, classroom and lecture hall usage is generally associated with the lecturer demonstrating a previously written program to the students in the lecture room as an integral part of the lecture. It may require one or two 10–15 min segments of a 50 min lecture. The lecturer is free to choose when and how it is used. The program may illustrate a particular concept or it might be a demonstration of a program to be used later by students as a part of a homework assignment. Experience has shown that for this type of use, bringing the computer to the classroom is more time effective than bringing the class to a computer equipped classroom. However, a computer classroom should be available when the lecturer desires this option.

Laboratory use requires a system capable of interfacing with a variety of measuring instruments as well as having the ability to control various aspects of the experiment. Analysis and graphical display are required. Because of the real time requirements associated with data acquisition and experiment control, a stand alone computer system is implied. Used in a real time environment, the results of an experiment may be analyzed as the experiment progresses. This helps to eliminate the problem of poor or inaccurate data acquisition due to instrumentation or procedural failures. It also allows using an experiment to teach the basic underlying physics and/or to perform experimental parametric studies within the length of a typical laboratory session (2–3 h).

In the design office or design course, computers and computer graphics can use previously written interactive graphics programs for analysis, surface description, geometric design, etc. Students should also be able to write their own individual programs to meet specific design requirements.

An integral part of any engineering program is the production of parts, test models, etc. A desire to provide students with actual experience in producing parts for, say, structural testing or models for wind tunnel or towing tank use, expecially as an end result of a design project, leads immediately to a requirement for numerical control. Facilities must be available for either direct CADCAM or traditional numerical control part programming. The objective is to make it possible for a student to produce, using CADCAM techniques, any part that can be drawn or described using computer graphics.

BUILDING DESIGN INTEGRATION

These requirements interacted significantly with the design of the building to house the new Engineering Studies Complex*. In particular, a complex of eleven rooms comprising some 7000 ft^2 of area was designated for Computer Aided Design/Interactive Graphics (CADIG). The rooms were equipped with raised floors and additional air conditioning. A large area in the machine shop (900 ft^2) was designated for numerically controlled machine tools. Further, every single room in the Complex, all classrooms, all laboratories, all faculty and staff offices, all conference rooms, etc., were wired with computer outlets. Connections to closed circuit television were also provided. All computer outlets, a total of some 460, were collected in the CADIG area in a patch panel. Approximately 100 lines from the CADIG patch panel into the Academy's in house time sharing system were provided. These lines are hard wired to the Academy's Honeywell 6060 Time Sharing system located approx. 4500 ft distant in another building. Several standard telephone lines were also brought to the patch panel. This configuration allows for provision of computer access, two way voice and visual communication at any location within the complex. The system also allows direct computer-to-computer interconnection either between the Academy's in house time sharing system or between mini-micro computers within the Complex.

EQUIPMENT

A wide range of computer graphics equipment is necessary to meet the requirements outlined above. In addition, a requirement for highly interactive Computer Aided Design (CAD) of relatively complex 3-D shapes and the need to simulate real time motions of complex 3-D shapes implies a sophisticated calligraphic refresh display and an associated support minicomputer. The need for large scale accurate high quality drawings of ships lines, engineering and manufacturing parts, etc. requires a plotter. Also, terminals are required to provide graphic output from the time sharing system of common engineering graphs, bar graphs, and histograms as well as to support lower levels of interactive design and analysis. These requirements resulted in the purchase and installation of the equipment shown in Table 1a in early 1975, concurrently with the opening of the new Engineering Studies Complex. The Computer Aided Design/Interactive Graphics (CADIG) Facility was fully operational for Academic Year 1975. Parts of the facility and equipment are shown in Figs 1–3. Additional facilities have been added since that time (Table 1b).

The work horse of the facility is the Tektronix 4051. The Tektronix 4051 is a stand alone microprocessor based computer graphics system. In stand alone mode, a Basic interpreter, line editor, tape cartridge mass storage, and up to 32K of user addressable memory are available. Provision is made

Fig. 1. Tektronix 4051 equipped classroom.

* Now called Rickover Hall.

Table 1a. CADIG equipment—original (1975)

40	Tektronix 4051 graphics systems with communications interface
20	Tektronix hard copy units
20	Tektronix 10 × 10″ data tablets
1	Tektronix 4016 graphics terminal
1	Tektronix 30 × 40″ digitizer
15	Spintronix 30 cps terminals
3	Centronix 120 cps remote printers
1	Evans & Sutherland Picture System I
	16K word refresh buffer
	Tablet
	8 Analog control dials
	16 Function switches
	Alphanumeric keyboard
1	Digital Equipment Corporation PDP-11/45
	32K words of memory
	256K word fixed head disk
	Two 1.2m word cartridge disks
	Dual DEC tape unit
	Paper tape punch
	Line printer
	Control console
	800 bpi magnetic tape unit
	Communication interface
1	Xynetics Model 1200 Flat Bed Plotter, 57 × 89″ drawing area
1	Pratt & Whitney Trimac XV Numerical Control Machining Center (54 × 28 × 24″)

Table 1b. CADIG equipment—additional

2	Tektronix 4014 graphics terminals
1	Tektronix 30 × 40″ digitizer
2	Tektronix 4054 graphics systems with refresh capability
2	Tektronix 4052 graphics systems
4	Tektronix 4907 floppy disc units
	Additional 96K words of memory for PDP-11/45
	Cache memory for PDP-11/45
	Communication interfaces
	Digital Equipment Corporation PDP-11/34
	128K words of memory
	Cache memory
	Two 1.2M cartridge disk units
	Paper tape punch
	Control console
	Communication interfaces
	Digital Equipment Corporation PDP-11/34
	128K words of memory
	Cache memory
	One 2M word cartridge disk unit
	Two 256K word floppy disk units
	Control console
	Communication interface
	Large screen video projection system
	Various data acquisition systems
	Autonumerics/Bridgeport numerical control milling machine (28 × 10 × 5″)
	Autonumerics/Bridgeport numerical control lathe (16″ dia. × 54″)

for additional features, such as matrix manipulation, extensive editing capabilities, and data acquisition through external ROM packs. It is equipped with an IEEE 488 standard instrument interface bus. This allows data acquisition from and control of laboratory experiments. It can also be used as a terminal on the time sharing system in a Tektronix 4012 emulation mode. It was chosen specifically for this flexibility.

The Evans & Sutherland Picture System I and its PDP-11/45 support computer, along with the Xynetics flatbed plotter, provide the central core of a high quality flexible three dimensional computer aided design/interactive graphics facility. A Pratt & Whitney Trimax XV machining center provided the nucleus for numerical control.

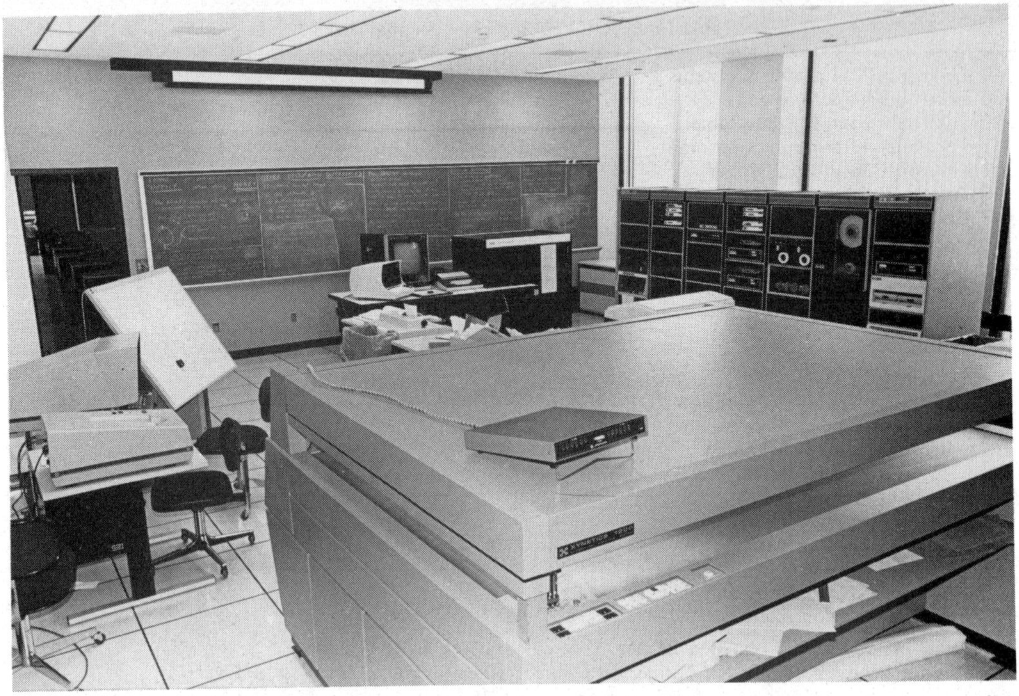

Fig. 2. Evans & Sutherland Picture System, PDP-11/45 and Xynetics flatbed plotter.

SUPPORT

In order to effectively develop and impliment a computer graphics program, high quality software and hardware support personnel are required. The CADIG Group consists of two professional computer programers, two professional digital electronics engineers and an electronics technician. Overall technical direction is provided by a faculty member. The need for software support is perhaps obvious. What is perhaps not so obvious is the need for electronic engineering support. Because the educational environment is unique and ill defined, commercial products are often not available, too sophisticated or too expensive to meet its requirements. Custom data acquisition systems, instrumentation interfaces and measuring systems are typical examples. The approach is generally to use off the shelf components with minimal custom board design to achieve the required result.

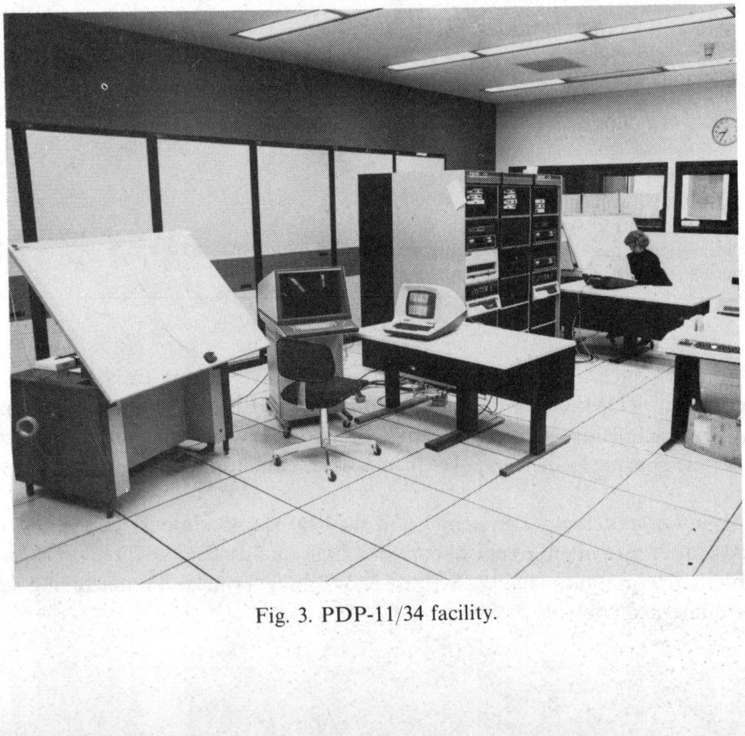

Fig. 3. PDP-11/34 facility.

With a large system such as this, maintenance can be a problem. Here, the approach is to maintain contracts on the large one-of-a-kind systems, namely the minicomputers, Evans & Sutherland Picture System and the Xynetics plotter. All other maintenance is performed in house by the electronics technician. This has worked well in practice with a very high degree of availability.

ECONOMICS

A facility such as described above is not inexpensive. However, in the context of modern engineering practice and of modern engineering education, it can be said that to a first approximation computation is free! Further, in comparison to the overall cost of computation, it can be said that to a second approximation computer graphics is free! Typically, excellent computational facilities will cost less than 2% and excellent computer graphics facilities less than $\frac{1}{2}$% of the overall university operating budget.

The initial investment in 1975 in the CADIG Facility was approximately one million dollars. Continued capital expenditures at the rate of approx. $75,000–$100,000 per year have occurred. Operating costs are approx. $100,000 per year, about half of which is for maintenance contracts. Personnel costs are approx. $125,000 per year. These costs are acceptable in the context of the overall operating budget of the school.

USAGE

Computer graphics is used in a variety of ways to enhance engineering education at the Naval Academy. Several of them are described below. All of the programs and software have been written by students, faculty or the CADIG staff of the Engineering & Weapons Division. In order to support this effort, a device independent graphics system called DIGS has been implemented. It is implemented as a subroutine suit. The primary implementation is in the Dartmouth Sixth Edition of BASIC on the time sharing system. Companion implementations exist in both BASIC and FORTRAN on the PDP-11 mini-computers. DIGS provides full three dimensional graphics capability.

Plotting

Frequently, a student's or, in fact, an engineer's first introduction to computer graphics is through a need to generate standard engineering plots. It is, therefore, important to make it easy for this new user. To this end, a plotting program has been developed for use with the various graphics devices. It is implemented in BASIC using DIGS. Principle use is with the Tektronix terminals on the time sharing system. Using this program, a student may obtain a complete scaled and labelled plot of a previously saved data file by interactively answering two simple questions. Data file techniques are taught all students in a required introductory computer programming course. This required format is simple and straightforward consisting of x,y pairs followed by a simple curve delimiter. Options, which may be interactively invoked, allow for selection of alternate axis type—linear, log-log, semi-log, scaling, overlay grid, character style, annotation, data fitting, etc. Hardcopy is provided by standard Tektronix hardcopy units. If a more elegant copy is required for professional papers, reports, etc. a standard display file (pseudo graphics file) may be created for subsequent plotting in ink on the flatbed plotter. Extensions to 3-D plots are possible. Examples of the standard default plots and an enhanced plot are shown in Fig. 4(a) and 4(b).

Computer aided ship hull design

The Naval Architecture Department at the Academy is one of five accredited undergraduate Naval Architecture programs in the United States. An integral part of the course of study is the design of ship hulls. Students are using interactive computer graphics to design ship hull shapes and numerical control machining techniques to generate models for subsequent testing in a towing tank. The program, called CAMILL (Computer Aided Milling), is more fully described in[3,4]. CAMILL is implemented in FORTRAN on the Evans & Sutherland Picture System and the PDP-11/45 minicomputer.

A ship hull surface is traditionally described by a net of lines formed by three orthogonal cutting planes through the ship. Preliminary lines for a ship can be generated either directly using CAMILL or by hand. If generated by hand, the lines are digitized and transferred to CAMILL. Fairing of the lines is interactively accomplished using a variety of techniques, e.g. cubic splines, parabolically blended, or B-spline curves (see Fig. 5a). Once the preliminary fairing is acceptable, waterlines and buttock lines are calculated and cross faired. During the cross fairing process, the ship hull is viewed in three dimensions, while using the hardware features of the Picture System to perform real time transformations, such as, rotations of perspective views of the ship hull (Fig. 5b). Any display on the

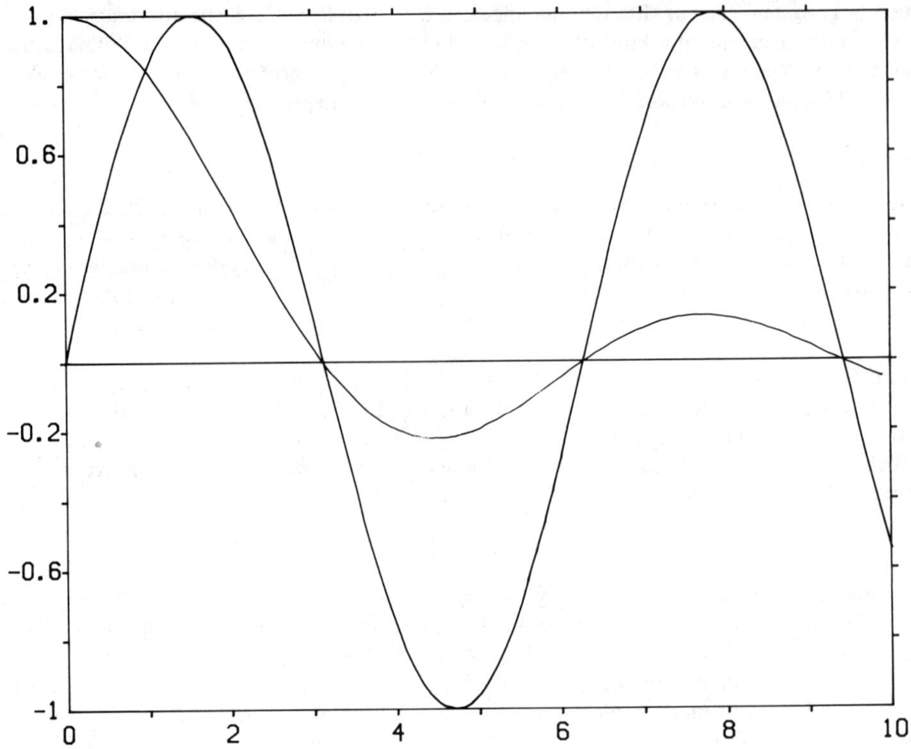

(a)

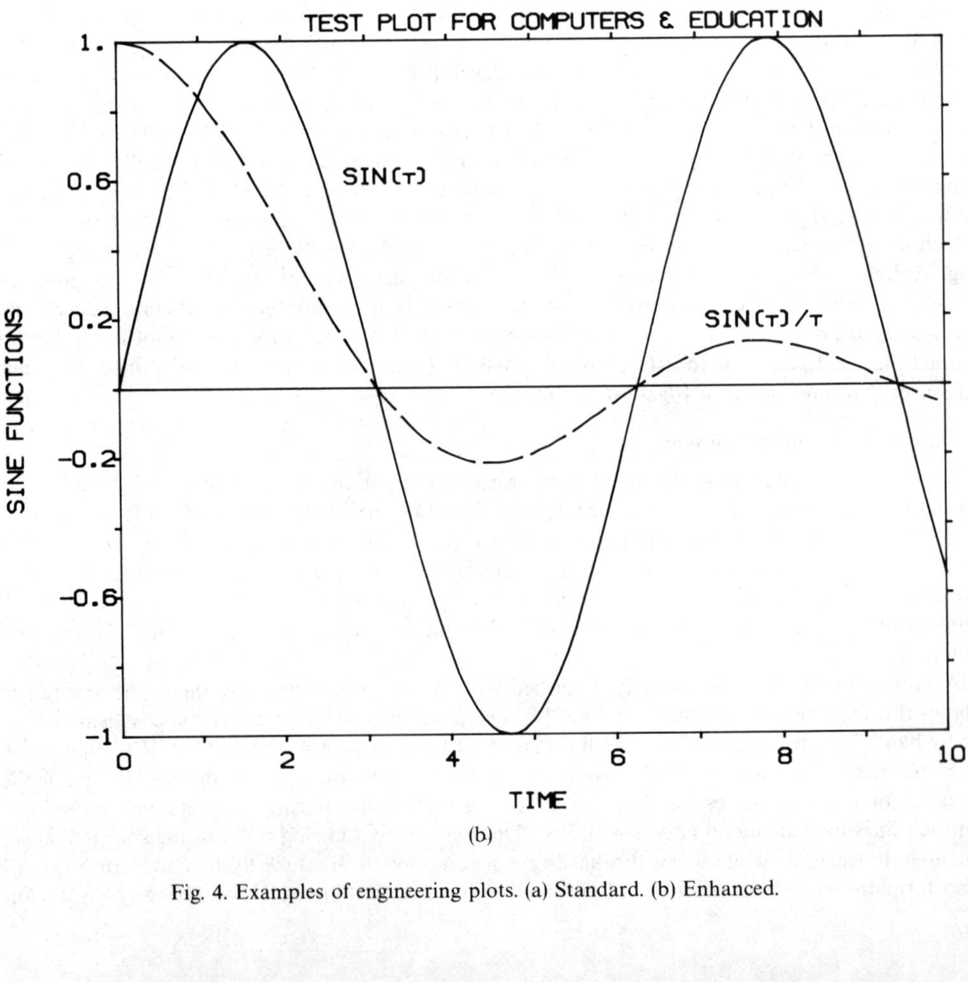

(b)

Fig. 4. Examples of engineering plots. (a) Standard. (b) Enhanced.

Picture system can be immediately obtained on the Xynetics flatbed plotter, on an associated Tektronix 4014 or saved for subsequent plotting. At any stage in the design process, the lines can be used to calculate the characteristics of the ship, e.g. the static stability. Several iterations are generally required before the student designer is satisfied.

Once the fairing of the hull is complete, a data file is created for the numerically controlled milling machine. The file consists of water lines sorted in order from the keel to the deck. This waterline data base is then transferred to the internal magnetic tape cartridge of the Tektronix 4051.

A Tektronix 4051 has been interfaced through its integral IEEE bus to the mini-computer used as a standard software controller for the numerically controlled milling machine. A simple custom designed interface is used to make the mini-computer controller think that the 4051 is a paper tape reader. Unplugging the interface cable automatically restores normal operation of the controller (Fig. 5c).

A BASIC program running in the 4051 assists the machine operator with set up and control, accesses the waterlines data base on the 4051's internal magnetic tape, calculates the necessary tool offsets, directly generates the necessary computer codes, and sends them to the controller to drive the machine tool. Simultaneously, it provides a graphical display for the operator, which is several steps ahead of the actual cutting operation. Full interactive control of the program is provided via the 4051's user definable keys. It should be noted that this is a true CADCAM (Computer Aided Design/Computer Aided Manufacturing) operation. No separate part programming takes place and, frequently, no detailed drawings exist of the ship other than in a computer file. Upon completion, hand finishing and painting, prepare the model for rigging and testing in the towing tank. Wind tunnel aircraft models can be done in a similar manner. This system allows a student to carry through a design from concept to testing.

Aircraft stability and control

One of the standard courses in any aerospace engineering curriculum is stability and control. Although static stability is relatively straight forward to calculate and understand, it is difficult for students to obtain a good physical and visual feel for dynamic stability. Basically, this is because, although straightforward, longitudinal and lateral dynamic stability calculations are more complex and time consuming. Hence, only one or two detailed calculations are attempted in a one semester course.

To assist in developing a physical feel and understanding of dynamic stability two programs have been implemented on the Evans & Sutherland Picture System. One handles longitudinal and the other lateral aircraft dynamic stability using small perturbation theory [5]. Each program allows the user to interactively change the parameters of the problem (stability derivatives) and observe the effects. Each program also allows the user to optionally display the various modes of motion either as a function of time or in the phase plane (Fig. 6a,b). Each program allows the user to view simulated motion of the aircraft in real time (Fig. 6c,d). The Picture System control dials can be interactively used in real time to change the view point, i.e. the motion, can be viewed from, say, directly ahead, directly abeam, or, say, from above, to the side and behind the aircraft. Simulated cockpit instrumentation depicts altitude, velocity and attitude changes during the motion.

Fluid dynamics

A BASIC program on the time sharing system uses cursor buttons, tablet, or thumbwheel input devices and a menu to allow students to interactively generate and graphically view the streamlines or potential lines for potential flow fields for arbitrarily located two dimensional point or line sources, sinks, vortices, doublets or uniform parallel fluid flows (Fig. 7). The program uses a unique and efficient method to generate the streamlines or potential lines [6]. The method involves the direct numerical integration of the streamline equations using a fourth order Range–Kutta numerical integration scheme. It has proven more efficient than previous methods.

In use, the student uses the interactive input device to first select the appropriate function from the menu, e.g. add point source, doublet, etc. (Fig. 7) by positioning the cursor in the appropriate box. The cursor is then moved to position the flow at the desired location. The characteristics of the flow are entered using the keyboard. Once the flow configuration is established, the cursor is used to select whether streamlines or potential lines are to be drawn. Subsequently, the cursor is used to select locations through which the appropriate type of line is to be drawn.

This program has a variety of classroom, laboratory and homework uses. For example, provision is also made for file input of previously defined flow fields. This allows the instructor to predefine a complex flow field and ask a student to investigate the effects of variations of one or two elements in the field. Students can now quickly and efficiently obtain valuable experience that would require

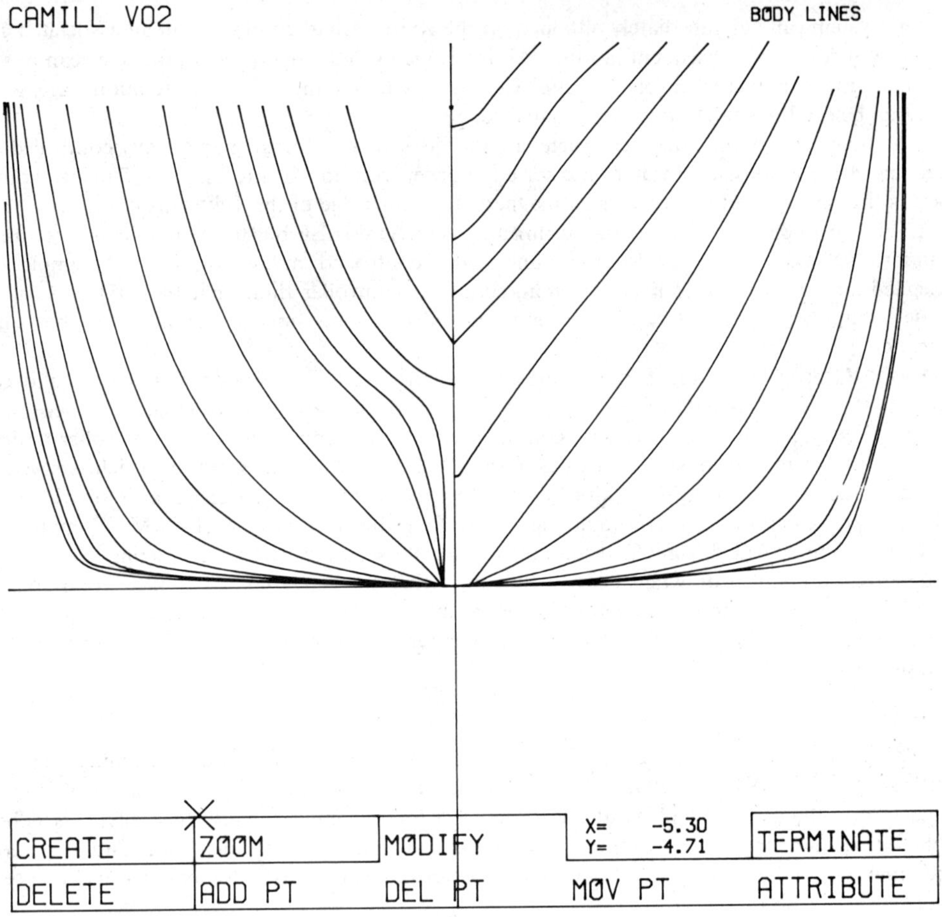
CAMILL V02
BODY LINES
CREATE
ZOOM
MODIFY
X= -5.30
Y= -4.71
TERMINATE
DELETE
ADD PT
DEL PT
MOV PT
ATTRIBUTE

Fig. 5(a).

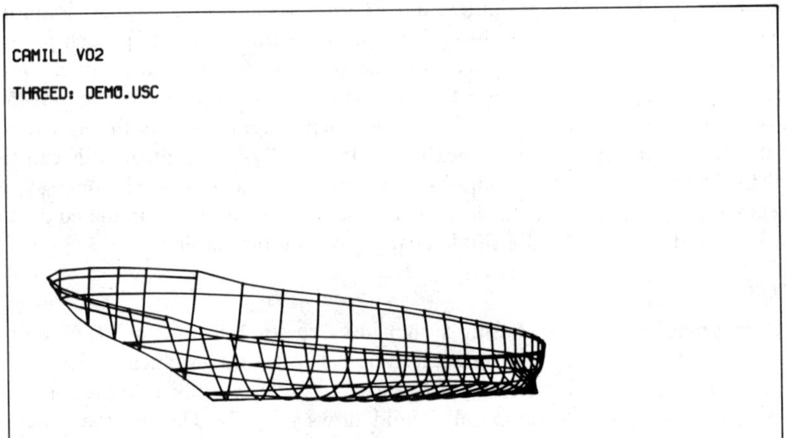
CAMILL V02
THREED: DEMO.USC
PERSPECTIVE
XTRN 5 YTRN 0 ZTRN 0 SCAL 71
XROT 0 YROT 48 ZROT 10 DIAL 35

Fig. 5(b).

Fig. 5(c).

Fig. 5. Computer aided hull design. (a) Faired body lines. (b) 3-D display. (c) Numerical control milling.

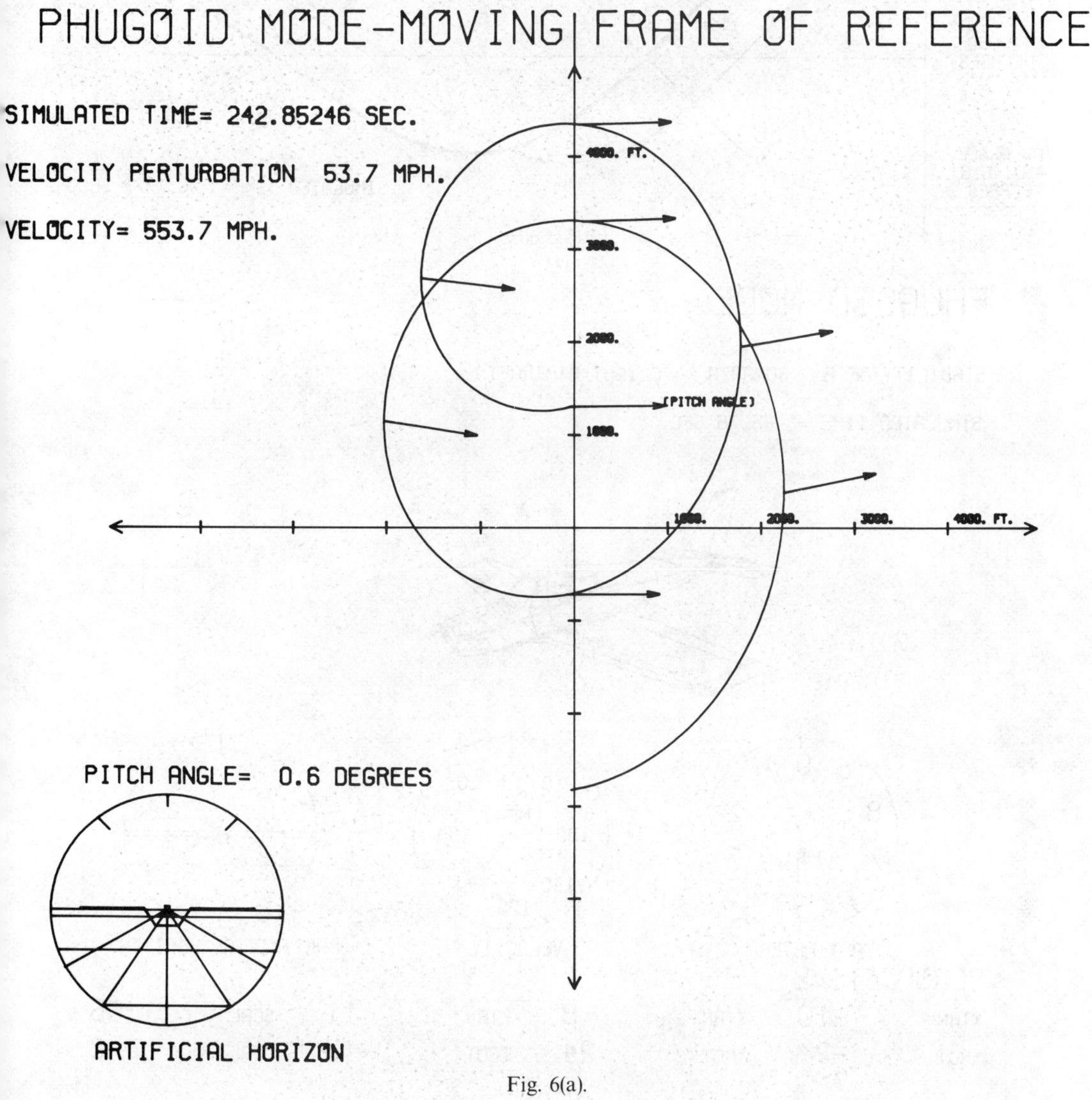

Fig. 6(a).

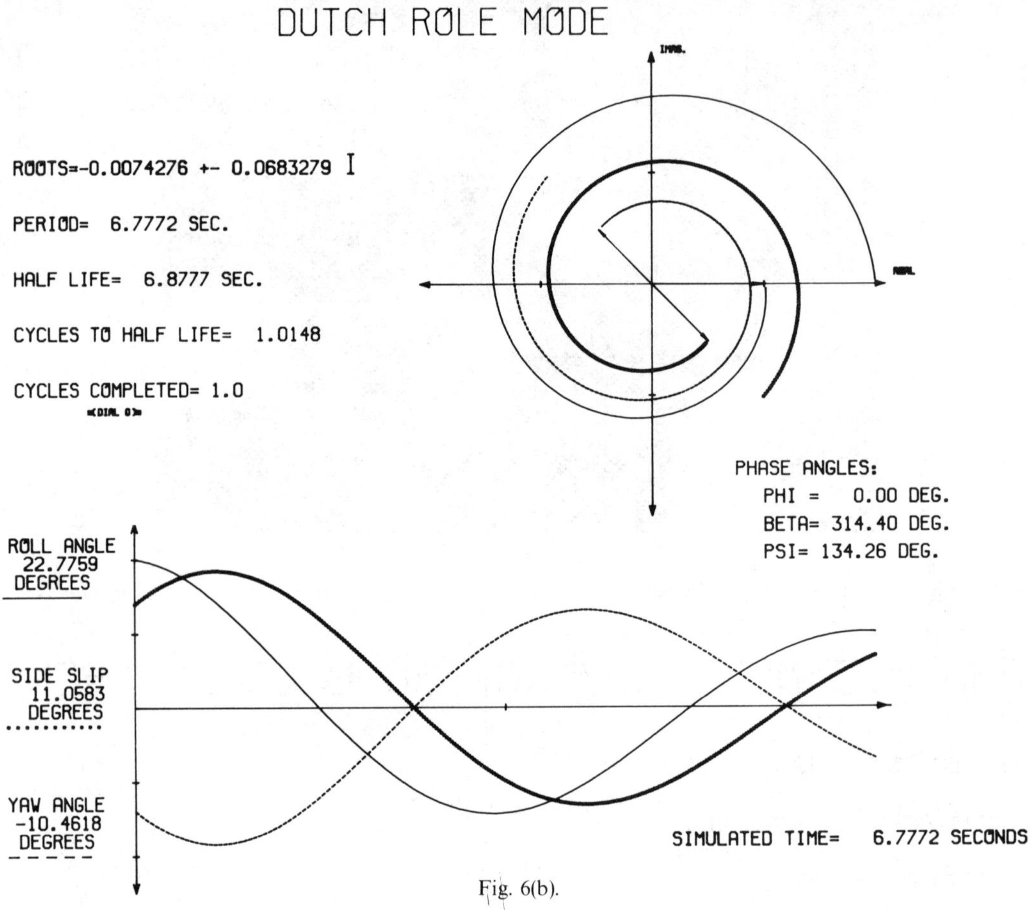
DUTCH RØLE MØDE
RØØTS=-0.0074276 +- 0.0683279 I
PERIØD= 6.7772 SEC.
HALF LIFE= 6.8777 SEC.
CYCLES TØ HALF LIFE= 1.0148
CYCLES CØMPLETED= 1.0
PHASE ANGLES:
PHI = 0.00 DEG.
BETA= 314.40 DEG.
PSI= 134.26 DEG.
RØLL ANGLE
22.7759
DEGREES
SIDE SLIP
11.0583
DEGREES
YAW ANGLE
-10.4618
DEGREES
SIMULATED TIME= 6.7772 SECØNDS

Fig. 6(b).

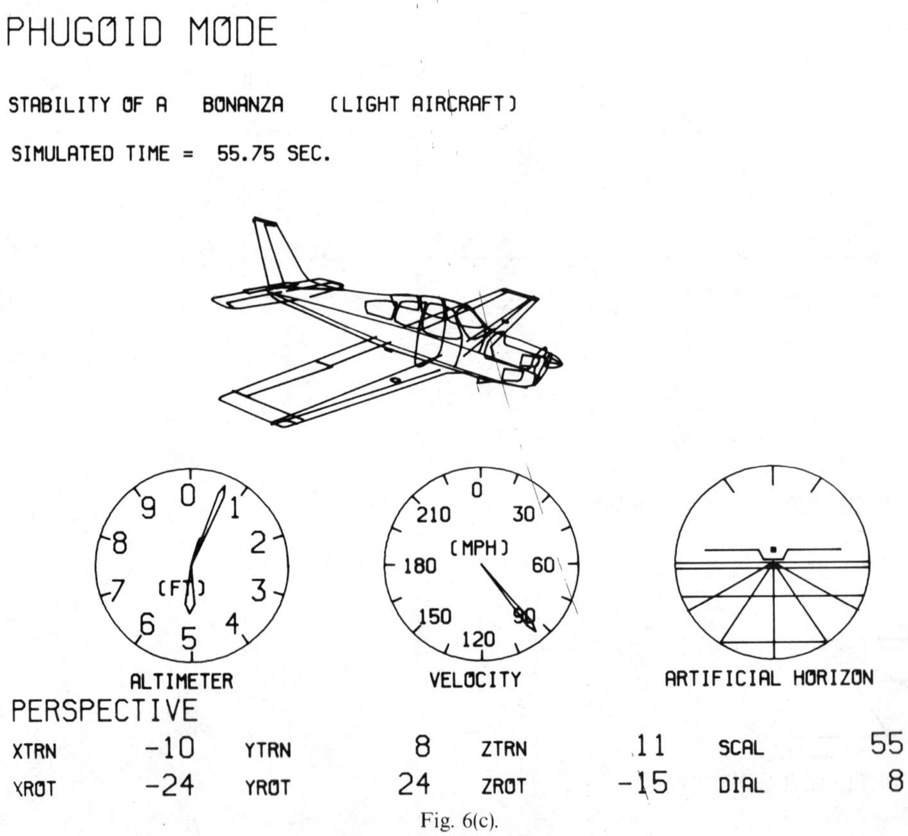
PHUGØID MØDE
STABILITY ØF A BØNANZA (LIGHT AIRCRAFT)
SIMULATED TIME = 55.75 SEC.
0
1
2
3
4
5
6
7
8
9
(FT)
ALTIMETER
0
30
60
90
120
150
180
210
(MPH)
VELØCITY
ARTIFICIAL HØRIZØN
PERSPECTIVE
XTRN -10 YTRN 8 ZTRN 11 SCAL 55
XRØT -24 YRØT 24 ZRØT -15 DIAL 8

Fig. 6(c).

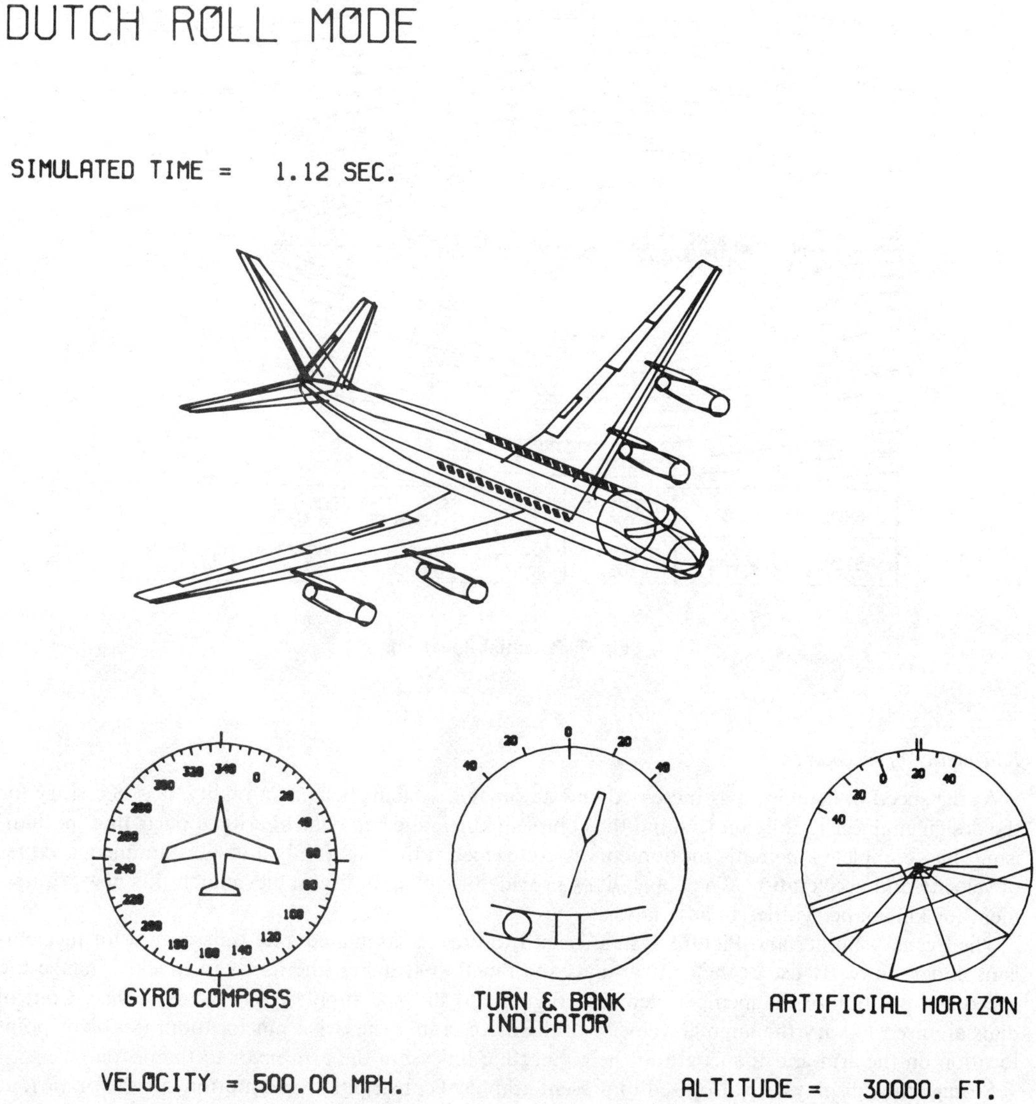

Fig. 6(d).

Fig. 6. Aircraft stability and control. (a) Longitudinal stability—phugoid mode in phase plane with climb angle. (b) Lateral stability—dutch roll mode. (c) Longitudinal stability—flight simulation phugoid mode. (d) Lateral stability—flight simulation dutch roll mode.

many man hours of work using traditional methods. The professor can now easily answer the ever present student question, "What if . . . ".

Uniform beam

One of the standard topics in any engineering curriculum is strength of materials. In particular, the rather useful uniform beam is studied in considerable detail. Generally, a number of methods are studied for solving for the bending moment, deflection, shearing stress, etc. in a beam under various loadings and for various support methods. In all of this the student frequently gets lost in the mathematics and fails to develop a physical feel based on experience.

An interactive graphics program implemented on the Evans & Sutherland Picture System seeks to alleviate this problem. It allows the student to arbitrary load and support a beam and calculate and graphically display the shear, bending moment, deflection and slope diagrams (Fig. 8a,b). Either statically determinant or indeterminant structures are possible using a specifically written finite element stiffness matrix analysis routine. The program is more fully described elsewhere in this issue.

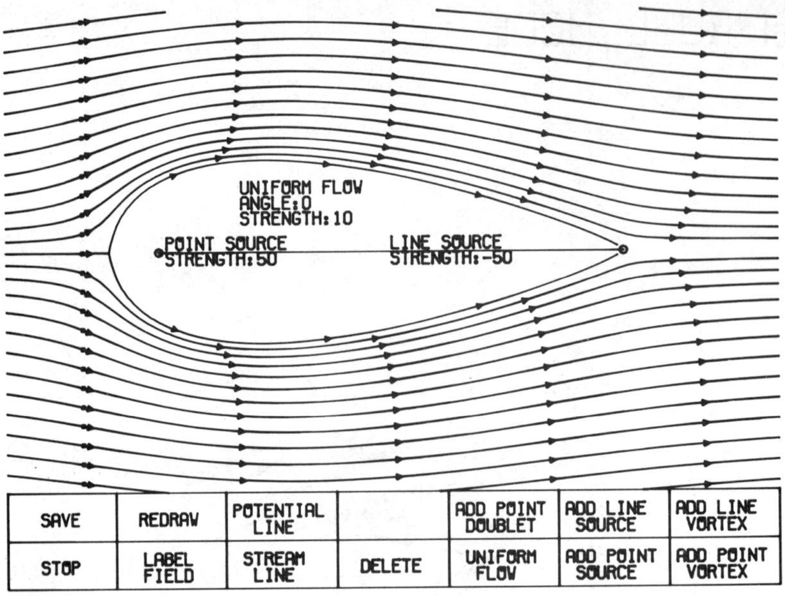

Fig. 7. Potential flow field.

Kinematics of mechanisms

As the speed of machinery is increased and automated systems become a reality, it is necessary for the design engineer to fully understand the complete kinematic behavior of critical parts in a mechanism. Thus, complete kinematic motion curves are needed rather than only a few instantaneous values of velocity and acceleration. The capabilities provided by computer graphics match this new requirement for kinematic synthesis and analysis.

The Evans & Sutherland Picture System is used to provide animated, real time output for mechanisms under study. By use of the control dials and function switches, the user can quickly change the speed and position of the member elements. Figure 9(a) shows a simple quick-return device. Control dials are used to vary the angular velocity of the drive crank, the drive pin location, the pivot point location on the arm and the length of the connecting link from the arm pivot to the piston.

Storage tube displays are also used to present graphical construction and motion curves for various configurations. Figure 9(b) shows that a very simple mechanism can have complex motion curves. Real time animation is not possible with the Tektronix 4051, but partial animation is being achieved on the new Tektronix 4054 terminals. The methods for obtaining the kinematic curves of motion and displaying the results are described elsewhere in this issue.

Wind tunnel testing

Laboratory experiments are an important part of any engineering curriculum. One of the classical aerodynamic or fluid dynamic experiments is the measurement of the pressure distribution about a two dimensional airfoil or wing to determine lift and the measurement of the energy loss in the wake to determine overall drag. Acquiring the data, reducing it by hand and performing the necessary area integrations is sufficiently time consuming that the experiment is normally done for only one angle of attack. Using computer graphics and modern data acquisition techniques along with a stand alone micro-computer based graphics system allows expanding the effort into a true experimental parametric study without an increase in laboratory time.

Specifically, a Tektronix 4051, an inexpensive custom designed data acquisition and control system, a scanning valve and a standard pressure transducer are combined into a modern data acquisition and analysis system (Fig. 10a). For the pressure distribution experiment, a parametric study is made as a function of angle of attack. For a given angle of attack, a BASIC program running in the 4051 sends a digital control signal to the custom data acquisition and control system via the IEEE bus. There, the digital signal is converted to the appropriate analog signal (voltage), which is sent to the scanning valve. The scanning valve resets itself such that it is reading the pressure at a known location on the airfoil. A specific number of pressure readings are then acquired at fixed time intervals,

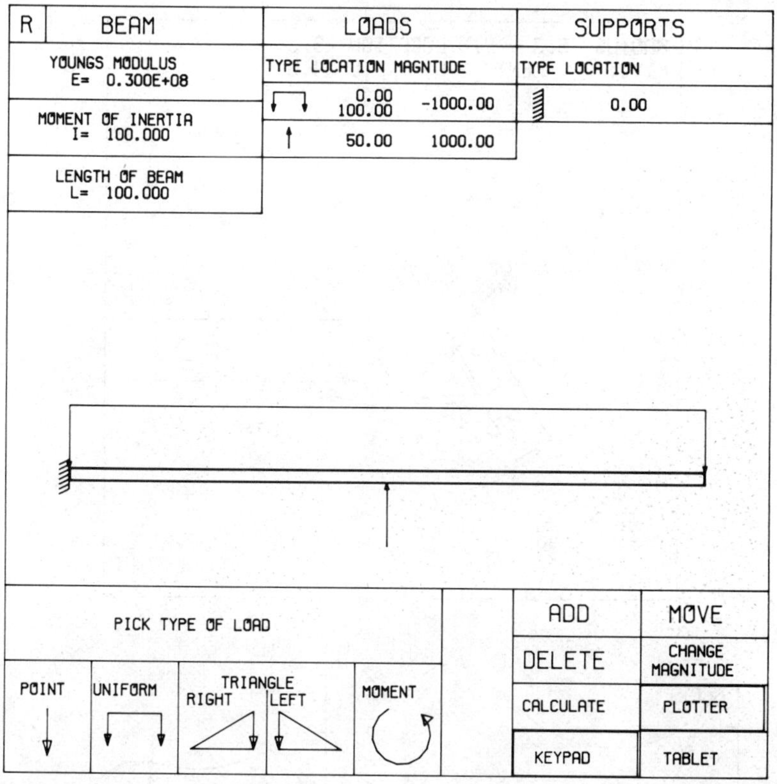

(a)

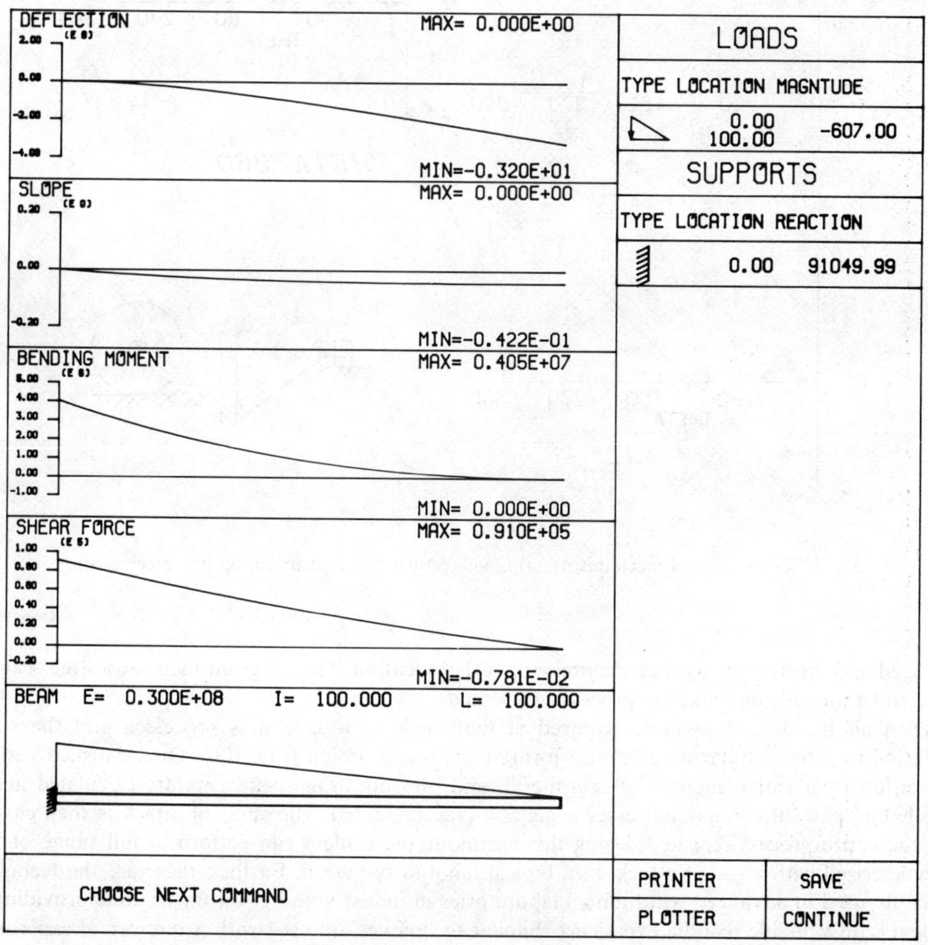

(b)

Fig. 8. Beam. (a) Configuration. (b) Results.

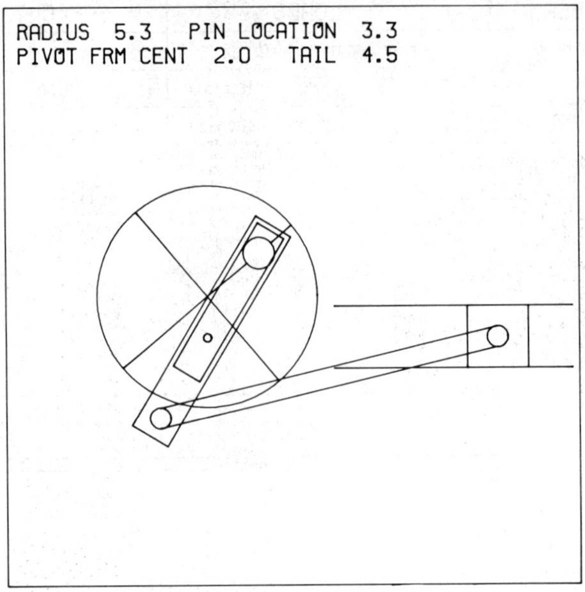

(a)

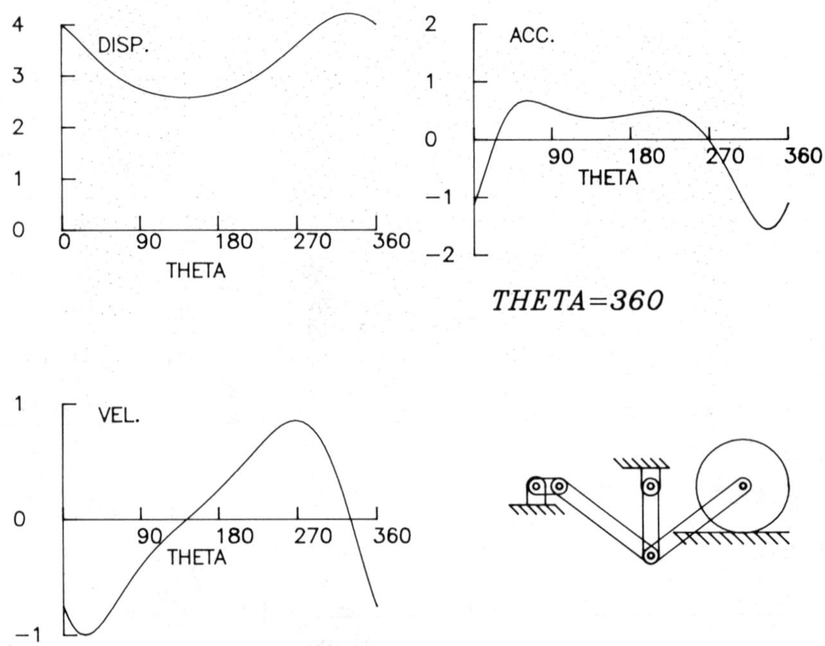

(b)

Fig. 9. Kinematics of mechanisms. (a) Quick return mechanism. (b) Simple mechanism.

averaged and the average used as the pressure at that location. The program then causes the scanning valve to be incremented and the process is repeated.

When all the data have been acquired at that angle of attack, it is processed and the results displayed in either tabular or graphical form at the user's option (Fig. 10b). Once satisfied with the results for a particular angle of attack, the lift and pressure drag coefficients are calculated and an updated graph of the functions verses angle of attack presented. The angle of attack is then changed and the entire process repeated. Using this technique the student can perform a full range of tests, parameterized with angle of attack, in a typical laboratory period. Further, these are the techniques generally used in advanced wind tunnel laboratories in industry and government, thus providing the student with valuable real life experience. Similar techniques are used with a number of experiments including the wake survey.

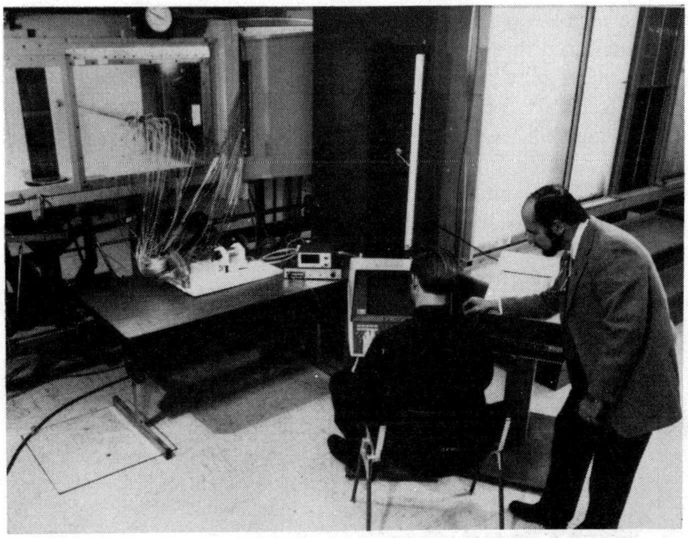

(a)

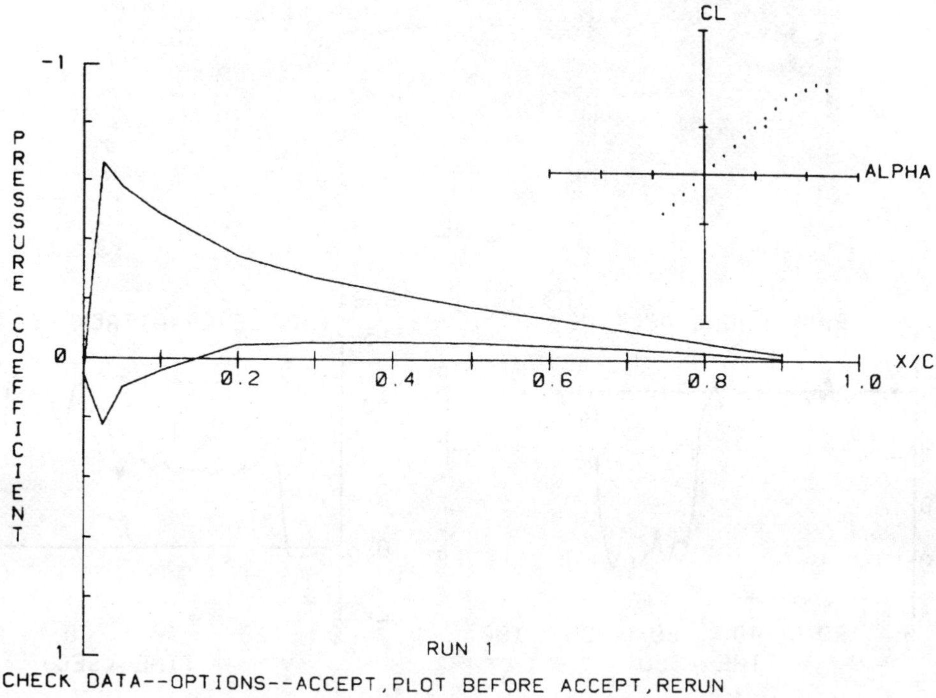

(b)

Fig. 10. Wind tunnel experiment. (a) Equipment set up. (b) Graphical results.

Student research—flight simulation study

The individual student research project is a vital part of an engineering curriculum. Computer graphics and computer aided data acquisition and analysis open up many new and interesting research projects. A recent one will serve as an illustration.

One of the fundamental dilemmas facing a pilot of a single engine airplane is: "What is the correct emergency procedure upon losing the engine at low altitude immediately after takeoff?". The standard approved answer is to continue straight ahead to an emergency landing. But what if a city or forest or water is straight ahead or it is night? Under these circumstances, the pilot will be tempted to turn back to the airfield. Is this feasible? What is the proper procedure?

Theoretical analysis indicates that the minimum loss of altitude in a gliding turn occurs for a bank angle of 45° at the stall speed of the aircraft. Is this maneuver practical for the average pilot? To answer this question, a small variable stability flight simulator already equipped with analog data output channels was interfaced to a Tektronix 4051 used in stand alone mode (Fig. 11a). Analog to digital conversion as well as data acquisition facilities were provided by a standard commercially available ROM pack. A BASIC program running in the 4051 was used as a controller. A large number of pilots of varying skill levels were asked to fly a series of prescribed turn back maneuvers after engine failure at low altitude immediately after takeoff. Eleven channels of data were acquired at one second intervals and stored on a floppy disc unit. Subsequent processing of the data yielded graphical plots of appropriate variables as well as two and three dimensional displays of the flight

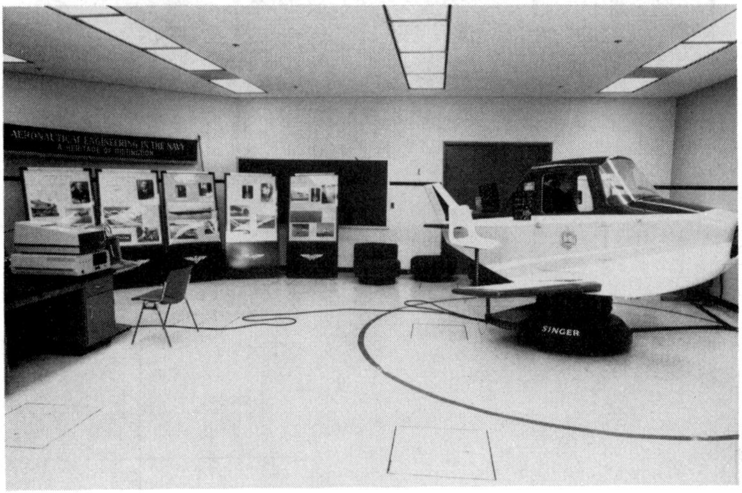

Fig. 11(a).

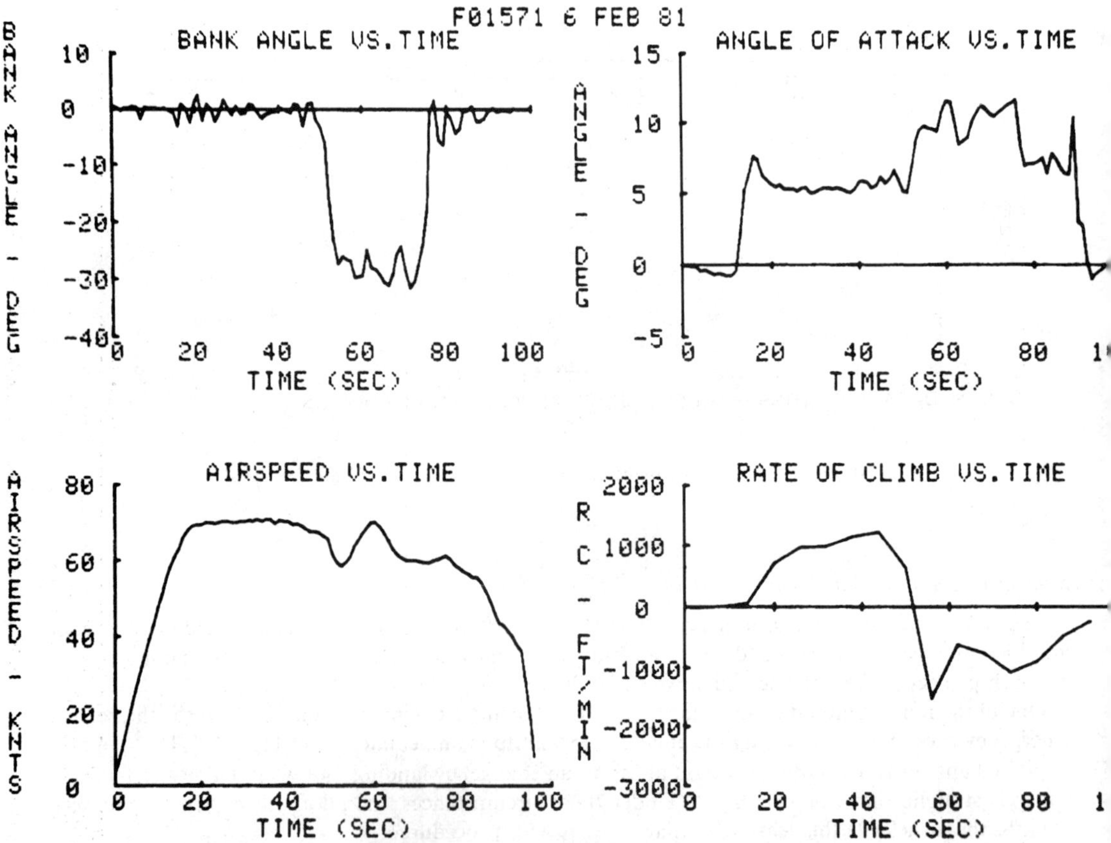

Fig. 11(b).

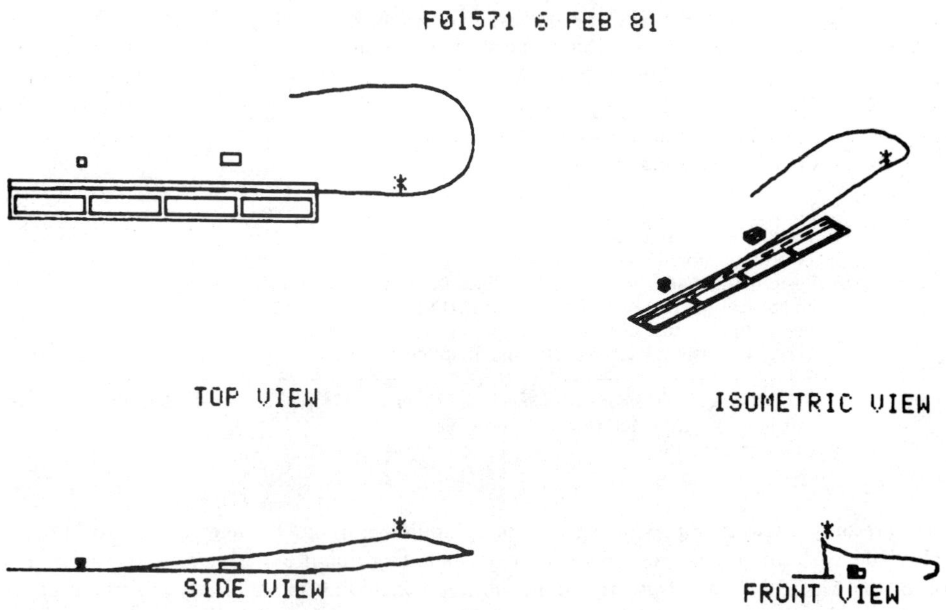

Fig. 11(c).

Fig. 11. Flight simulation. (a) Equipment set up. (b) Graphical results. (c) Graphical flight path display.

path during the turn back maneuver (Fig. 11b,c) for analysis. The experimental results confirmed the theoretical predictions but also indicated that a smaller bank angle of 30° yielded near optimum results with a higher margin of safety [5].

COURSES

Every student at the Naval Academy is required to complete an introductory computer programming course, which covers the elements of BASIC. This course also introduces the students to the standard plotting program described above. Two elective courses in computer graphics are offered. One, offered in the Mechanical Engineering Department, uses computer graphics as a vehicle for a study of the kinematics of mechanisms. Approximately 30% of the course is devoted to computer graphics, specifically Chapters 1–4 Ref. [8], with the rest devoted to the kinematics of mechanisms (Table 2). The second course, offered in the Aerospace Engineering Department, combines computer graphics and numerical control to effectively offer a CADCAM course. Approximately 75% of the course is devoted to computer graphics including all of Ref. [8]. The remaining time is devoted to computer aided manufacturing including the elements of APT and the concept and execution of a direct CADCAM system. Each student actually programs and manufacturs two simple parts, one using APT and one using direct CADCAM techniques. The course outline is shown in Table 3.

Table 2. Course outline. Kinematics of mechanisms with computer graphics

Topics
Computer graphics hardware and software
Two dimensional transformations
Three dimensional transformations including perspective
Two dimensional curves (conics, splines, B-splines)
Loop equations
Kinematic motion curves
Velocity and acceleration of planar mechanisms
(Whitworth quick return, 4-bar, crank and slot gearing, etc.)
Geometric properties (centroids, moment of inertia, etc.)

Textbook: *Mathematical Elements for Computer Graphics* (by D. F. Rogers and J. A. Adams). McGraw–Hill, New York (1976).

Table 3. Course outline. Computer graphics, computer aided design, computer aided manufacturing

Topics
Computer graphics hardware and technology
Computer graphics software
Two dimensional transformations
Three dimensional transformations including perspective
Techniques for refresh display
Two dimensional curves—conics
Basic mathematics for circles and lines in numerical control
Numerical control/APT PROGRAMMING
Three dimensional curves (cubic splines, Bezier, B-splines)
Three dimensional surfaces (Coons, B-splines)

Textbook: *Mathematical Elements for Computer Graphics* by D. F. Rogers and J. A. Adams. McGraw–Hill, New York (1976).

These are only a few examples of the uses of computer graphics in engineering education at the Naval Academy. Many other programs and areas, including fracture mechanics, experimental verification of the classical stress–strain relations, vibration including modal analysis, structural testing, and supersonic wind tunnel and towing tank data acquisition, benefit from computer graphics. Modern engineering education can and does significantly benefit from computer graphics, computer aided analysis and modern data acquisition techniques.

REFERENCES

1. Rogers D. F. and Adams J. A., American Society of Engineering Education Annual Meeting, Paper No. 53 (1969).
2. Rogers D. F. and Adams J. A., *Proceedings of the Twenty-First International Astronautical Congress*, p. 1045. North-Holland, Amsterdam (1971).
3. Satterfield S. G., Rodriguez F. and Rogers D. F., *Comput. Graphics* **11**, (1977).
4. Rogers D. F., Rodriguez F. and Satterfield S. G., *Proceedings of the 16th Design Automation Conference, IEEE*, pp. 207 (1979).
5. Etkin B., *Dynamics of Flight*. Wiley, New York (1959).
6. Siddon R. L., USNA Division of Engineering & Weapons Report EW-1-78 (1978).
7. Jett B., Middle Atlantics Section AIAA Student Paper Conference (1981).
8. Rogers D. F. and Adams J. A. *Mathematical Elements for Computer Graphics*. McGraw-Hill, New York (1976).

Comput. & Educ. Vol. 5, pp. 183 to 192, 1981
Printed in Great Britain

0360-1315/81/040183-10$02.00/0
Pergamon Press Ltd

KEY ISSUES IN INSTRUCTIONAL COMPUTER GRAPHICS

MICHAEL J. WOZNY
Center for Interactive Computer Graphics, Rensselaer Polytechnic Institute, Troy, NY 12181, U.S.A.

INTRODUCTION

The integration of computer graphics into the undergraduate instructional engineering program is not a recent idea. The University of Illinois pioneered this concept with the PLATO (Programmed Logic for Automated Teaching Operations) system more than 15 years ago [1]. The cognitive and pedagogical reasons for instructional graphics were well known at that time. Although computer graphics usage was found to be very beneficial in engineering curricula, one could not conclusively prove that computer graphics was significantly "better" than more traditional instructional techniques [2]. Consequently, university efforts limped along for 10 years with only sporadic attempts to incorporate graphics widely into the instructional program, most notably at the University of Michigan [3,4] and the U.S. Naval Academy [5,6].

Clearly, one could not justify this expensive technology purely on pedagogical grounds. The low cost per terminal promised by PLATO never materialized, and the concept of managed instruction using computers, CAI (Computer Aided Instruction), was never widely adopted by engineering schools. Finally, the "theoretical" space age orientation of most engineering programs could not reconcile the "design" nature of graphics usage in industry, where it was used for "mundane" work like drafting.

However, the situation changed dramatically in the 1976–1977 time frame. The decline in U.S. industrial productivity was acknowledged to be a national crisis. The high cost of labor and the demand for shorter design-to-manufacturing lead times made "computerization" necessary. The turnkey graphics system suppliers which had plodded along since 1969 suddenly became the premier growth industry. Computer graphics interpreted in its broadest sense, has become a vital link in the nation's quest for increased industrial productivity. All projections indicate that this rapid growth will continue well into the next decade.

This explosion has created a large industrial demand for engineering graduates who understand computer graphics. Instead of an expensive toy with inconclusive cognitive and pedagogical value, computer graphics has become an indispensable tool of the engineer. The whole question of computer graphics in engineering education must be re-examined.

This paper addresses a number of key issues facing universities which plan to establish instructional computer graphics facilities. The issues are presented in a generic sense, but are based on four years of experience in directing the RPI Center for Interactive Computer Graphics.

Appendix A gives a brief overview and equipment configuration for the Center. More detailed information on specific faculty experiences in developing and using instructional software appears in Refs [7–29] and elsewhere in this issue. Appendix B lists the courses which used computer graphics during the 1980–81 academic year including the number of terminal-hours involved.

COMPUTER GRAPHICS AND CAD/CAM

From a functional point of view, a computer graphics terminal is simply a pictorial communication medium for manipulating and interpreting data. The graphics software package controls where and how the data is presented on the display, by drawing lines.

Engineering requires a higher level of interpretation than lines, namely geometry. For example, a box connotes something more than the twelve lines which comprise the edges, and a tangent means something more than a line which terminates on a circle.

Consequently, engineering uses of graphics require, in general, additional software to create and maintain a geometrical model. An image on a graphics display is simply one or more views of a geometric model.

The geometric model may have attributes associated with it, like material properties or fabrication costs. The totality of this information must be organized in a data base so that the appropriate geometry and information can be accessed interactively. Finally the data base must allow the user to interface analysis and other utility programs to the geometry.

When properly structured, this total software system handles the mundane tasks of a design, allowing the engineer to concentrate on the creative and judgmental aspects.

Depending on the application and industry, many levels of sophistication exist for graphics display software, geometric modeling capability, data base architecture, analysis programs, communication/networking, and the manufacturing interface. This complete structure is called a CAD/CAM (Computer Aided Design/Computer Aided Manufacturing) system. The ultimate CAD/CAM system implies a totally automated and integrated design/manufacturing environment.

Strictly speaking, the term "computer graphics", when used in an engineering context, refers to the "front end" of a CAD/CAM system. However, we shall use the term more generically to imply part or all of the software/hardware components of the CAD system defined above. This conforms with popular engineering usage.

ROLE IN CURRICULUM

The role of computer graphics in the engineering curriculum is to provide a creative environment in which to learn. It must focus on those aspects which are fundamental enough to sustain a graduate through a 40 year career. Computer graphics allows students to visualize and more clearly understand complex geometric concepts associated with many engineering disciplines. The ability to visually interpret complex relationships and understand global trade-offs as parameters are varied is basic to an engineering education.

The key to achieving this role is a highly interactive system. The system must respond quickly and the software must be configured to handle all mundane details. In essence, the software represents a computer model or logical structure of a given phenomenon which the student is attempting to understand. Understanding is achieved through a decision process consisting of sequentially inputting new parameters based on the interpretation of results from the previous iteration. This approach is generally called computer aided learning as opposed to the managed instruction philosophy of computer aided instruction.

Since graphics is a methodology, it should not displace conceptual material in the curriculum but enhance it. This can be achieved by overlaying graphics throughout the entire undergraduate program and across all disciplines like icing on a cake.

In addition to understanding concepts, students should also be familiar with industrial quality equipment and current industrial uses of computer graphics. Consequently we are faced with the traditional long term versus short term goals in an engineering education. The use of industrial systems and software should be approached with the following cautions.

Industrial systems have been developed for the experienced user to accommodate sophisticated design through many options. The beginning student generally does not understand the meaning of the options and ultimately becomes a button pusher. Such systems are also configured for solving large problems and therefore have a high overhead requiring large amounts of computer time, even for simple problems. Finally, most industrial training courses consist of 45–60 h just to become familiar with the system capability. Translated to a university environment, this means that an entire semester would be used to teach button-pushing on a system which will be obsolete in a few years. One must weigh these trade-offs very carefully. Obviously, there are compromises.

Teaching computer graphics programming is important and should be done. However, there are two aspects to this issue. On the one hand, many engineers in the near future will have small desk top microcomputers with graphics displays for solving small problems and plotting simple results, just like calculators today. On the other hand, it is important for a student to realize that computer graphics in engineering is generally a tool, a means to an end and not the end itself. Most commercial turnkey graphics systems have more than 500 man-years of development invested in their software. A student is not going to rewrite such programs. He must learn to use such large programs intelligently. For example, he must realize that the quality of the solution is only as good as the underlying computer algorithms. Furthermore, he must avoid the temptation to create so much data that the desired result is totally masked in a sea of information pollution.

HARDWARE ISSUES

The extremely rapid changes which are taking place in computer graphics hardware today have made people reluctant to purchase a new system because something better may be just around the corner. This concern is precisely correct. Something better is around the corner. In fact there will always be something better around the corner. Consequently, the best advice is to jump in and get started by making a sound decision on the best available data. This experience will place you in a knowledgeable position the next time around—and there will certainly be a next time because the field is moving very rapidly.

However, enough terminals should be available so that the student can get on the system with minimum delay. RPI has 36 terminals servicing roughly 2000 engineering undergraduate students per semester in 30 courses (see Appendix B). The number of terminals required depend on the instructional goals. Except when the terminals are reserved for a large class, students can generally find an empty terminal sometime during the 16 h per day that they are available to undergraduates. All 36 terminals are needed for large classes (like the computing fundamentals class for freshmen engineers consisting of 720 students) and at peak periods (like the last 5 weeks in the semester).

Equipment sophistication depends on local needs and budgets. Experience has shown that students tend to grow to fit the sophistication of the equipment. Each incoming freshman class is more computer literate than the previous one. Consequently, we found that each successive offering of the freshmen computing fundamentals course dealt with more sophisticated graphics programming concepts. The same is true in courses using canned programs. The programs became more sophisticated as students became more proficient in using the terminals and as the faculty responded by incorporating additional concepts into the programs.

Unfortunately, these increasingly sophisticated programs require more computational power. The computational power required to run graphics is very deceiving. RPI totally underestimated the computational power required in its original configuration, even with industrial consultant input. Consequently, an upgrade of twice the CPU power and memory was made in September, 1980. The lack of computational power becomes evident in the poor response time of the graphics terminals. Students begin to complain and lose interest once the response drops below several minutes.

Choosing the appropriate display technology (vector, raster, storage) is a trying experience. No single technology provides all the desired functionality. The selection criteria must be based on a thorough understanding of the intended areas of application. Although not specifically intended for this application, see Ref. [31] for an informative article on equipment selection.

CRT display devices provide two basic capabilities. At one end is a very dynamic line drawing capability, and at the other is a color photographic quality rendition of an object. The user must decide which display device offers the best compromise to fit the intended use.

Vector refresh displays provide a high quality line drawing capability coupled with high interactivity, but are relatively expensive. If too many vectors are drawn on the screen, the display will flicker. (Most instructional programs are not complex enough to cause flicker even on the low cost vector terminals.)

A storage tube display (DVST) offers line quality comparable to a vector display at a cheaper price. However, it lacks comparable interactivity. Storage tubes can display an extremely large number of vectors without flicker.

Although the above comparisons are true in general, recent advances in all technologies have blurred the distinctions. A good method of tracking the technologies is through the various vendor exhibitions associated with the national computer graphics and CAD/CAM conferences. However, the user must have specific applications in mind for making a valid comparison. See Refs [32–34] for an introduction to display technology and additional resource material.

RPI chose vector refresh displays because they provided the required interactivity to reinforce intuition. The ability to easily change parameters and get fast responses for comparison cannot be underestimated in an instructional environment.

SOFTWARE ISSUES

Software is the most critical component in instructional computer graphics. Well designed software enhances the problem solving process by allowing the student to concentrate on the creative aspects while the computer handles the mundane aspects. The software, in some sense, must reflect the thought process of the user, providing the proper information at the right time and in the right format. For example, the graphics software should allow a user to enter a set of parameters, obtain a result, then change one parameter without re-entering the others, obtain a second result, and finally compare the two results. Various extensions to this idea include placing the solutions on a stack where selective results can be recalled for comparison, or placing the solutions on disk for long term storage and later recalled. The bottom line is maximum flexibility for manipulating data but based on a rational process. The logic structure which defines the interactive capabilities of a given program must be thought through very carefully.

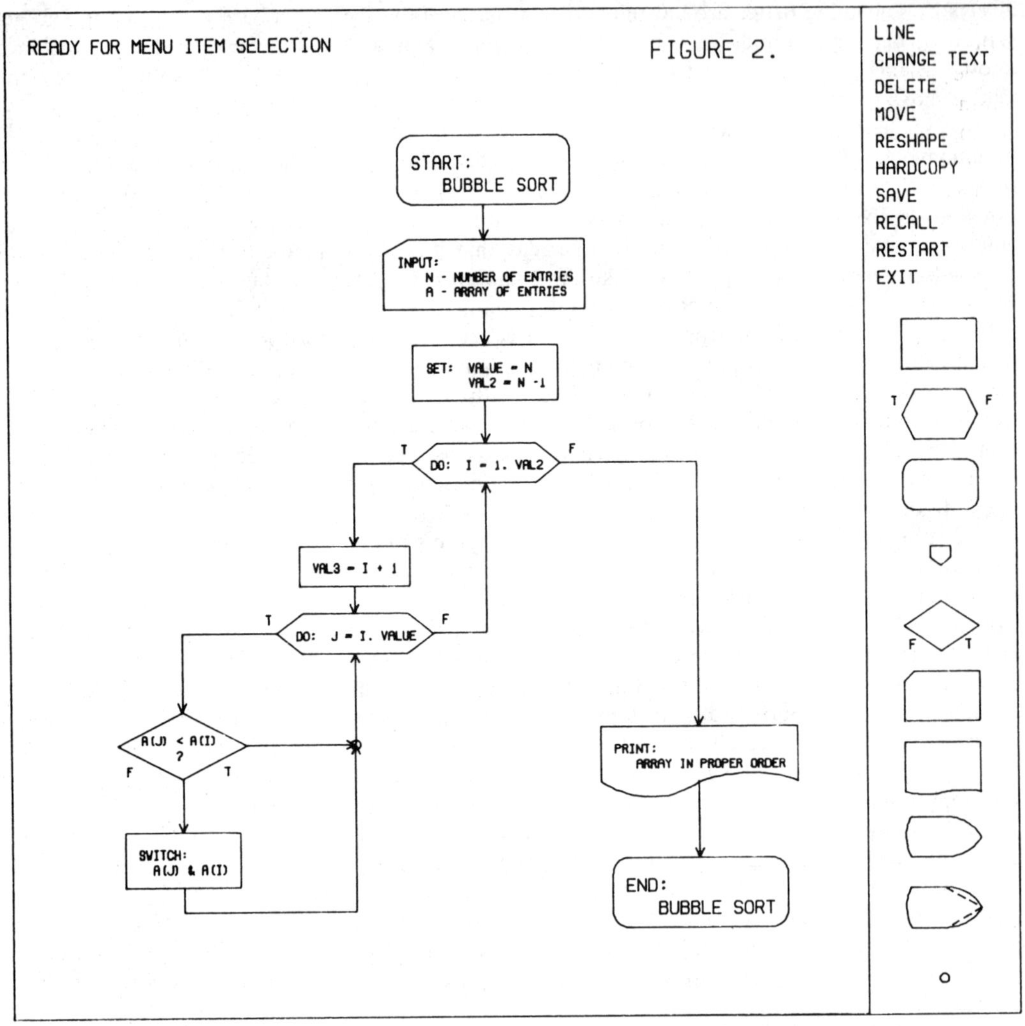

Fig. 1. Example of flowchart program.

The example shown in Fig. 1 illustrates some of these points. The blocks of the flow chart are selected from a menu structure making the program easy to use. There is no need to be precise about lining up the blocks in a vertical or horizontal direction because the computer handles this mundane job. The computer also determines the size of each box after the text is typed in; another mundane detail. Finally, the program has a crude routing algorithm which allows the user to simply point to a starting point and ending point with the light pen, and the software picks a candidate path. If the path is unsatisfactory the user has the option to easily change it with the light pen.

Obtaining instructional computer graphics software from other sources is difficult, because the software is not generally transportable. Most terminals have their own graphics language and specific functionality. For example, many terminals use local intelligence to achieve a high level of interactivity. A transportable graphics software package would have to emulate this capability in the host, making the response a lot slower, and consequently less interactive. Graphics programs written in the Tektronix Plot 10 software are perhaps the most transportable and are easily modified for other terminals. However one may have to add more interactive capability to the converted program. Recent announcements by Tektronix indicate that their new software is ACM Siggraph core compatible [35] which represents a significant enhancement over Plot 10. RPI currently maintains eight different graphics software packages.

Although RPI was able to get some of its software from other universities only a small portion of that software was directly applicable in the instructional program. Much of it was too narrow in concept and too rigidly structured, offering only a single path to the answer. Students quickly became bored with such packages because they offered no challenge—much the same way as young children discard TV games after a week.

At the other end of the scale are industrial quality analysis programs. These programs contain large arrays and are very CPU intensive. Consequently, they require a lot of computer resources even for simple problems. They also contain extensive lists of input parameters, important in real problems, but most of which the students did not understand. Although this latter problem can be overcome by writing a special front end program which prefilters the data, the overall execution is still unnecessarily slow. Industrial software is generally useful for the senior and graduate years. Special subsets must be developed for the other undergraduate classes.

In the final analysis most of the instructional software is being written at RPI. In-house software development raises a host of operational issues. Students are very adept at writing good code but seldom document their work thoroughly enough, making it difficult to maintain after they graduate. Most useful graphics programs require a programming effort comparable to a Master's Thesis. Who will maintain the instructional software? The professor who developed it or the graphics facility operations staff? What about transportability? Are you willing to accept a slower response in order to make the programs usable by other schools? There are no pat answers for any of these questions. The role of graphics standards is a key issue in instructional software and is being investigated by a group from a number of universities under a NSF DISE grant [36]. This grant is also sponsoring the development of a number of instructional modules.

WRITING INSTRUCTIONAL SOFTWARE

There are many reasons and uses of graphics software in the instructional program. This section will only touch on some general ideas found useful at RPI. Furthermore, only canned software will be discussed, realizing that in some courses it is more appropriate to have students write their own programs. An ideal instructional module is one which accommodates user growth. For example it should be easily used by the novice who understands only a few commands and yet has enough richness that an advanced user who has the complete command structure at his disposal also finds it useful.

A graphics software module should be self-contained with a definite objective, similar to a laboratory experiment. It should require active participation on the part of the student, that is, the student should perceive some type of trade-off in the problem. Entering certain values of one or more parameters increase the result while other values or other parameters decrease the result. The student is caught in a conflict type situation. He does not know the answer, but by going through several iterations of the solution he has learned enough to give him confidence that he is converging to an answer. Examples of this structure are discussed in the references cited in the Introduction.

Such a module must have certain interactive features. First of all it should be easy to use. We must assume the student has some background in the discipline, and the purpose of the software is to provide an environment for enhancing intuition and for obtaining a more complete understanding of the underlying concepts. Consequently, the screen and the interactive menus should be laid out so that the student immediately sees a first step. All additional steps give him more information about the legal structure and the interaction. There should always be a help command available for more detailed information about any part of the program. Note that this is a "conversational" approach to interaction.

Other features apparent on the screen should be a prompt message so that the user knows exactly where he is in an interactive sequence. Some highlighting features such as blinking or boxing a menu command or object after it is picked can be used. Status information is very important in an interative environment. A list of parameters currently in use is a common piece of status information.

Finally, no structure is complete without an error message area. These messages range from system errors to choosing a menu item out of sequence.

All software packages should maintain as neutral an educational philosophy as possible, for maximum transportability. We must avoid the situation of creating an analogy to a "programmed text" which has so much of its writer's soul in it that it cannot be adapted for anyone else's use.

As software packages are developed they should be tied into some type of data base which simply creates a common accessing structure or may allow data to be passed between analysis programs.

Every program should be accompanied by a complete set of documentation consisting of a user's manual and a systems manual. Most programs end up being enhanced sometime in the future.

GETTING FACULTY INVOLVED

Faculty will become involved in graphics once they see its potential benefits. The most effective means for revealing these benefits is through graduate student programming support. A graduate student can quickly translate a professor's idea into a demonstrable program. Using this software in the classroom and observing the positive student response will convince even the most hardened skeptic of its pedagogical value. At this point the professor is usually looking for more graduate students to develop extensions to the original software. Although computer graphics is a very motivational medium, one cannot expect all faculty to write their own programs. Faculty involvement in instructional computer graphics requires substantial support.

This responsibility generally falls on the graphics staff to provide good documentation, student consultants to handle operational difficulties, guidance on writing easy to use instructional software, and reliable system performance.

Finally, no instructional graphics operation will be successful without support from higher administration. Faculty must know that their efforts will be recognized.

OPERATIONAL ISSUES

Although the operational issues of a graphics center are similar to any university computing center, there is one major difference. University computer centers tend to provide a computing service based on purchased commercial software. A graphics center acts like a software house coordinating the development of extensive instructional software.

Although systems software is provided by the host computer vendor its effective use in a graphics environment requires local expertise. A computer graphics terminal is a sophisticated computer in its own right and places heavy demands on the operating system if good performance is desired. Either a full time professional programmer or a graduate student must accept this responsibility. Using graduate students is risky because they graduate every few years.

Maintaining account information and security is another problem area. Most supermini computer operating systems can be penetrated by students so that one must develop software to guard against such intrusions. Accounting and billing information must be maintained if the computer system is to be used on any government research contracts.

Hardware maintenance is another key issue. All of RPI's instructional equipment is covered by maintenance contracts. The center must guarantee an operational environment to its 2000 students using the system every semester. Faculty must be able to plan their computer assignments and expect deadlines to be met.

Finally, the center must provide an applications support capability. Applications software must be organized and maintained in an applications library. This software must be documented and enhanced as the need arises. Student consultants must be available to help users with specific problems. Minicomputer systems and graphics devices are not very forgiving. Cryptic error message will result if the commands are not entered precisely as described in the user manuals. Knowledgeable students and staff must be available to help faculty and in some cases train new teaching assistants for classroom needs. Finally, staff must be available to handle the large number of visitors.

RESEARCH ISSUES

The RPI graphics center maintains an extensive research program in conjunction with the instructional program. The research program, called University–Industry Cooperative Research Program, is supported by NSF [37] and 18 industrial affiliates.

The tight coupling between the graduate research assistants and the operations staff has created a nice channel for funneling useful industrial practice and knowledge in computer graphics into the instructional program. Consequently, the undergraduate program is kept current. This approach also helps recruit bright undergraduates into the research program and eventually into graduate school.

The research program also maintains high performance state-of-the-art graphics equipment which is available in special cases to the instructional program.

SUMMARY

Computer graphics will become an essential ingredient of an engineer's formal education. It will extend his creative insights by allowing him to configure and analyze designs which exist only in his imagination. The highly interactive response will allow him to quickly and easily try many alternative solutions to a problem so that he not only understands the concept thoroughly, but also understands the sensitivity of the solution to the range of parameters chosen.

The display technology of the future will probably be some combination of vector and raster capabilities. The instructional need for high interactivity implies vector displays. However, the line quality of the relatively new 1024 × 1024 pixel raster devices seems to be quite acceptable for engineering work. In addition, several raster terminals have vector (line drawing) processing capability in the front end to increase interaction. If we now take a 2048 × 2048 pixel color raster display (which will be available in the near future), couple it with a fast vector processing front end, and add a powerful 32 bit virtual memory microcomputer with several megabytes of memory under user control, we have the best of both worlds. I expect that the graphics equipment being ordered today will be obsolete before this hypothetical terminal of the future becomes fast enough and cost effective. Consequently, don't sit tight waiting for an impending announcement!

Good instructional graphics software is a major need. One aspect of graphics software development is programmer efficiency. Generic graphics functions like creating menu structures, or file structures need to be developed. There is no reason why every graphics programmer must work at the lowest line drawing level to create, for example, a menu structure.

The other key aspect of graphics software is transportability. The exchange of good instructional computer graphics programs between universities will continue to be inhibited until the programming effort required to convert software is greatly reduced. Several commercial "transportable" graphics software packages are available, but are somewhat expensive for university budgets. Several NSF funded efforts are underway to study this question for instructional use.

The final issue is funding. Computer graphics equipment is very expensive. A number of universities have been successful in attracting government, industrial, and foundation support to develop graphics capabilities. RPI provided substential university funding to establish the graphics center. The strong industrial interest for students with computer graphics experience has made industry more willing to work with universities to obtain equipment and software. Unfortunately, the government funding picture is very cloudy with large impending cuts in educational spending. One possibility is to have several schools share resources.

Acknowledgements—Portions of the material discussed in this paper are based upon work supported by the National Science Foundation under grants ISP 79-20240-01, SED 79-20085, and the industrial sponsors. Any opinions, findings, and conclusions or recommendations expressed in this publication are those of the author(s) and do not necessarily reflect the view of the National Science Foundation, nor the industrial sponsors.

Special thanks is given to the faculty and graduate students who developed and shared their experiences regarding the instructional packages referenced in this paper.

REFERENCES

1. Sugarman R., Computer-Aided Instruction. *IEEE Spect.* (1978).
2. Wozny M. J., An experiment on the use of computer graphics in the teaching selected topics from automatic control theory. *Proceedings of the Purdue Symposium on the Applications of Computers to Electrical Engineering Education.* Purdue University, Lafayette, IN (1971).
3. McMullen M. J., Use of computer graphics in EM field courses. *IEEE Trans. Educ.* (1974).
4. Volz R. A., Denver M., Johnson T. J. and Conliff D. C., COINGRAD—Control Oriented Interactive Graphical Analysis and Design. *IEEE Trans. Educ.* **E-17,** (1974).
5. Adams J. A., A comparison of methods for cubic spline curve fitting. *Comput.-Aided Design* **6,** 1–9 (1974).
6. Adams J. A., Computer graphics in mechanical engineering. *Proceedings of the 1978 ASEE Annual Conference,* Event No. 2582 (1978).
7. Wozny M. J., Interactive computer graphics for engineering education. *Prof. Engn* (1978).
8. Musgrave W., Training: CAD courses for RPI students. *Datamation* (1980).
9. Wozny M. J., Computer graphics in universities. 1979 Midcon Professional Program, paper session 28, Chicago, 6–8 Nov. (1979). Available through Electronic Conventions, Inc., 999 North Sepulveda Blvd, El Segundo, CA 90245.
10. Wozny M. J., The RPI interactive computer graphics center after one year. *Proceedings of the 1978 Frontiers in Education Conference,* Lake Buena Vista, FL, 23–25 Oct. (1978).
11. Wozny M. J., Interactive computer graphics for a multi-discipline CAD engineering program. *Proceedings of the First Annual Conference on Computer Graphics in CAD/CAM Systems,* MIT, Cambridge, MA (1979).
12. Gerhardt L. A. and Carlson A. B., Instructional computer graphics in electrical and systems engineering. *Proceedings of the 1978 Frontiers in Education Conference,* Lake Buena Vista, FL, 23–25 Oct. (1978).
13. Frederick D. K., An implementation of NDTRAN on an interactive computer graphics system. *Proceedings of the Tenth Annual Pittsburgh Conference on Modeling and Simulation,* Pittsburgh, PA (1979).
14. Flanagan K. J., Renegades—A computer aided instruction system for electromagnetic theory using interactive graphics. Masters Project Report, Rensselaer Polytechnic Institute (1979).
15. Frederick D. K. and Waag G. L., An interactive graphics program for assistance in learning convolution. *Trans. Comput. Educ. Div. A.S.E.E.* **XII,** (1980).
16. Frederick D. K., Kaufman H. and Wozny M. J., The role of computer graphics in control system studies. *Proceedings of the 1978 Summer Computer Simulation Conference,* Newport Beach, CA, (1980).

17. Wozny M. J., Instructional computer graphics in control system design. *IFAC Symposium on Computer-Aided Design of Control Systems*, Zurich. Pergamon Press, Oxford (Plenary session paper) (1979).
18. Chin C. Y., SLAP—an interactive computer program for analyzing single loop systems. Masters Project Report, Rensselaer Polytechnic Institute (1980).
19. Killeavy W., Interactive computer graphics program for linear systems analysis and optimization. Masters Project Report, Rensselaer Polytechnic Institute (1978).
20. Frederick D. K. and Gerhardt L. A., A computer graphics program for the analysis and design of digital filters. *Proceedings of the 1980 International Conference on Cybernetics and Society*, Cambridge, MA (1980).
21. Kunz R. J., An adaptation of a recursive digital filtering program to classroom use. Masters Project Report, Rensselaer Polytechnic Institute (1980).
22. Kaufman H., Sadeghi T. and Wozny M. J., Interactive graphics simulation for linear quadratic regulator design. *Proceedings of the 1979 Summer Computer Simulation Conference*, Toronto, Canada (1979).
23. Nelson W. E., A streamlined user interface for the UMIST computer-aided control system design suite. Masters Project Report, Rensselaer Polytechnic Institute (1979).
24. Levinn M., Graphics pre and post- processors for SPICE. Term Project for ICAD course, Rensselaer Polytechnic Institute (1980).
25. Frederick D. and Wozny M. J., Computer graphics in electrical engineering at Rensselaer. *Proceedings of the ASEE Annual Conference*, Los Angeles, CA (1981).
26. Feeser L. J., Educational use of computer graphics at Rensselaer Polytechnic Institute. *Proceedings of SHARE 54*, New York, NY (1979).
27. O'Rourke M. J., Johnson R. and Feeser L. J., Computer graphics in education: a case study. *Proceedings of the 2nd Conference on Computing in Civil Engineering*, ASCE 458–460 (1980).
28. Shephard M. S., RPIFEP—an interactive finite element package. *Proceedings of the 1st Chautaugua on Finite Element Modeling* (edited by J. H. Conway) (1980).
29. Shephard M. S., The university's role in meeting industry's CAD/CAM needs. *Proceedings of the 1981 ASEE Annual Conference*, Los Angeles, CA (1981).
30. McKenzie J., Eaton L. and Lewis R., *Interactive Computer Graphics in Science Teaching*. Halstead Press (1978).
31. Bliss F. W. and Hayman G. M., Selecting and implementing a turnkey graphics system. *IEEE Comput. Graph. Applic.* **1**, (1981).
32. Machover C., Neighbors M. and Stuart C., Graphics displays. *IEEE Spectrum* **14**, (1977).
33. Machover C., Neighbors M. and Stuart C., Graphics displays: factors in systems design. *IEEE Spectrum* **14**, (1977).
34. Machover C., A guide to sources of information about computer graphics. *IEEE Comput. Graph. Applic.* **1**, (1981).
35. Status report of the graphics standards planning committee. *IEEE Comput. Graph. Applic.* **13**, (1979).
36. NSF grant SED79-20085. Computer graphics in engineering education, Dr. Gregg Edwards, Program Manager, Division of Science Education Development and Research.
37. NSF grant ISP79-20240-01. University–industry cooperative research center in computer-aided design, Dr Robert Colton, Program Manager for University/Industrial Research, Industrial Program, Division of Intergovernmental Science and Public Technology, NSF.

APPENDIX A

Overview of Center for Interactive Computer Graphics

The Center for Interactive Computer Graphics was established in 1977 as part of the School of Engineering. It exists as a separate administrative unit in the School of Engineering with a commitment: (1) to coordinate the integration of interactive computer graphics into the entire undergraduate curriculum, across all engineering disciplines; (2) to provide a facility for graduate instruction and research; and (3) to develop with heavy industrial support a vigorous research program in computer graphics and CAD/CAM. The Instructional facility in the Center consists of two Prime 750 supermini's and 36 Imlac vector graphics (refresh type) terminals. The remainder of the equipment was obtained as part of the research program and is available only for special instructional programs for funded research.

The research program in the Center for Interactive Computer Graphics is officially called the University–Industry Cooperative Research Program in Computer Graphics and CAD/CAM. It is supported with a 5-year grant from the National Science Foundation [25] and 18 companies to jointly attack important computer graphics and CAD/CAM research questions, as well as address the organizational issues of effective collaboration. Research areas include:

Interactive graphics systems
Geometric design systems
Graphics/Analysis software interface
CAD/CAM interface
Manufacturing applications of graphics
Specific industrial graphics applications
Geometric surface and solid modeling
Geometric data base
Computational geometry

The Center also supports a number of major software packages for analysis and design used in various research projects. Two examples are the NASA IPAD (Integrated Programs for Aerospace-Vehicle Design) software and the Lockheed design software CADAMTH. Currently, four faculty, four full-time research staff, and

Table 1. Equipment complement

Two Prime 750 computers, each with $1\frac{1}{2}$ megabytes (MB) of memory, and a total of three 300 MB disks
36 Imlac Dynagraphic 6220 vector refresh graphics terminals each with 16 K buffers tied to the Prime 750's over 9600 Baud serial lines
A Versatec 1200 A electrostatic printer/plotter and a CALCOMP 1051 4-pen 36 inch plotter tied to the Prime 750's for hard copy
IBM 370/148, with 2 MB memory, 1600 MB disk storage and a channel to channel link to the Central Campus IBM 3033 computer
Two IBM 3250 vector refresh terminals and three IBM 3277 Graphics Attachment storage type terminals with hard copy, all attached to the 370/148
One Prime 500 with 1 MB memory and a 300 MB disk
Two Applied Dynamics Light 50 color raster graphics terminals with 512 × 512 × 8 image memory, and a Lexidata 3400 raster system, all tied to the Prime 500
A DUNN 631 camera system for 35 mm slide, 8 × 10 in. Poloroid, and 16 mm movie films tied to the ADI Light 50 color raster video signal

23 graduate research assistants are directly funded by the research program. An additional 32 faculty support the graphics center through their own funded research projects.

The equipment complement in the Graphics Center is listed in Table 1.

APPENDIX B

Instructional usage 1980–1981

Tables 2 and 3 list the Engineering courses which used computer graphics during the 1980–1981 academic year. They also includes the total terminal hours used and the number of students in each class. Over the two semesters, 4535 students in scheduled classes accumulated 20,239 h on the graphics terminals for an average of 4.5 terminal-hours per student.

No listing is given for students using the system for individual project courses, nor for sponsored research projects.

Table 2. Course usage of CICG computer graphics: Fall 1980

Title and level of course	Number of students	Total terminal hours
General engineering:		
Computing fundamentals (Frosh)	35	427
Thermodynamics I (Soph)	152	57
Mechanics I (Soph)	480	21
Lumped parameter systems (Soph/Jr)	254	365
Electromagnetic theory (Soph/Jr)	137	549
Heat transfer (Soph/Jr)	22	2
Civil engineering:		
Advanced finite element (Grad)	6	105
Soil dynamics (Grad)	11	168
Earth structures and slopes (Grad)	8	85
Foundation engineering (Soph)	22	98
Electrical and systems:		
Computer applications laboratory (Sr)		7
Control systems engineering (Sr)		3
Linear systems (Sr)	83	19
CAD (Sr)	75	3870
Software engineering (Sr)	66	478
Electromagnetic engineering (Sr)	10	12
Discrete time systems (Sr)	161	147
Readings in computer science (Sr)	15	262
Mechanical aeronautical:		
Vibrations (Sr)	17	29
Mechanisms (Sr)	29	217
Computer aided manufacturing (Sr)	15	568
Nuclear engineering:		
Applied atomic and nuclear I (Grad)	12	36
Naval science:		
Naval operations (Soph)		10
TOTAL	1610	7535

Table 3. Course usage of CICG computer graphics: Spring 1981

Title and year	Number of students	Total terminal hours
General engineering:		
Computing fundamentals (Frosh)	683	3531
Thermodynamics I (Soph)	473	25
Mechanics I (Soph)	84	32
Engineering laboratory I (Soph)	300	31
Lumped parameter systems (Soph/Jr)	382	320
Electromagnetic theory (Soph/Jr)	48	452
Heat transfer (Soph/Jr)	261	1
Chemical and environmental:		
Chemical process control (Sr)	116	115
Civil engineering:		
Computer techniques in civil engineering (Sr)		398
Finite elements (Grad)	34	923
Advanced finite element (Grad)	34	73
Electrical and systems:		
Computer applications laboratory (Sr)	80	574
Control systems engineering (Sr)	40	1460
Linear systems (Sr)	167	137
Advanced CAD (Sr)		740
Artificial intelligence (Grad)	56	1079
CAD (Sr)		1663
Digital systems processing (Grad)	21	359
Software engineering (Sr)	66	80
Readings in computer science (Sr)	15	421
Mechanical aeronautical:		
Vibrations (Sr)		83
Design with composite materials (Sr)	20	2
Computer aided manufacturing (Sr)		163
Nuclear engineering:		
Applied atomic and nuclear I (Grad)		1
Naval science:		
Naval operations (Soph)	45	41
TOTAL	2925	12,704

Comput. & Educ. Vol. 5, pp. 193 to 200, 1981
Printed in Great Britain

0360-1315/81/040193-08$02.00/0
Pergamon Press Ltd

LOW COST COMPUTER GRAPHICS IN ENGINEERING EDUCATION

RICHARD L. PHILLIPS
Computer, Information, & Control Engineering, The University of Michigan,
Ann Arbor, MI 48109, U.S.A.

Abstract—The Apple II is a personal computer which provides 6 color, raster graphics via a 280 h × 192 v frame buffer. A user-programmable MOS Technology 6502 CPU addresses 48 K bytes of RAM, 12 K of ROM, and 4 K of memory-mapped I/O. This system has been evaluated in a variety of applications for which one normally assumes higher resolution, higher cost graphics devices are needed.

Examples were drawn from computer aided design, color microfilm previewing, cartography, and aircraft synthesis. The results were encouraging; low resolution raster scan graphics is surprisingly effective for a wide range of applications. As a result, a computer graphics laboratory, with a cluster of 10 Apples as its nucleus, was formed and has been functioning successfully for 4 terms.

INTRODUCTION

Overview

There are never enough terminals—a familiar refrain for anyone who teaches interactive computer programming. The terminal shortage is especially acute for courses in computer graphics, mostly because each unit costs at least $5000. I teach a course in "highly interactive" computer graphics where a student will spend between 30–40 h at a terminal for each problem. With a class size of 50 students, the demand for terminal access is feverish.

Several months ago, I set out to remedy the terminal shortage problem by investigating the personal computer as a possible display device. The main attraction of personal computers is their price. If they can be made to do useful work, there is a real potential for cost effectiveness. In our context, usefulness is measured in terms of demanding scientific problem solving for teaching and research. Computer graphics plays an important role in this process. This paper presents the results of a several month evaluation of the potential of a personal computer for doing serious work.

The Apple II computer

One has only to leaf through a recent copy of BYTE magazine to appreciate the bewildering array of personal computers now available. The "big three" among these are the TRS-80, Commodore Pet and the Apple II. The Apple II was selected for our purposes because it assumes a minimum user naivete and provides true computer graphics capability (beware of alphanumeric manipulations masquerading as graphics). Other Apple II features that appeal are:

1. a versatile resident monitor.
2. 48 K bytes of user-programmable RAM.
3. 12 K bytes of user-redefinable ROM.
4. two 8 K byte frame buffers for defining raster scan images of 280 h × 192 v resolution. These frame buffers can be context switched under program control to produce animation effects.
5. a full BASIC interpreter with graphics extensions.
6. a variety of peripherals including a floppy disk, printer, light pen, PROM programmer, and communications interface.

The basic Apple II price is about $2000 including a communications interface and a floppy disk. While this is not exactly an "out of pocket" amount, it is nonetheless an attractive price to an educator who would otherwise have to pay about $5000 (Tektronix 4010) simply for a graphics terminal with no computing power.

Project goals

The goals of the evaluation project were to:

1. Determine the range of applications for which the low, 280 × 192 graphics resolution is acceptable.

2. Evaluate the stand alone computing power of the Apple II for "real" problems.
3. Study the Apple II as a distributed computing element in a time sharing system.

STAND-ALONE CAPABILITIES

Capacity and speed

The full BASIC interpreter has a complete complement of string capabilities, mathematical functions, and graphics commands. In principle, any problem that is solved on a large system can be solved on the Apple. There are, however, the practical limitations of program size and speed of solution to consider. Even with 48 K bytes of user RAM, indefinitely large programs cannot be constructed. But Apple BASIC uses dynamic memory management (better than FORTRAN!) and stores the program text in a compressed, tokenized form so that 100 variable, 1000 statement programs are certainly feasible. Speed is another thing, however. As with any interpreter, speed of execution can be somewhat slow, requiring perhaps minutes for a problem that would take a few seconds on a large system. (This comparison may not be too unfavorable, however, if one is dealing with a heavily loaded host.)

Examples

Two problems from computer aided design were chosen to exemplify stand-alone capabilities of the Apple II. These problems, as others described later, have a heavy graphics emphasis, both on input and output. Both examples are described by Chasen[1] and are representative components of more extensive programs used in industry.

Often one wishes to approximate roughly defined two-dimensional contours by a series of blended analytic functions; ellipses are a common choice. Figure 1* shows the layout of such a problem. The user has been prompted to specify Y1 and X3, the points where the two ellipses will cross the y and x axes, respectively. The line y = Y2 is the ordinate of the blending point and X2B is the minimum abscissa where the blending may occur. Once the x value is selected, blending can take place within a range of limiting slopes. At this point the two ellipse segments are drawn.

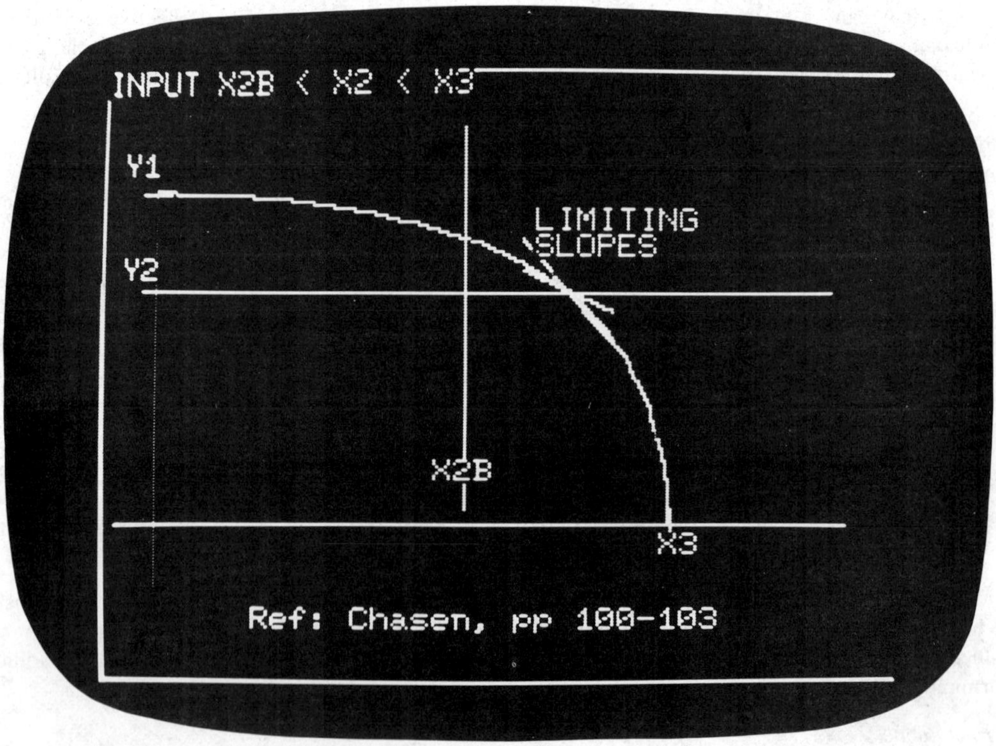

Fig. 1. Blended ellipses.

* All figures have been produced by directly photographing the Apple display screen.

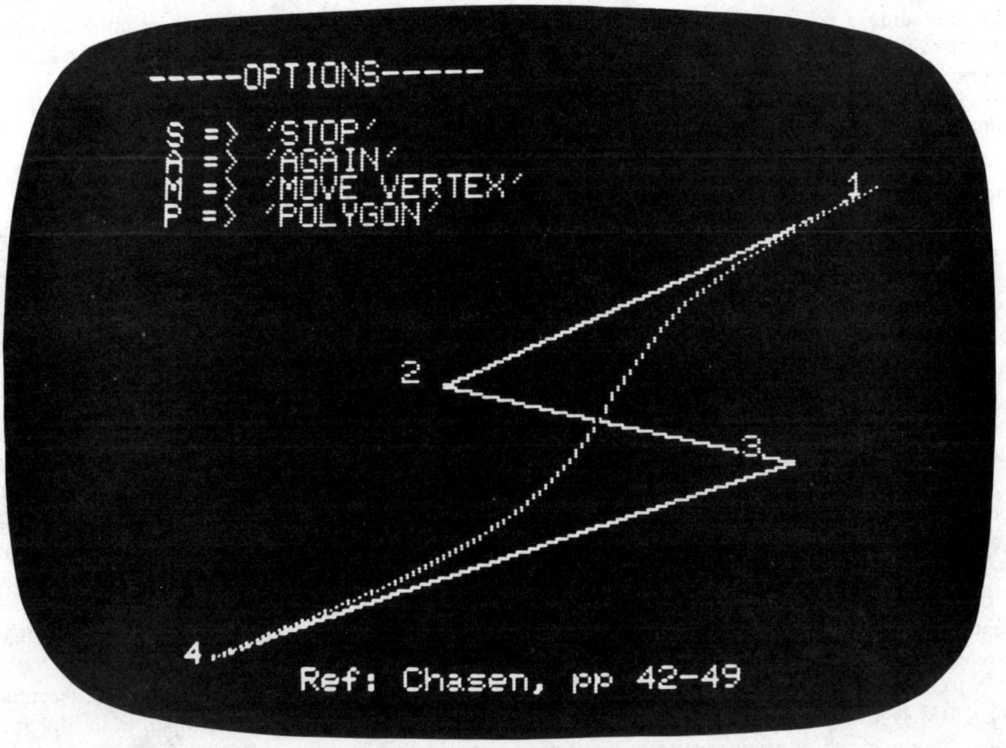

Fig. 2. Bezier polynomial.

All input necessary to produce Fig. 1 was done graphically by rapidly moving a non-destructive cursor to the desired point and striking a key. The curves are computed and displayed in less than a second, making the entire process highly interactive. On a color display the two ellipses are drawn in red and blue to facilitate distinction.

Another example of two dimensional curve manipulation is shown in Fig. 2. Bezier polynomials are defined by a control polygon; points 1–4 denote its vertices. The Bezier polynomial thus determined will be a smooth curve passing through the first and last vertices where it is also tangent to the initial and final line segments. By moving any of the control vertices, the designer can rapidly develop the desired curve; the value of the technique depends on a high degree of interactivity.

In Fig. 2 the control vertices were imput graphically. The computation of the Bezier curve requires repeated evaluation of the factorial function and for the case shown required about 10 s to compute and draw. This is too slow to be considered interactive. One would like to be able to move a selected vertex around and have the new Bezier curve follow it almost immediately. Here is a case, then, where the computing power of the Apple II (really the BASIC interpreter) is not sufficient to the task. The situation could be improved if a compiled program were being run or, of course, if the time critical portions of the algorithm were coded in 6502 assembly language.

Yet another possibility is to program the Apple to behave as a graphics terminal, do all computation on a large host system, and send the coordinates of the computed curve to the Apple. Unless the communications bandwidth is sufficiently high, however, plotting the curve can be as slow as doing the entire task on the Apple. An alternative possibility is to devise a division of labor between the host and the Apple that optimizes interactivity. This approach is discussed later.

TERMINAL CAPABILITIES

Communicating with a host

With little difficulty the Apple II can be programmed to function as a computer terminal, provided a communications interface is available. There are several suppliers for these boards; they range in price from $60 to $180. Because of the farsighted Apple design it is possible to access the communications board from a BASIC program as well as directly from an assembly language program. Thus, all sorts of information transfer possibilities exist; sending data and programs back and forth between host and terminal; running an Apple program that reads data from a host file, and vice-versa; and down loading a cross-assembled program from host to Apple. All of the above examples suggest transfer of just character information. Since the Apple II has graphics capabilities, however, its use as a graphics terminal has been investigated.

Simulating a Tektronix terminal

Apple II computer graphics is of the raster scan[2] variety. An 8 K byte region of RAM is designated as the graphics bit map or frame buffer. The frame buffer can be thought of as a memory mapping of the video screen. Each point on the screen that is illuminated corresponds to a bit being "on" in the frame buffer. The resolution afforded by an 8 K frame buffer corresponds to approx. 280 columns × 192 rows of potentially lighted dots, or pixels, on the screen. By context switching, the Apple can be directed to graphics mode whereby its video output reflects the contents of the frame buffer. Since the frame buffer is user RAM it can be written in by a program. In fact, a line between any two points in the 280 × 192 grid is produced by turning on those pixels in the frame buffer that give the best approximation to the line. The user need not do this directly; low level software is provided for this purpose. To operate as a graphics terminal, then, data sent by a host computer that describes a line must be passed to the Apple software for pixel mapping in the frame buffer.

The line-producing data sent by the host could be designed specifically for an Apple, but this would be restrictive and short-sighted. The Apple could function as a graphics terminal only on those host computers having that special program. Rather, the approach was to develop a program for the Apple that causes it to emulate all terminals in the Tektronix 4010 family. Software to drive Tektronix terminals abounds; any host computer that supports graphics probably supports the Tektronix. It matters not whether the resident software is PLOT-10 (a Tektronix product) but only that the data stream sent to the terminal is in Tektronix format[3].

A ROM-based interpreter called TEKSIM* allows the Apple II to behave as a Tektronix terminal. TEKSIM is sensitive to the special mode characters that cause a Tektronix to operate in alphanumeric mode, graphics mode, graphics input mode, etc. Naturally, not all Tektronix features can be emulated, most notably the resolution which ranges from 1024 × 1024 to 4096 × 4096. On the other hand, the Apple has features such as color, which amount to an enhancement of graphics capabilities. These will be discussed later.

Figures 3 and 4 are examples of Apple emulations of graphics output that was originally designed for Tektronix terminals. The range of applications for which Apple graphics resolution is acceptable is clearly depicted. Figure 3 is typical output from a general aviation synthesis program [4] and shows a three-view of a proposed airplane design. Figure 4 is an example from cartography and shows that distinguishing features of counties and lakes are clearly identifiable.

Extensions to Tektronix software

The Apple II can produce graphics in 6 colors and TEKSIM supports this capability. To use this feature requires modification of host computer software because existing Tektronix programs would not normally provide for color selection. This modification is usually a trivial task, however, because to send color information to the Apple through TEKSIM requires only that 3 characters be sent by the host. In line with the Tektronix convention, these are an ESC (escape), DC2 (device command 2), and an ASCII integer from 0–5. Any lines drawn after this command will be in the color specified by the third character (a look-up table maps this integer into a corresponding color). Substituting a DC3 for the second character in the above sequence causes the screen background to be set to the specified color upon next erasure. Tektronix PLOT-10 software provides an easy way to send such character sequences via the TOUTST subroutine [5]. Other host graphics libraries provide similar capabilities.

Figure 5 is an example of using the color select features (reproduced here in black and white) of TEKSIM where the Apple was used to preview a slide that was to be produced on an FR-80 film recorder. The pie chart in Fig. 5 was shaded by individual lines and required many minutes of connect time at 300 baud. Since a sector of a circle can be specified by center location, radius, and limiting angles, only that information need be sent to the Apple and the shading could be done locally. This leads to the notion of distributed computing.

DISTRIBUTION OF TASKS

Graphic output primitives

In deciding on tasks to distribute among computing elements, one criterion is to select those operations that do not require feedback. That is, a small amount of information can be sent from host

* TEKSIM is available from ABW Corporation, Ann Arbor, MI. EDUCOM members are entitled to a special purchase arrangement.

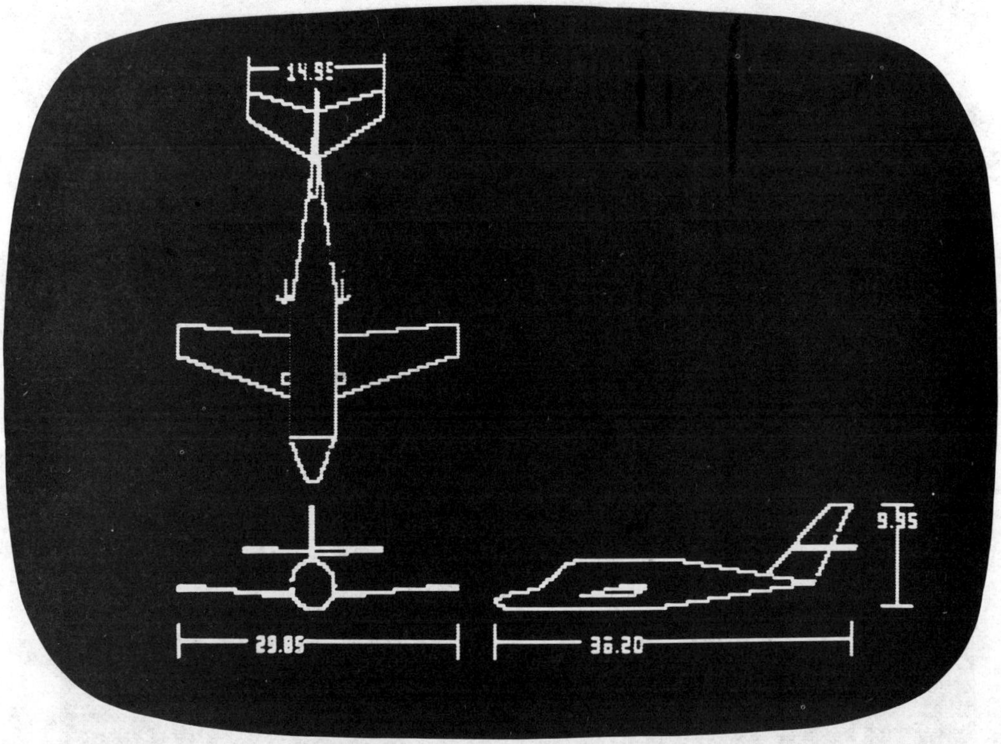

Fig. 3. Airplane synthesis

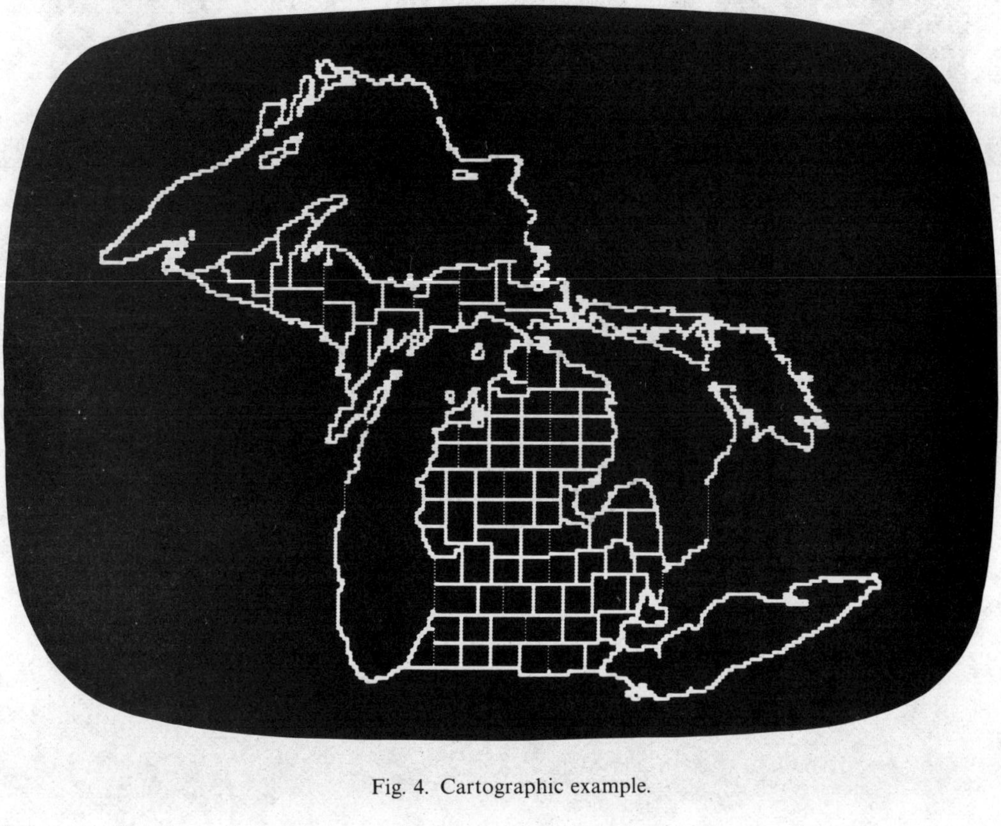

Fig. 4. Cartographic example.

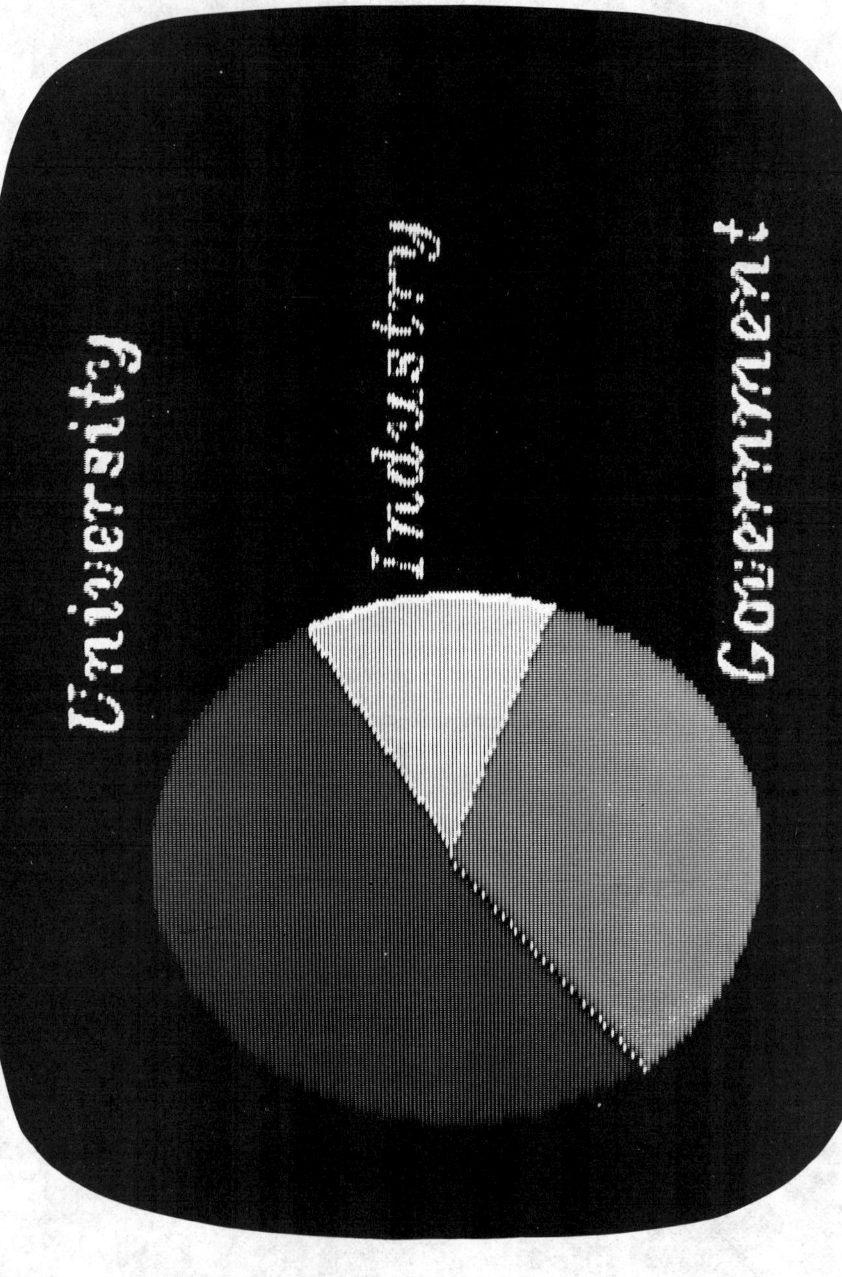

Fig. 5. Color slide preview.

to terminal, say, and the task specified can go to completion without further communication. In graphics there are many candidates for such tasks; they involve inherently graphical operations and we call them graphic primitives. Obvious candidates for primitives are a rectangle, a circle, conic sections, etc. Shaded figures such as bars, pie charts, and general polygons are even more useful primitives because of the time involved in the shading process. Several of these primitives have been implemented in conjunction with TEKSIM resulting in a significant speed increase over straight terminal performance. So far the bar, circle, and pie chart have been implemented as primitives. This means that when a certain character sequence is received from the host, TEKSIM jumps to an external routine to produce the requested graphical output. An example of such a routine is the one that implements the algorithm of Badler [6] for drawing a shaded circle. This algorithm requires only addition, subtraction and shifting to produce a pie chart, so it is ideal for a microprocessor environment. The algorithm is fast; for the Apple a disk covering the entire screen is drawn in less than a second. By contrast, sending the shading lines from a host, using the same algorithm, requires 5 min!

Additional output primitives are planned for use with TEKSIM. In addition to a shaded general polygon, an axis generation routine for graph drawing is being developed. By sending only the extrema of the dataset to be plotted, the primitive will lay out an axis system, determine "nice" scale intervals for each axis, and apply corresponding tick marks and labelling. Then, one or more datasets can be plotted using different symbols or line colors.

Graphic input primitives

TEKSIM supports graphic input through the use of a joystick which propels a non-destructive tracking cross around the screen. Through a software "hook", however, any other graphic input device can replace the joystick. Upon command from the user an appropriate machine language module is downloaded from the host. TEKSIM then accesses this module whenever the host application program requires graphical input. In this way we can support graphic input from a light pen, a variety of graphic tablets and, for a handicapped student who can only use a mouth stick, from the keyboard.

CONCLUDING REMARKS

Findings

There is no doubt that the Apple II can do serious, constructive work in an educational and research environment. The notion of task distribution has proven extremely useful, especially for computer graphics. Moreover, the graphics resolution of the Apple II appears to be satisfactory for a wide range of applications. Only a few cases have been encountered where information is lost because of resolution.

The Apple II graphics Laboratory

Armed with the above findings and a modest amount of money we marshalled all the resources needed to assemble a computer graphics laboratory with a nucleus of ten Apple II computers. All Apples are equipped with TEKSIM and are connected to our Amdahl 470V/8 through a special front-end computer called a *remote data concentrator* (RDC). Each Apple communicates with the host at 9600 baud and has its own floppy disk for local file storage. The laboratory also includes a CORVUS 11A 10 mb hard disk system. All Apples in the cluster can communicate with a special "disk mother" Apple through the RDC for rapid file transfer. The Corvus system provides the equivalent of 87 Apple disks of on-line storage. Finally, a specially modified Houston Instrument COMPLOT electrostatic copier provides the cluster with hard copy capability. Each Apple has direct queued access to the copier through remote switching.

The future

This is really just a beginning. While the laboratory was initially established to teach computer graphics, it has been used by many courses having both graphical and non-graphical requirements. It is widely used by freshman computing classes, by design classes and for teaching engineering graphics.

Being interested in computer graphics, I am looking forward to enhancing the capabilities of the cluster beyond just emulating Tektronix terminals. This involves using the local processing power of the Apple to do such things as selective erase, dynamic graphics, local zoom and pan, graphics scrolling, and improved color manipulation.

I expect to see this cluster concept replicated manyfold, not just at Michigan but elsewhere. It represents considerable capability for a modest investment.

REFERENCES

1. Chasen S. H., *Geometric Principles and Procedures for Computer Graphics Applications.* Prentice–Hall, Englewood Cliffs, NJ (1978).
2. Newman W. M. and Sproull R. F., *Principles of Interactive Computer Graphics*, Second Edition, Chapters 15–19. McGraw–Hill, New York (1979).
3. Anon, *Tektronix 4014 and 4014-1 Computer Display Terminal Users Instruction Manual.* Tektronix Inc., P.O. Box 500, Beaverton, OR.
4. Galloway T. L. and Smith M. R., General aviation design synthesis utilizing interactive computer graphics. Society of Automotive Engineers Business Aircraft Meeting, Wichita, KS (1976).
5. Anon, *Tektronix PLOT-10 Terminal Control System Users Manual.* Tektronix Inc., P.O. Box 500, Beaverton, OR.
6. Badler N. I., Disk generators for a raster display device. *Comput. Graphics Image Process.* **6,** 589 (1977).

Comput. & Educ. Vol. 5, pp. 201 to 217, 1981
Printed in Great Britain

0360-1315/81/040201-17$02.00/0
Pergamon Press Ltd

THE UNIFORM BEAM

DAVID F. ROGERS[1], DAVID CHALMERS[2]* and J. D. RICHARDSON[3]

[1]Aerospace Engineering Department, U.S. Naval Academy, Annapolis, MD 21402, U.S.A.,
[2]RCNC Office, Mechanical Engineering Department, University College London,
Torrington Place, London WC1 E7JE, England and
[3]Computer Aided Design/Interactive Graphics Group, Division of Engineering and Weapons,
U.S. Naval Academy, Annapolis, MD 21402, U.S.A.

Abstract—The development and use of a minicomputer-based interactive graphics program for a uniform beam arbitrarily loaded and arbitrarily supported. The program uses the linear stiffness matrix technique to solve for the reactions, bending moments, shear stress and deflection in the beam and supports. At University College London the program is implemented in FORTRAN on a PDP 11/40 using a VT 11 display. Interactively loading, supporting, changing the characteristics of the beam is accomplished using a light pen. At the U.S. Naval Academy the program is implemented in FORTRAN on a PDP 11/45 with an Evans and Sutherland Picture System. Interactively loading, supporting, changing the characteristics of the beam is accomplished using an analog tablet. The stiffness matrix analysis subroutine is the same in the two implementations; the graphics is, of course, similar in concept but different in implementation. In both cases the programs are educationally oriented. At UCL the program is presently being used with first and second year students. At the U.S. Naval Academy the program is used in Strength of Materials at the sophomore/junior level.

INTRODUCTION

At the university level computer aided design and interactive graphics can be an effective tool for providing experience. As an example, consider the title problem of the paper. The uniform beam or, in its more complex form, the non-uniform beam, is met by engineering students in many guises, e.g. the ship as a beam, an aircraft wing as a beam, etc. Generally the uniform beam is first met in a course in strength of materials. Here the student is taught a variety of methods for solving for the support reactions, bending moment, shear distribution, etc. He is generally asked to do a half dozen problems for each method. In this way he masters the calculation procedure. However, the student seldom develops physical or engineering intuition with respect to the effects of changing types and/or location of supports, moving loads, changing moment of inertia, length of beam, etc. under these circumstances. It is neither practical nor reasonable to require the student to hand calculate enough problems by whatever method to develop this intuition. Interactive computer graphics can be used to overcome this lack, i.e. it can be used to foster engineering experience or intuition in undergraduate students.

By using a highly interactive computer graphics program, a student can easily solve and analyze 100 problems in an hour. These problems can be posed to him in a very logical way and in a logical order. For example, the student might be asked to determine what happens to the reactions, bending moment, shear, etc. on a uniform beam simply supported at the ends with two concentrated loads at $\frac{1}{3}$ and $\frac{2}{3}$ span when the right hand load is incremented from its initial value to some final value. Similarly, he might be asked how many concentrated loads are required to approximate the effects of a uniform load. If the program is highly interactive, all this can be accomplished in very short order indeed. This will encourage the student to ask his own "what if" questions and explore the answers. The end result will be greater physical and engineering intuition and knowledge.

ANALYSIS OF BEAM

Concept

It is clear from the requirements of the program that the analysis of the beam needs to be as general as possible to cope with any distribution of loads and supports of different types. It was therefore decided to treat the beam as an assembly of finite beam elements, the nodes being arranged at supports and at any discontinuity of load. At the development stage it was adequate to have a prismatic beam and so it was possible to build the beam model interactively on the display and then arrange the program to search for nodes and carry out the necessary sorting into elements. With the

* Present address: Ministry of Defence, Ship Department, Room 21, Block B, Foxhill, Bath BA1 5AB, England.

nodes defined, it is then possible to calculate the stiffness of elements between nodes. The boundary conditions and external loads are then used to solve the set of simultaneous equations to give the displacements and rotations of the nodes. Retracking is then carried out to find the bending movement and shear force at the nodes. Interpolation is used to find responses at points between nodes.

The stiffness matrix

The beam element between nodes is defined in Fig. 1 with orthogonal x and y axes as shown and nodes numbered 1 and 2. At each node there are two degrees of freedom: a translation positive in the y direction and a rotation, positive anti-clockwise. For an isotropic elastic material, the Young's Modulus, E, is constant and for a prismatic beam the second moment of area of a section about the z axis, I, is also constant so the stiffness k of the element may be written in matrix form as

$$\mathbf{K} = EI \begin{bmatrix} \frac{12}{l^3} & \frac{6}{l^2} & \frac{-12}{l^3} & \frac{6}{l^2} \\ \frac{6}{l^2} & \frac{4}{l} & \frac{-6}{l^2} & \frac{2}{l} \\ \frac{-12}{l^3} & \frac{-6}{l^2} & \frac{12}{l^3} & \frac{-6}{l^2} \\ \frac{6}{l^2} & \frac{2}{l} & \frac{-6}{l^2} & \frac{4}{l} \end{bmatrix}$$

The degrees of freedom in order are

Translation at node 1
Rotation at node 1
Translation at node 2
Rotation at node 2.

With all the nodes and consequently the lengths of each element defined, the stiffness matrices for each element are calculated and merged into the beam stiffness matrix **K** as shown below for 3 elements, (a, b, and c) and 4 nodes, and thus 8 degrees of freedom.

$$\mathbf{K} = EI \begin{bmatrix} \mathbf{K}_{a11} & \mathbf{K}_{a12} & \mathbf{K}_{a13} & \mathbf{K}_{a14} & 0 & 0 & 0 & 0 \\ \mathbf{K}_{a21} & \mathbf{K}_{a22} & \mathbf{K}_{a23} & \mathbf{K}_{a24} & 0 & 0 & 0 & 0 \\ \mathbf{K}_{a31} & \mathbf{K}_{a32} & \mathbf{K}_{a33} + \mathbf{K}_{b11} & \mathbf{K}_{a34} + \mathbf{K}_{b12} & \mathbf{K}_{b13} & \mathbf{K}_{b14} & 0 & 0 \\ \mathbf{K}_{a41} & \mathbf{K}_{a42} & \mathbf{K}_{a43} + \mathbf{K}_{b21} & \mathbf{K}_{a44} + \mathbf{K}_{b22} & \mathbf{K}_{b23} & \mathbf{K}_{b24} & 0 & 0 \\ 0 & 0 & \mathbf{K}_{b31} & \mathbf{K}_{b32} & \mathbf{K}_{b33} + \mathbf{K}_{c11} & \mathbf{K}_{b34} + \mathbf{K}_{c12} & \mathbf{K}_{c13} & \mathbf{K}_{c14} \\ 0 & 0 & \mathbf{K}_{b41} & \mathbf{K}_{b42} & \mathbf{K}_{b43} + \mathbf{K}_{c21} & \mathbf{K}_{b44} + \mathbf{K}_{c22} & \mathbf{K}_{c23} & \mathbf{K}_{c24} \\ 0 & 0 & 0 & 0 & \mathbf{K}_{c31} & \mathbf{K}_{c32} & \mathbf{K}_{c33} & \mathbf{K}_{c34} \\ 0 & 0 & 0 & 0 & \mathbf{K}_{c41} & \mathbf{K}_{c42} & \mathbf{K}_{c43} & \mathbf{K}_{c44} \end{bmatrix}$$

The matrices within the dotted lines are the element stiffnesses and these are summed with the overlapping parts of the adjacent element matrix within the solid lines. The extension to any number of elements is obvious.

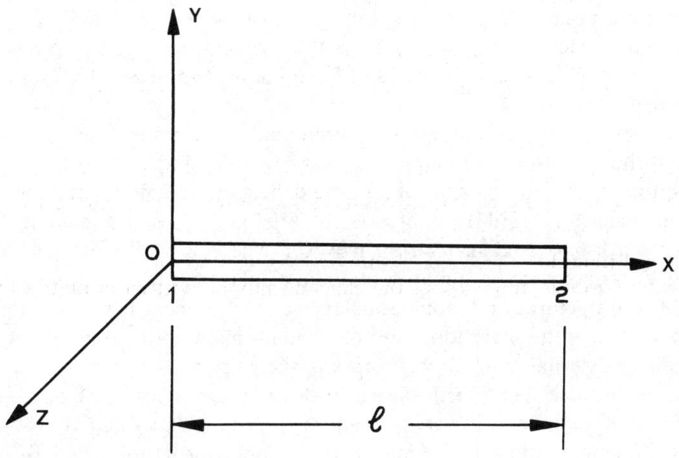

Fig. 1. Beam element.

Only a linear solution may be obtained from such an approach but it was felt that that was all that was necessary for undergraduate teaching. If it is required to analyze a beam with anisotropic properties or large deflections then the purpose of the analysis would be different and a completely fresh approach to the problem would almost certainly be justified.

Types of Support

Within the context of the simple beam problem, three types of support are allowed.

Pinned—allows rotation but not translation
Sleeve—allows translation in the y direction but not rotation*
Fixed—neither translation nor rotation allowed.

At the beginning of the analysis these are only used to suppress relevant degrees of freedom. For n nodes, the general problem has $2n$ degrees of freedom and so there will be $2n$ simultaneous equations to solve. The supports constrain certain of these degrees of freedom. For the solution, where these are to be suppressed, the relevant rows and columns of **K** are set to zero off the diagonal and 1 on the leading diagonal. Equivalent nodal loads are also set to zero. This avoids the tedious requirement of repacking the beam stiffness matrix after deleting suppressed degrees of freedom.

Types of loads

Three types of loads can be specified:

Point
Uniformly distributed
Triangular (linearly varying distributed loads).

The first speaks for itself, and is used directly as a nodal load. The latter two are not directly usable as the method implicitly can only accept external loads at the nodes. It is necessary to calculate the equivalent nodal forces and moments which give the *same nodal* translations and rotations as the distributed load: these nodal loads may then be used in the analysis to obtain the *nodal* displacements. The nodal loads may be found statically by taking a beam element with the required distributed load but with *fixed* ends: the fixed end support forces and moments are then equal and opposite to the equivalent applied nodal forces and moments. To find displacements between nodes, it is necessary at the end of the analysis to add the displacements due to the distributed load between fixed ends to those calculated from the nodal loads.

Calculations

The means of setting up the parameters to obtain a solution have now been described. Specifically we have a stiffness matrix **K** for the beam with non-existent degrees of freedom suppressed, and a set of nodal loads which may be defined as a column matrix **P**, with, in general, a force and moment at each node, but with these being zero where a support is encountered. It will be noted that as the problem is defined, there will be nodes only at supports and loads so for n elements we will have in general $2n$ loads, i.e. **K** is $2n \times 2n$ and **P** is $2n \times 1$. The solution in the form of displacements (a

* This is not an ideal description of an unlikely support case, but is adequate in the context.

translation and rotation at each node) can be found from inverting $\mathbf{P} = \mathbf{K}\,\mathbf{R}$ where $\mathbf{R}$ is the $2n \times 1$ column matrix of displacements, i.e. $\mathbf{R} = \mathbf{K}^{-1}\,\mathbf{P}$. As the problem is set up and provided the beam is at least statically supported (i.e. sufficient degrees of freedom are suppressed to hold the beam in space) $\mathbf{K}^{-1}$ will always exist.

We now have a full set of translations and rotations at the nodes and it is only necessary to interpolate between these (noting that slope must vary with x^2 and deflections with x^3), and to add displacements due to distributed loads, to obtain the deflection and slope diagram for the beam. The other two diagrams, shear force and bending moment, are found by first calculating the internal nodal forces and moments $\mathbf{p}$ for each element from $\mathbf{p} = \mathbf{K}\,\mathbf{r}$ where $\mathbf{K}$ is the element stiffness matrix as previously defined, and $\mathbf{r}$ is the column matrix of nodal displacements identically equal to the relevant constituents of $\mathbf{R}$. From the force and moment balance at each node, the support forces and moments may be calculated, and then the shear force and bending moment at any point along the beam may be found from the known external and support forces in the conventional way.

A FORTRAN subroutine called STIFF based on these concepts was developed. This subroutine is used without change in both the University College London (UCL) and the United States Naval Academy (USNA) implementations of an interactive graphics program called BEAM. The graphics portions of the programs are different because of different graphics hardware.

UCL OPERATING ENVIRONMENT

Computer hardware

The UCL program BEAM is implemented on a DEC PDP 11/40 with 32K core operating under RT11 version 2C. With the size of core, some of which has to be permanently set aside for a graphics buffer, it is necessary to overlay subroutines in the store, and in fact there is a very small root segment program whose only function is to pass control to one of three overlay segments in one overlay region under implicit commands from the operator, depending on what function is wanted. The three overlaid segments contain subroutines to:

Set up the initial graphics display with a "menu" of available supports and loads.
Carry out the analysis of the beam displayed.
Scale and plot the required results on the screen.

The graphics display attached to the PDP 11/40 is a DEC VT11 with unswitched light pen. This has a display matrix of 1024 × 1024 points on the screen giving adequate definition for this type of

Fig. 2. UCL facility.

problem. However, to change the display it is necessary to change the display buffer from the program and replot; to facilitate this the picture is built up of subpictures which are deleted and redrawn independently.

Attached to the computer are two RK05 disc drives, a line printer, and Decwriter keyboard. The Decwriter is only required for initial setting up and for numerical input, and one disc drive is needed to hold the program disc. A Calcomp plotter is available onto which the picture on the graphics display may be dumped (via a second PDP 11) but so far this facility has not been needed. The facility is shown in Fig. 2.

UCL graphics program

The graphics displayed on the screen consist basically of three parts:

The menu of options and commands.
A picture of the beam with its supports and loads to be analyzed.
A plot of the solution.

All commands are activated by pointing the light pen at the required word on the screen. A typical display is shown in Fig. 3. Note that as the light pen is not switched, it is easy to activate the wrong command and the CONFIRM command at the bottom of the screen is a necessity. The process is to point to a command which then flashes with the CONFIRM command; if it is correct, point to the YES command (which can be reached easily) and the action is carried out. Where possible the program is written so that illogical commands cannot be activated when the light pen points to them.

When the program is started only the menu is displayed (see Fig. 3). The commands on the right of the screen are those required to set up the beam model. The sequence is commenced by pointing to INITIALISE and then entering Young's Modulus, second moment and length of beam via the keyboard. The values displayed in the top right corner are then changed from the default values to those entered. The beam is shown on the screen as a line of standard length 250 screen units and the resultant scale factor is used for all further x direction scaling.

The beam model is completed by pointing to the SUPPORT or LOAD commands in any order followed by the required type of support or load. Numerical magnitudes of load and lengths of distributed loads are input from the keyboard on request from the program. A typical completed model is shown in Fig. 3. Loads are scaled relative to each other, the first load drawn being made 50 screen units high.

On completion of the model the analysis is carried out by pointing to the command CALCULATE, and when this is done the program responds with "Calculated" on the keyboard. Any of the display commands on the left of the screen may now be used in any order. The process is to point to

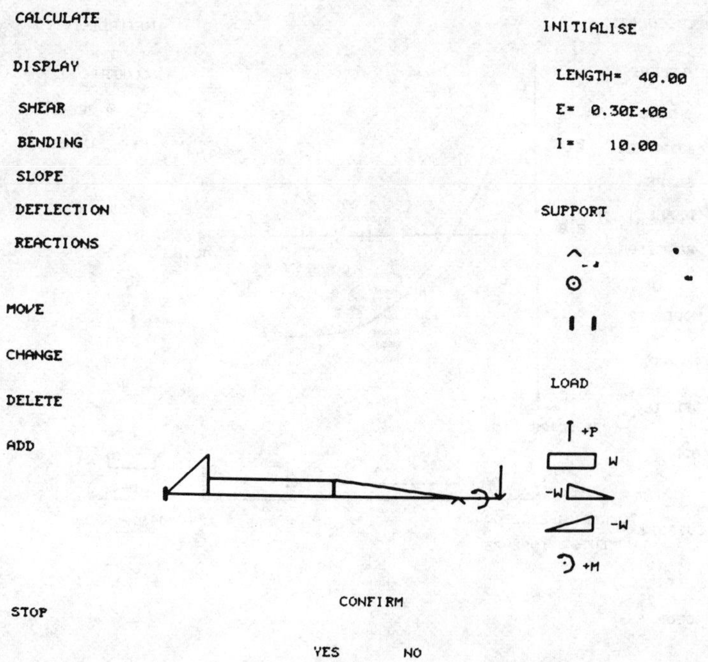

Fig. 3. Typical UCL display with command menu and completed beam model.

DISPLAY and then the required display type. The curve is then drawn to scale above the beam. The sequence of displays from Shear Force to Deflection is shown in Fig. 4(a)–(d). Note that the display type command remains bright as a reminder of what is displayed; also the values of the reactions may be displayed beneath the beam at any time. The reaction values will be erased when any changes are made to the beam model but can be restored at will. The curve displayed will change with changes to the beam model. The vertical scale of the curve displayed is arranged so that the curve fills as nearly as possible a scale of −1, −2 or −5 to 0 to +1, +2 or +5 times some power of 10. This will be apparent from a study of Fig. 4. The curve is drawn from 100 vectors which gives sufficient definition.

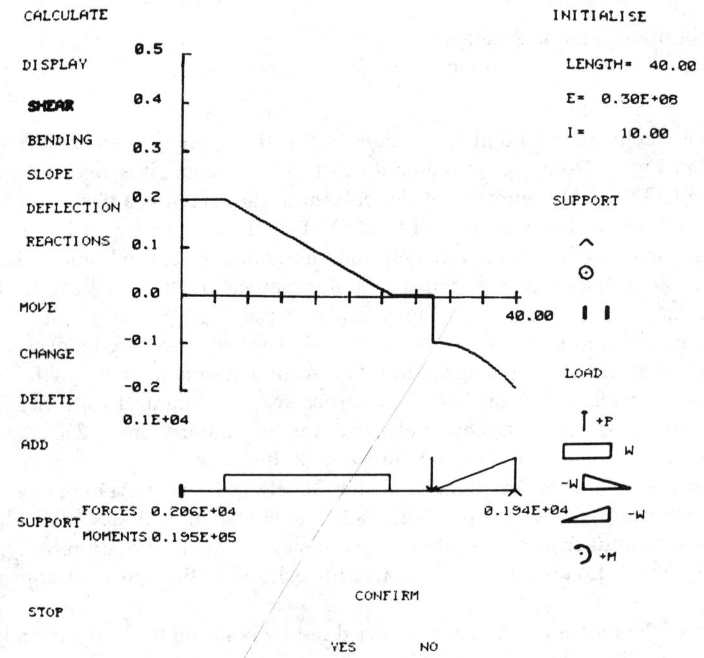

(a)

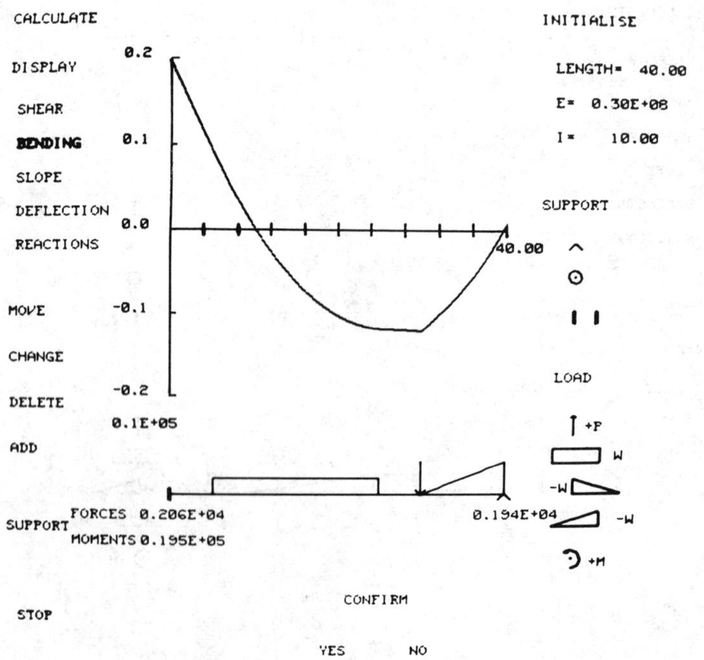

(b)

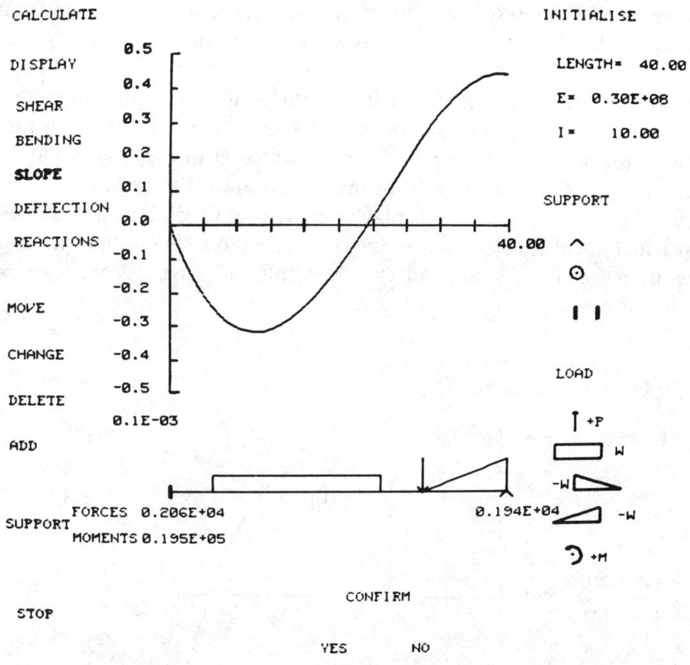

(c)

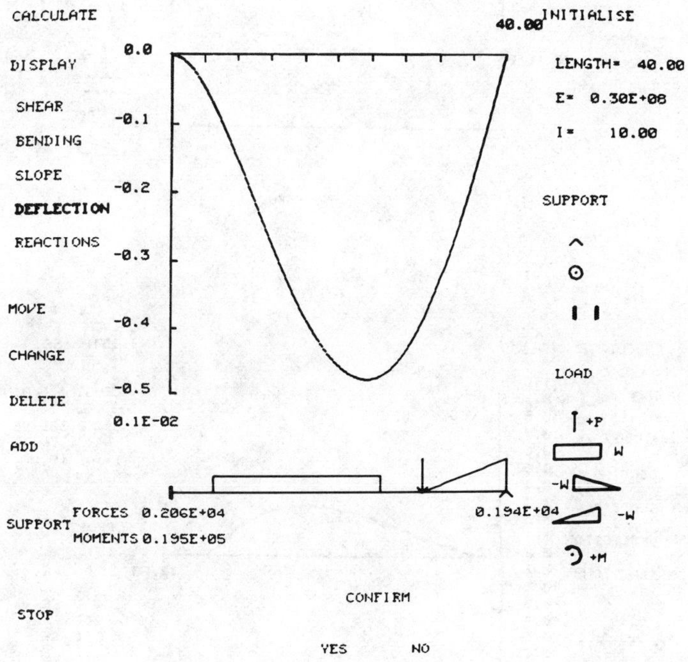

(d)

Fig. 4. UCL graphical display of calculated results.

When the beam model is complete and a curve displayed, the model may be changed by pointing to one of the commands on the lower left. DELETE allows any load or support to be removed by pointing to that load with the light pen. ADD transfers control back to the right side of the screen for a support or load to be added. The CHANGE command enables the magnitude of a load or the length of a distributed load to be changed by entering a new numerical value from the keyboard; the load is identified on the screen by pointing to it with the light pen. It is important at this stage to make sure the beam is adequately supported or the program will fail on inverting the stiffness matrix. After each of these commands is completed the displayed picture of the beam will be updated, and the curve displayed above will be rescaled and replotted accordingly. Other current curves may be displayed at any time. (All are held concurrently in an array and are transferred as required to the display buffer.)

The MOVE command works a little differently. On activation of that command it is necessary to point to a support or *point* load load on the beam and then to a new position on the beam to which it is to be moved. Once this is done, the new position is printed at the keyboard and the support or load moves in 25 screen unit increments (i.e. 1/10 beam length) until it reaches the required position. As it moves it is redrawn on the beam and the displayed curve replotted at each increment. The time delay of approx. 1.5 s per increment is solely that required to re-analyze the beam. The scale is not replotted so if not used with care it is easy to send the curve off the screen. This very powerful facility is illustrated as well as it can be statically in Fig. 5.

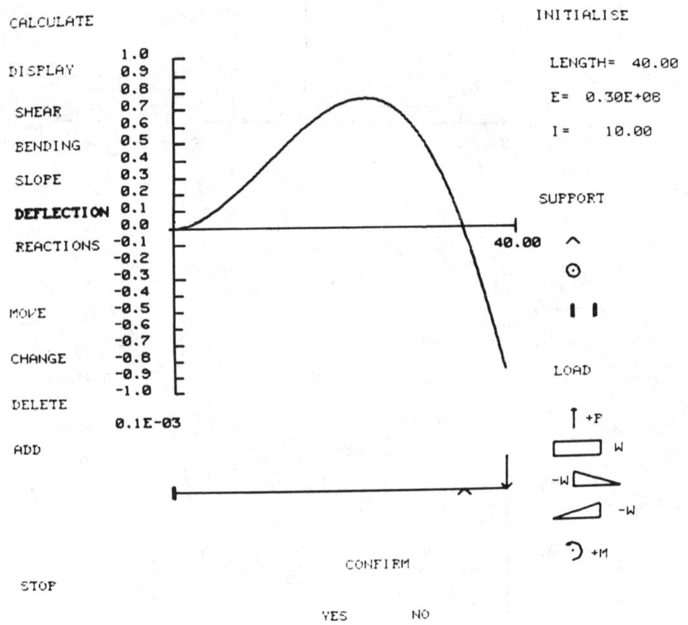

(a)

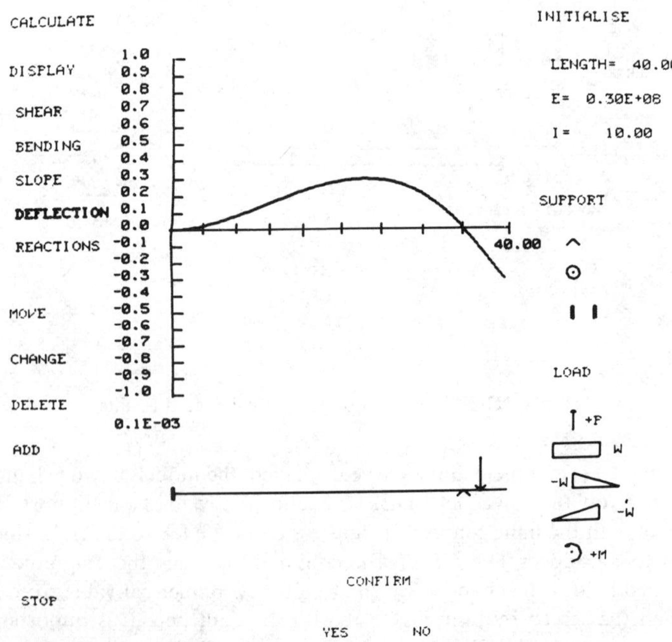

(b)

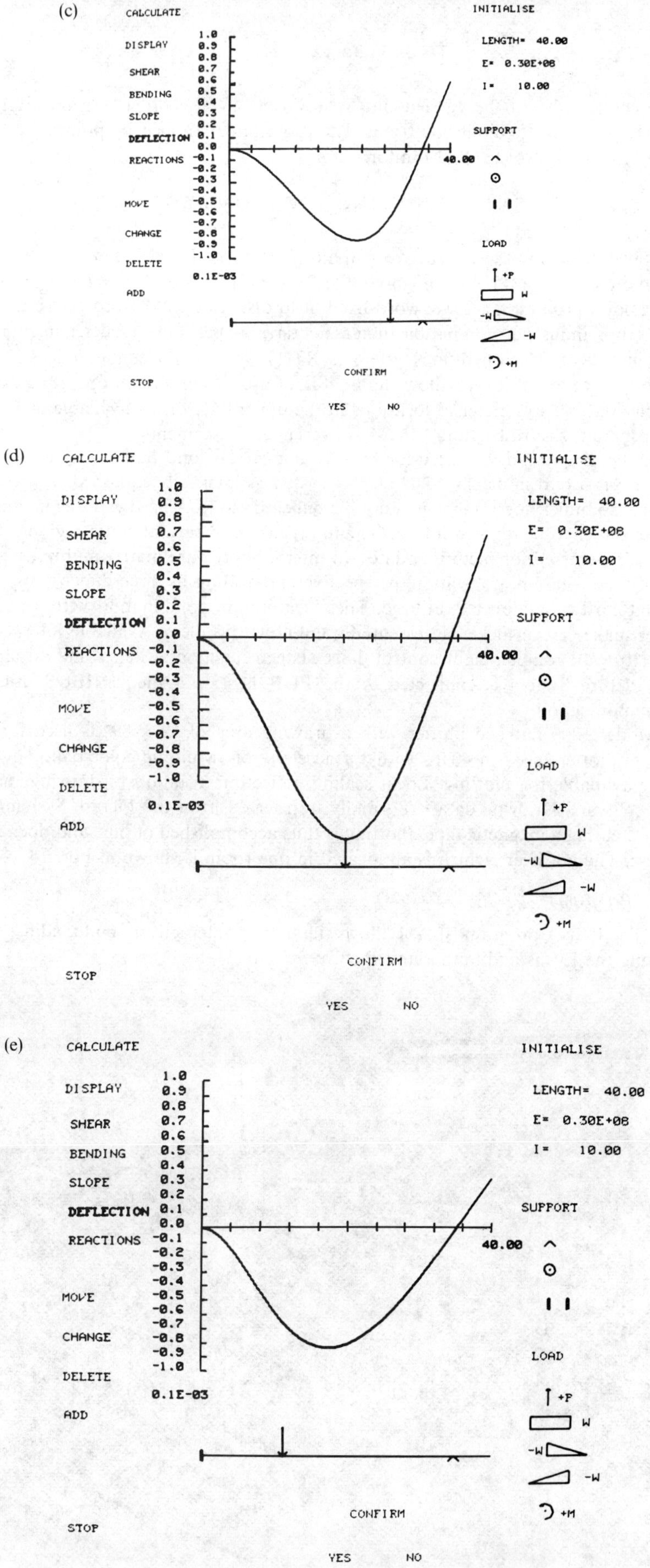

Fig. 5. UCL effect of moving a load along the beam.

All the above commands can be carried out at any time in any order, the only limit being a maximum of 20 beam elements along the beam. The program is stopped by pointing to the STOP command which returns control to the Monitor.

USNA OPERATING ENVIRONMENT

Computer hardware

At the U.S. Naval Academy the interactive graphics portion of BEAM is written in FORTRAN and implemented on a PDP 11/45. As configured, the PDP 11/45 has 64K core memory, a 1K Cache memory, floating point processor, a 256K word fixed head disc, two 1.2M word cartridge discs, DEC tape, 9 track 800 bpi industrial compatible magnetic tape, paper tape reader/punch and various communication interfaces. The operating system is RT-11 version 3B configured as a single user system. This implementation of RT-11 allows up to 28K of user program and operating system in the lower memory plus data arrays assigned locations in the upper 36K of the available 64K of memory. Because of this program size restriction, BEAM is overlaided in segments.

The 3-D computer graphics device used for BEAM is an Evans and Sutherland Picture System I. The Picture System is a refresh display. The display system is internally equipped with 16K of 36 bit refresh buffer. Refresh buffer operation is in a double buffered mode. A hardware segmentation option allows the refresh buffer to be divided into a dynamic region and several static regions. The regions may be individually accessed for picture update. An internal hardware matrix multiplier provides for fast, efficient real time rotation, translation, perspective and scaling in three dimensions. An internal three-dimensional hardware clipper is utilized. These features in combination with separate update and refresh rates make screen flicker an essentially unknown problem. Available interactive devices include a small (10 × 10″) tablet, eight control dials, sixteen function switches and an alphanumeric keyboard. The Picture System is connected to the PDP 11/45 via the UNIBUS utilizing DMA transfers for communication.

A Xynetics Model 1200 flat bed plotter with a drawing area of 59 × 89″ is used for hard copy output. Maximum plotter speed in 40 ips with 1 *g* acceleration. Multiple color ballpoint, wet ink or felt tip pens are available for plotting. Local scaling, reflection, rotation of drawings are available through plotter software. Drawing data is normally transferred from the Picture System/PDP 11/45 to the plotter by creating a magnetic tape. Plotting is thus accomplished off-line and does not "tie-up" the design system. The hardware which is all located in one room is shown in Fig. 6.

USNA Graphics Program

General outline. The USNA program BEAM allows the user to interactively build, adjust, and solve a simple beam using the Evans and Sutherland Picture System.

Fig. 6. USNA facility.

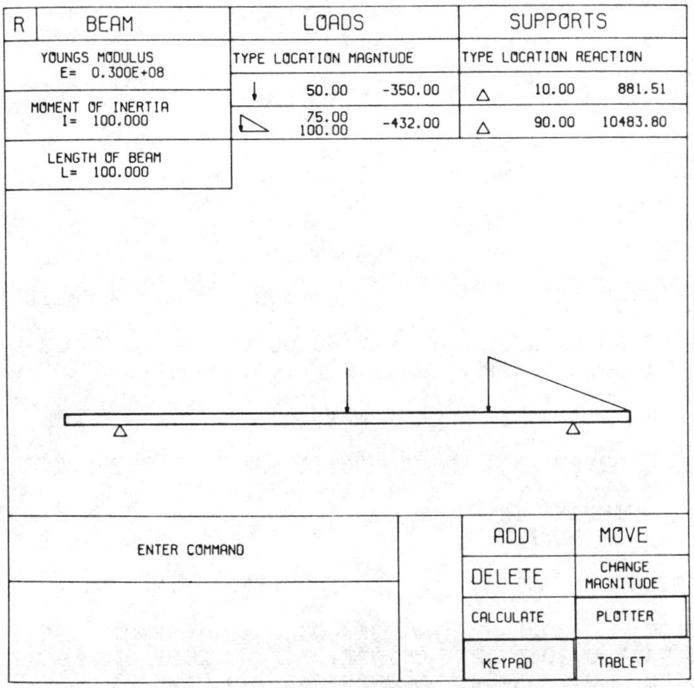

Fig. 7. USNA Xynetics plotter copy of display.

A beam is built by inputting its characteristics and selecting and positioning loads and supports along its length. These beam characteristics, supports and loads can be interactively changed at any time during this building process. The program can then be directed to solve the beam, at which time it calculates and displays the reactions at each support along with the shear force, bending moment, slope and deflection curves for the beam. Maximum values for these curves are also listed.

At any time during the building of a beam its current configuration values may be saved on a disc file for reloading in subsequent runs. This capability allows the user to accumulate a repertoire of beam problems for demonstration purposes or the study of a class of beam problems by saving those characteristics common to the class of beams and adding the distinguishing characteristics for each member of that class.

A plotter copy of the display picture (see Fig. 7) and/or a printer listing of the current beam data (see Fig. 8) can be generated at any time during the program run.

After a solution is displayed, the user can interactively change specific characteristics of the beam, its loads and supports and then quickly obtain the solution for the new configuration. During a program run, the current values of the beam characteristics and the values and locations of the supports and loads are displayed at all times.

Options. Three characteristics of a beam can be set by the user; its length, its Young's modulus and its moment of intertia. The types of supports which can be built are fixed, pin and roller (sleeve), and the types of loads available are point, uniform, triangular right, triangular left distributed loads, and concentrated moment. The user may add, delete or move supports and loads and change the magnitude of the loads and beam characteristics. There are two methods for setting positions and magnitudes. The first simply asks the user to point to a position on the display using the tablet and pen of the Picture System. This action indicates a location along the beam or a value according to some current scale. The second method incorporates the use of a keypad simulation routine. With this option the user is presented with a keypad menu and can enter exact mixed number values by pointing with the tablet pen to the digits and symbols which make up that number. TABLET and KEYPAD input modes are set by the appropriate command menu selection.

Interactions. The user has the Picture System tablet and pen along with the PDP-11 console as input and interactive devices. Most interactive input can be accomplished using the tablet and pen.

When the program is run it first asks the user whether he is building a new configuration or wants to start with data saved from a previous run. If he is using old data the program will ask for the file name, open that file, load its data and update the display to represent the beam configuration at the time the data was saved. The user may then continue from that point with changes, deletions, additions, etc.

BEAM PROGRAM RUN 31-JAN-80

YOUNGS MODULUS= 0.300E+08
MOMENT OF INERTIA= 100.000
LENGTH OF BEAM= 100.000

LOADS

TYPE	POSITION	MAGNITUDE
CONCENTRATED	50.00	-0.3500E+03
TRIANGULAR LEFT	75.00 100.00	-0.4320E+03

SUPPORTS

TYPE	POSITION	REACTION
SIMPLE PIN	10.00	0.8815E+03
SIMPLE PIN	90.00	0.1048E+05

POSITION	DEFLECTION	SLOPE	BENDING MOMENT	SHEAR FORCE
0.00	0.292E-02	-0.292E-03	-0.469E-01	-0.781E-02
2.94	0.206E-02	-0.292E-03	-0.239E-01	-0.781E-02
5.88	0.120E-02	-0.292E-03	-0.919E-03	-0.781E-02
8.82	0.344E-03	-0.292E-03	0.221E-01	-0.781E-02
10.00	-0.931E-09	-0.292E-03	0.312E-01	-0.781E-02
10.03	-0.860E-06	-0.292E-03	-0.253E+01	0.882E+03
14.71	-0.137E-02	-0.289E-03	-0.415E+04	0.882E+03
17.65	-0.221E-02	-0.284E-03	-0.674E+04	0.882E+03
20.62	-0.304E-02	-0.276E-03	-0.933E+04	0.882E+03
23.56	-0.383E-02	-0.265E-03	-0.119E+05	0.882E+03
26.47	-0.459E-02	-0.252E-03	-0.145E+05	0.882E+03
29.44	-0.531E-02	-0.237E-03	-0.171E+05	0.882E+03
32.38	-0.599E-02	-0.219E-03	-0.197E+05	0.882E+03
35.32	-0.660E-02	-0.198E-03	-0.223E+05	0.882E+03
38.26	-0.715E-02	-0.175E-03	-0.249E+05	0.882E+03
41.21	-0.763E-02	-0.149E-03	-0.275E+05	0.882E+03
44.15	-0.803E-02	-0.121E-03	-0.301E+05	0.882E+03
47.09	-0.834E-02	-0.905E-04	-0.327E+05	0.882E+03
50.00	-0.856E-02	-0.572E-04	-0.353E+05	0.882E+03
50.00	-0.856E-02	-0.571E-04	-0.353E+05	0.532E+03
52.94	-0.867E-02	-0.218E-04	-0.368E+05	0.532E+03
55.88	-0.868E-02	0.150E-04	-0.384E+05	0.532E+03
58.82	-0.858E-02	0.534E-04	-0.399E+05	0.532E+03
61.76	-0.837E-02	0.934E-04	-0.415E+05	0.532E+03
64.71	-0.803E-02	0.135E-03	-0.431E+05	0.532E+03
67.65	-0.757E-02	0.178E-03	-0.446E+05	0.532E+03
70.59	-0.698E-02	0.222E-03	-0.462E+05	0.532E+03
73.53	-0.626E-02	0.268E-03	-0.478E+05	0.532E+03
75.00	-0.585E-02	0.292E-03	-0.485E+05	0.532E+03
75.00	-0.585E-02	0.292E-03	-0.485E+05	0.529E+03
79.41	-0.441E-02	0.362E-03	-0.444E+05	-0.235E+04
82.35	-0.328E-02	0.401E-03	-0.349E+05	-0.408E+04
85.29	-0.206E-02	0.429E-03	-0.205E+05	-0.567E+04
88.24	-0.775E-03	0.440E-03	-0.172E+04	-0.710E+04
90.00	0.140E-08	0.437E-03	0.115E+05	-0.789E+04
90.00	0.129E-05	0.437E-03	0.115E+05	0.259E+04
94.12	0.178E-02	0.427E-03	0.358E+04	0.132E+04
97.06	0.303E-02	0.425E-03	0.821E+03	0.583E+03
100.00	0.428E-02	0.425E-03	0.170E+00	-0.122E-01

Fig. 8. USNA printer listing of the beam configuration.

If the user is building a new beam configuration the program assumes he will first want to set the characteristics of the beam to be studied. The keypad menu is displayed and the user asked to enter the Young's modulus, moment of inertia, and length of his beam, as shown in Fig. 9. If he skips to the selection of another command at this point, default values are inserted for these characteristics.

The user adds or changes the configuration of his problem by first selecting from a command menu and then following instructions as they are displayed. For instance, if the ADD command is selected, the user is next asked to choose from a menu whether he wants to add a support or load to the beam. If he indicates his intention to add a load, a menu of the five load type symbols is presented (Fig. 10a) with instructions to select one. Similarly for ADDing a support (Fig. 10b). Once a load type is selected, the input mode (tablet or keypad) determines the procedure. If tablet mode is in effect, the corresponding symbol becomes the screen cursor and the user is instructed to position it along the beam. When it has been positioned appropriately, the user sets its position by closing the pen switch. With a double ended load the left side is positioned first, the load symbol "rubber banded" along the beam and the right side set. After a load position is set its magnitude is rubber banded in the vertical direction and is set by closing the pen switch when the magnitude is at the desired value. During this process the load position and magnitude values are listed in the top center of the display and the values for the load being currently set are dynamically updated in this list. An initial load magnitude scale is set and it is adjusted dynamically so that the current largest load magnitude fits into the beam display area.

If keypad input mode is in effect the program will display a keypad menu and ask the user to input position and magnitude values by building the corresponding numbers with the keypad.

The selection and positioning of supports is accomplished in the same manner as with loads. Support position values are listed at the top right side of the display and the currently active support

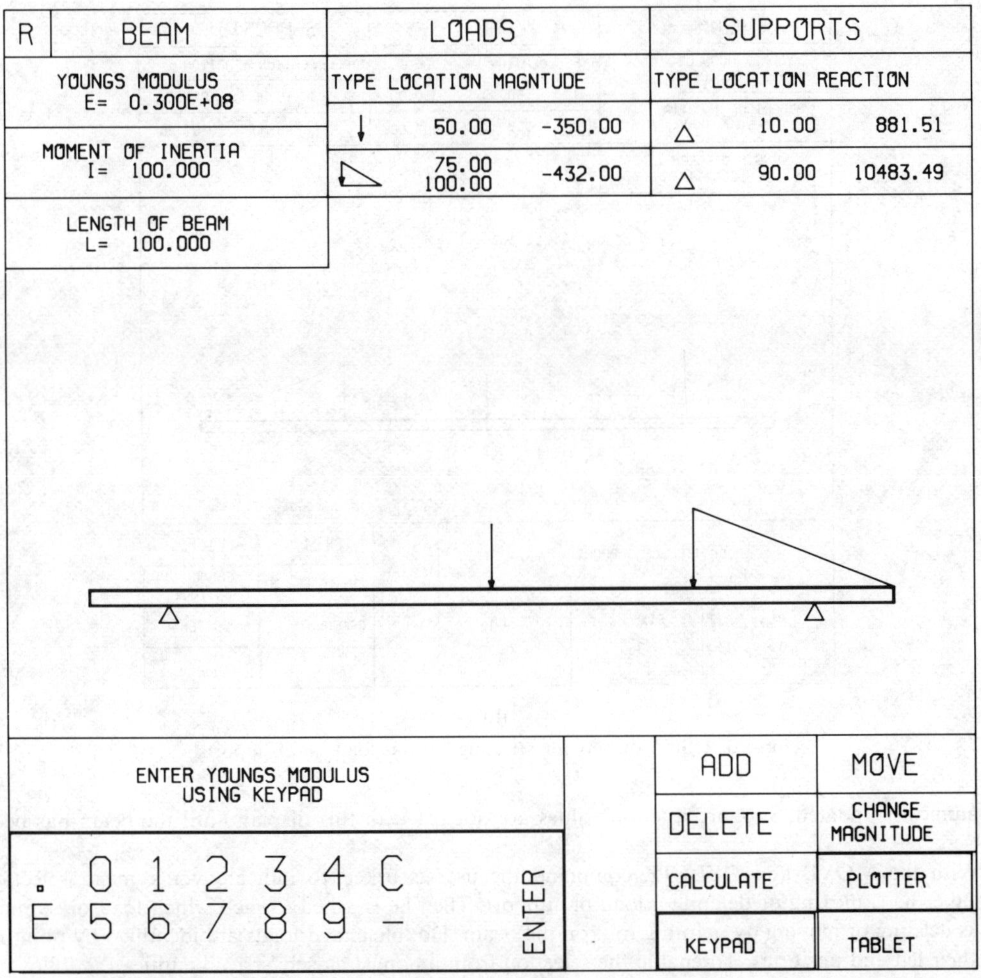

Fig. 9. USNA keypad input.

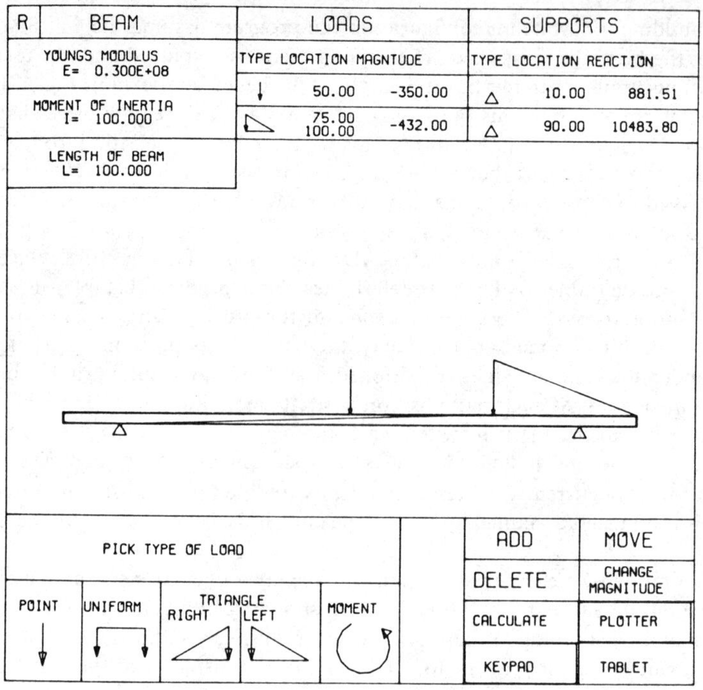

(a)

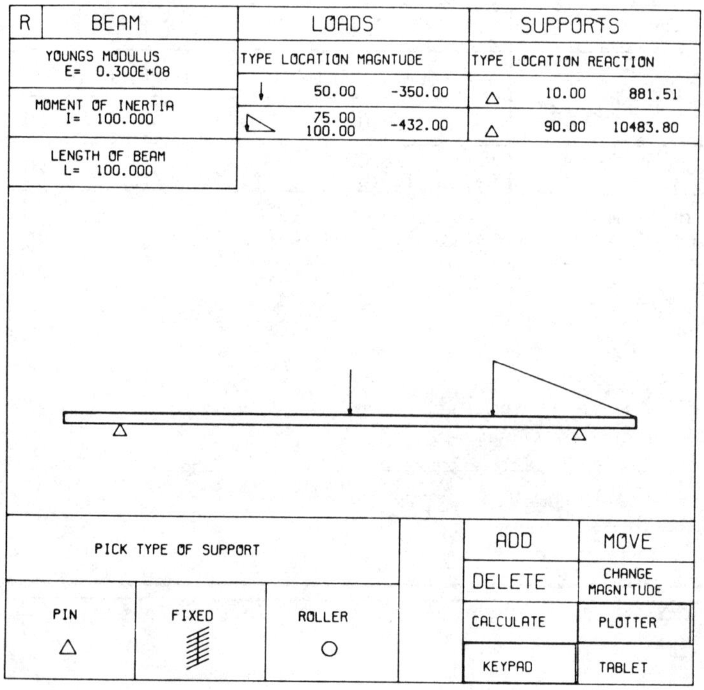

(b)

Fig. 10. USNA display for selecting various loads and supports.

dynamically updated. Support reaction values are not listed in this display until the beam has been solved.

With the MOVE and DELETE command the user is asked to indicate via a menu selection whether he is moving or deleting a load or support. Then he is asked to pick which load or support he is deleting or moving by pointing to it on the beam. Double ended loads are identified by pointing at their left end positions. To enable the selection from amongst closely spaced entities the following verification sequence is used. The indicated load or support just selected is blinked. The user is asked to verify the blinking symbol as his choice as shown in Fig. 11. If he indicates that it is not, the blinking load or support is temporarily removed from consideration and the user is asked to select again. When a selection is finally verified, the program continues. If the command is DELETE the selected entity is deleted. If the MOVE command is active and the keypad method has been selected, the keypad menu is displayed and is used to set the new position. If the direct tablet method is active, the load or support symbol picked becomes the screen cursor and is repositioned in the same manner as with the ADD command.

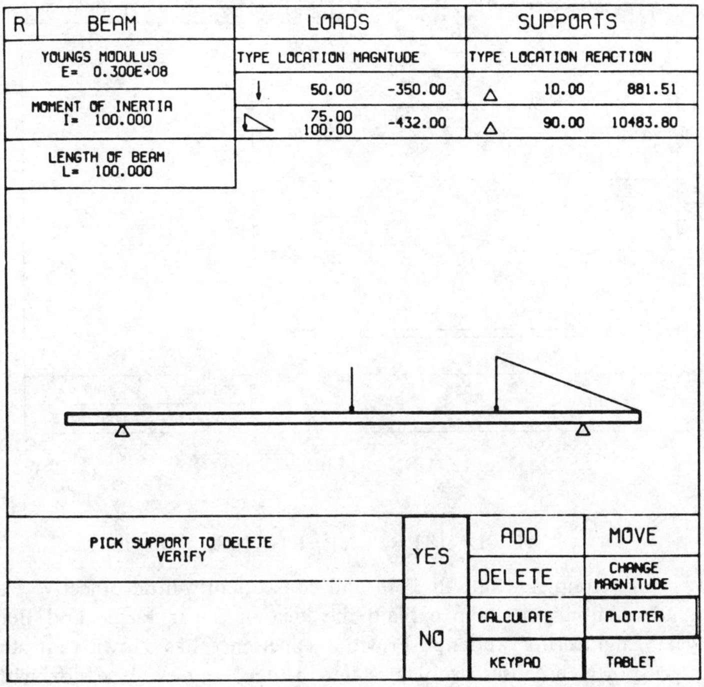

Fig. 11. USNA display showing $\substack{Y\\N}$ verification menu.

Selection of the CHANGE MAGNITUDE command allows the user to change the beam characteristics or load values. The beam characteristics can only be changed using the keypad method, load magnitudes can be changed with either the keypad or direct tablet methods.

The PLOTTER command lets the user make a hard copy plot on the Xynetics plotter of the current display. When this command is selected the user is asked to enter the file name for an intermediate display file to be created on disc. The current Picture System display data is then written to this file which can be further processed to generate the plot.

Picking the CALCULATE command instructs the program to solve the beam as it is then configured. If enough data has not been supplied, a message to that effect is displayed. When sufficient data is available the program solves the problem and changes to a second display as shown in Fig. 12. This second display, called the solution display, lists the loads and supports as in the first display but includes the reaction forces at each support. The deflection, slope, bending moment and shear force curves are also displayed along with a listing of their maximum values. A smaller version of the beam configuration is also displayed under the curve plots.

With this solution display another command menu is provided for generating Xynetics plots, for obtaining a printer listing of the current configuration data, and for saving a disc file of the current data for later use. A fourth command, CONTINUE, allows returning to the initial display.

During the execution of the program command menu selections are global. That is, if the user selects a new command in the middle of another command sequence, the old sequence is discarded and the new one initiated. No values are permanently updated until a command sequence is completed. The program can be restarted at any time by picking the RESTART command block in the upper left corner of the display.

The program uses values as they are entered. The user is therefore responsible for using consistent units in his input values and for interpreting the units of the output values.

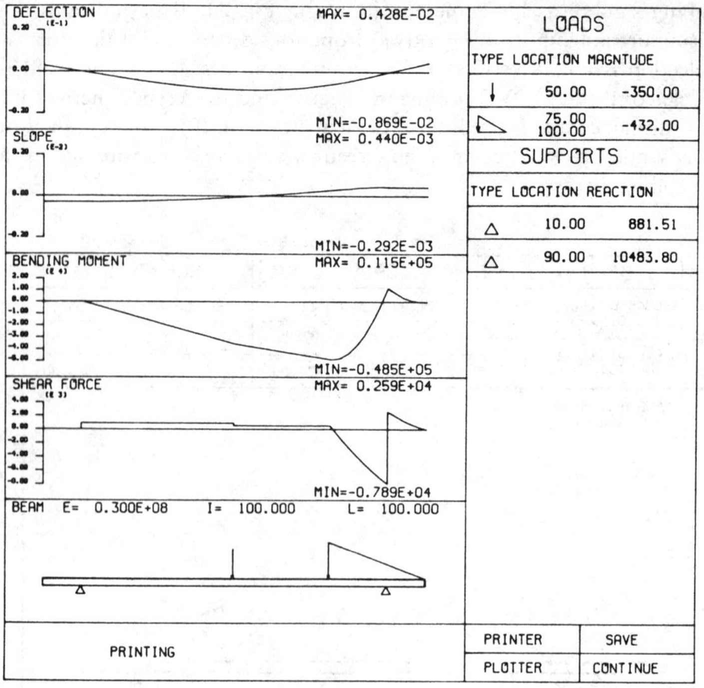

Fig. 12. USNA solution display.

UCL USER EXPERIENCE

The program was only completed late in 1978 and consequently little objective experience is yet available. It is intended initially to help explain the idea of Shear Force and Bending Moment diagrams to first year Engineering students. Previous experience has shown that students find the concept difficult to grasp, which causes problems later in their courses. A session with a member of staff manipulating the program followed by some time trying it out individually appears to be helping, but with only limited experience, it is not possible to be more definite. Certainly it does no harm, and simply taking students out of the normal lecture theatre environment to see something different raises their enthusiasm.

One particular aspect which bears fruit is the demonstration of a single point load moving along a simply supported beam. Displaying first the deflection diagram and then the slope diagram dispels forever the student myth that the maximum deflection is immediately below the load!

The program will continue to be used in the years ahead for first year students and possible also for other groups and it will then be seen if the effort was worthwhile. However, indications so far are that the program is very effective.

USNA USER EXPERIENCE

The graphics part of the BEAM program was completed in late 1979 and immediately used (complete with minor bugs) in a Strength of Materials class with some 130 students and 6 instructors. The program was demonstrated to groups of 20 students by the individual instructors during normally scheduled laboratory sessions. Although not required to do so, students were encouraged to return and use the program on their own time. A member of the computer graphics staff was made available to assist them. Some 19 students utilized the program on a voluntary basis. These students plus the course instructors accounted for some 26.5 h of usage. A typical student session lasted 30–45 min. In all cases, both students' and instructors' comments have been very favorable.

During the spring semester the program is being used with some 200 students in the same Strength of Materials course. Based on the previous semester's usage, a more organized approach is being used. For example, the demonstration during the scheduled laboratory period is organized to illustrate specific concepts and points made previously in the classroom, to reinforce the results of a previously conducted hands-on laboratory experiment by building a beam which allows comparison with the experimental results. The voluntary individual sessions are being more forcefully encouraged by providing a set of specific problems and variations on these problems to get the student started.

Again, as in the case of the usage at UCL, it is too early to provide objective experience on the educational use of the program. However, it can probably safely be said that it can't hurt.

CONCLUSIONS

Two different implementations of graphics programs based on a single analysis subroutine have been successfully completed at two different locations using two significantly different graphics devices.

The difficult and time consuming part of the implementation is the graphics display program, not the analysis routine.

The program represents an excellent demonstration to both engineering and non-engineering students of the power of computer aided design and interactive graphics.

Although it is too early to quantify results, reaction from both students and faculty to the use of the program has been very favorable. Correctly and carefully used, it appears as if programs such as this can be effective teaching tools.

Comput. & Educ. Vol. 5, pp. 219 to 227, 1981
Printed in Great Britain

0360-1315/81/040219-09$02.00/0
Pergamon Press Ltd

COMPUTER GRAPHICS IN CIVIL ENGINEERING AT RPI

MARK S. SHEPHARD

Center for Interactive Computer Graphics, Rensselaer Polytechnic Institute, Troy, NY 12181, U.S.A.

Abstract—The use of interactive computer graphics in civil engineering education at RPI is discussed. Emphasis is placed on how specific software packages are used in courses to increase a student's understanding of basic problem behavior and to reduce the effort required to generate meaningful problem inputs for computer solution.

INTRODUCTION

Since its opening, approx. 3 years ago, RPI's Center for Interactive Computer Graphics[1,2] has played a constantly increasing role in our students' education. All RPI engineering students are introduced to computer graphics in their freshman year and continue to use it throughout their entire undergraduate education. This paper discusses some of the specific applications of interactive computer graphics in the civil engineering curriculum.

As is the case with any computer terminal, an interactive computer graphics terminal represents an interface between the computer and the user. However, an interactive graphics terminal represents a superior interface because it allows the user to communicate with the computer via means as simple as pointing and can display volumes of results in the form of easily understood pictures. Therefore, computer graphics represents an important tool that can be used in education to both teach the student and to increase their working efficiency.

There are two key ingredients required before computer graphics can be incorporated into a curriculum. First, there is the computer hardware. This includes the computer, the graphics devices, hardcopy device, and input devices. (The hardware of the RPI graphics center is discussed in Refs[1,2].) Second, is the software, that is the computer programs needed to make the hardware do what is desired. Thus, after a university has purchased the required hardware, it must still obtain the required application software. This is not a simple task since there is not a large amount of good educational graphics software available and its development is time consuming and expensive. However, through the efforts of interested faculty and students it is possible to develop such software and make it available for student use. The following subsections discuss how some graphics software packages, developed primarily at RPI, are used in civil engineering education.

PRE-ENGINEERING

Before a student has even selected civil engineering as his major, he will have used interactive computer graphics in several courses. Each engineering freshman is required to take a computing fundamentals course. A substantial portion of this course is devoted to teaching the basics of computer graphics and having the students write some simple graphics programs. In addition, the students will use instructional graphics programs in several other pre-engineering courses. Of particular interest to prospective civil engineers are the programs used in the mechanics, statics and dynamics courses. The instructional graphics programs used in these courses are:

1. A program that takes user defined position and force vectors and displays the moment in components and vector form.
2. A program that calculates the frictional forces present in a block and cylinder on an inclined plane system that the user has defined.
3. A program that lets the student generate shear and moment diagrams for a beam subjected to user defined systems of loads.
4. A simple truss analysis program that displays the internal forces in a nine-bar truss interactively loaded by the user.
5. A path motion program that shows how the radius of curvature, the tangential acceleration and normal acceleration change along a set of preprogrammed or user defined curves.
6. A program that demonstrates the use of moving reference frames by displaying the velocities of user selected points on a rotating disk in both a fixed and rotating reference frame.

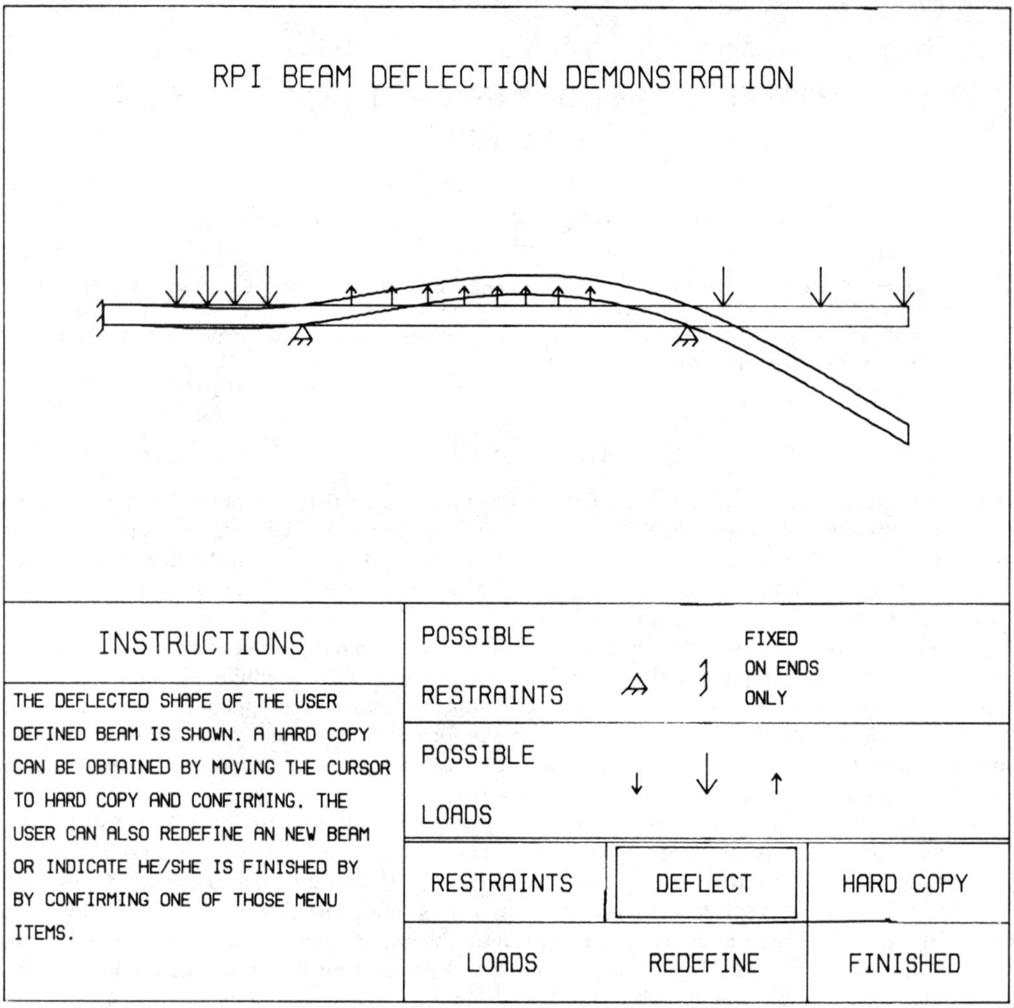

Fig. 1. Beam deflection demonstration program.

CONTINUOUS BEAMS

The computerized analysis techniques of today can quickly solve complex problems. However, they have the disadvantage of not giving the students the behavioral insight that is obtained solving problems manually. Computer graphics techniques can be used to remove this disadvantage and to give students this insight by graphically displaying the analysis results. An example of such a capability is a beam deflection program that the students can use to see how a continuous beam will deflect under various loading and boundary conditions (Fig. 1). In this program students can easily define and analysis various sets of loads and boundary conditions. This program is an example of what could be referred to as an interactive demonstration program, which is a specific purpose program that is simple to operate (it gives its own operation instructions) but has a limited set of procedures it can perform and demonstrate.

FRAME STABILITY

An interactive graphics package that demonstrates the overall stability behavior of steel frames is used in the steel design course. This program traces the displacement history (Fig. 2) and the internal force distribution history as a portal frame is loaded to failure. Various factors that are accounted for in the analysis include nonlinear connection behavior, member instabilities, material yielding and overall frame instability. By selecting various sets of parameters the students can see how the overall structural behavior is affected and by watching the animation of the displacement history can see which behavioral aspects control the design through the loading history.

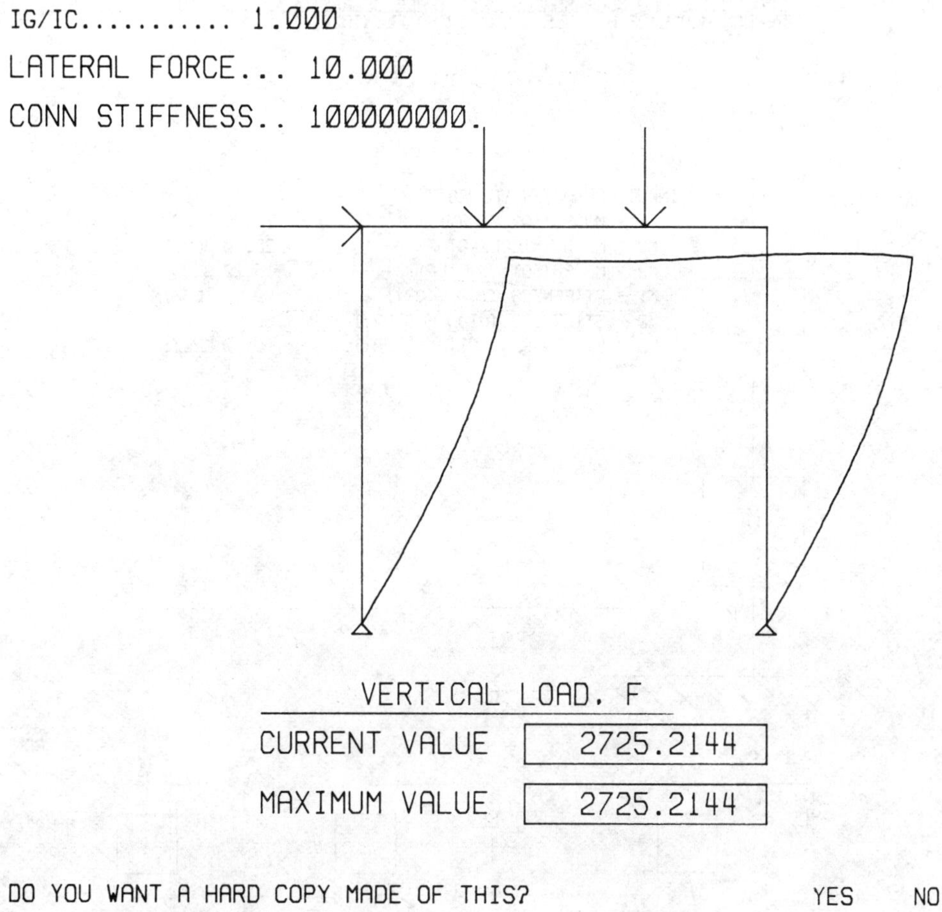

Fig. 2. Frame stability program (programmed by Professor Michael H. Ackroyd).

STRUCTURAL DYNAMICS

It is difficult to give students a good intuitive "feel" for the behavior of structures subjected to dynamic loads because this "feel" can only be obtained through the experience of seeing how various structures behave. In an effort to give the students this experience, a series of seven interactive graphics modules [3] have been developed for use in the structural dynamics courses. The individual modules are:

1. Response of a 1 DOF (degree of freedom) system to harmonic excitation;
2. Response of a 1 DOF system to impulse excitation;
3. Fourier decomposition of a periodic force;
4. Response of a 1 DOF system to a periodic forcing function;
5. Response of a 1 DOF system to earthquake excitation;
6. Response of a 3 DOF system to harmonic excitation;
7. Response of a 3 DOF system to earthquake excitation.

In addition to working out problems by hand, the student's homework assignments require the use of these modules to solve various problems by varying specific parameters and to discuss how the behavior was affected by the variations. Figure 3 shows the use of module 6 to obtain the natural frequencies and mode shapes of a 3 DOF structure. Once this is obtained the student can request an animated sequence of the structure for any of the solved for modes.

SLOPE STABILITY

The basic technique used to determine the stability of a soils slope is to calculate the factor of safety for each one of various possible failure surfaces and select the most critical (the one for which the factor of safety is a minimum). A graphics interface has been developed for such a slope stability

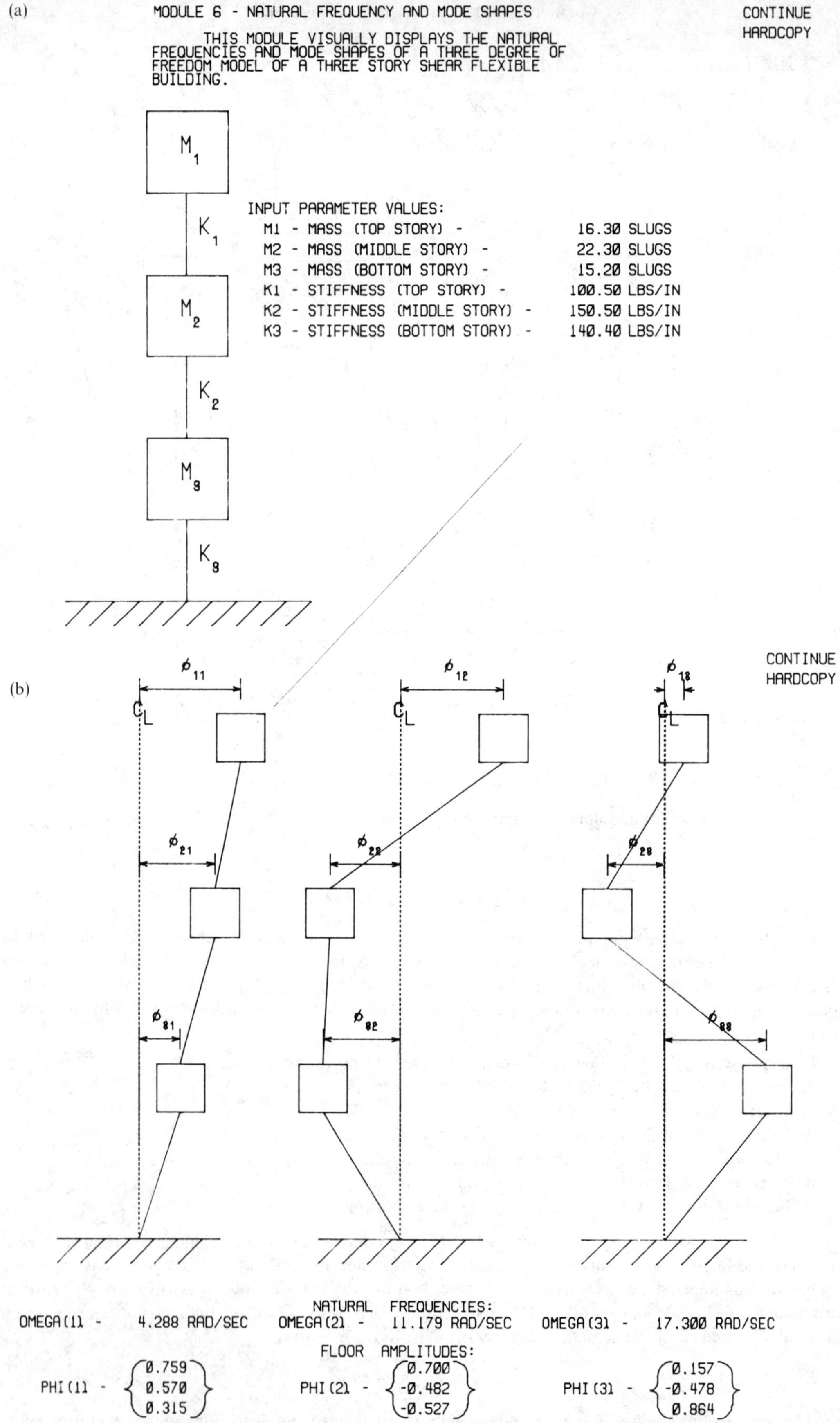

Fig. 3. (a) User defined 3-DOF system. (b) Natural frequencies and mode shapes for 3-DOF system. Structural dynamics programs (programmed by Robert U. Johnson).

program that shows the failure surfaces and the factors of safety for the various cases tested. Students in a soils structure course use these displays to gain some insight into the behavior of various soil slopes. This insight is very useful when designing a slope and assuring that its factor of safety against failure is large enough.

COMPUTER TECHNOLOGY FOR CIVIL ENGINEERING

Recently a new course has been developed to demonstrate how current computer technologies can be employed in civil engineering applications. A major part of this course is a term project. Many of the projects selected involve the development of interactive graphics software for use in civil engineering design. Some of the projects from the first offering of this course that used interactive computer graphics include:

1. Plate girder design,
2. Truss design and analysis,
3. Raft foundation design, and
4. Design of reinforced concrete beams.

FINITE ELEMENT SOFTWARE

The finite element method is a numerical analysis technique used in many civil engineering applications. One of the difficulties confronted in teaching finite element analysis is in providing the

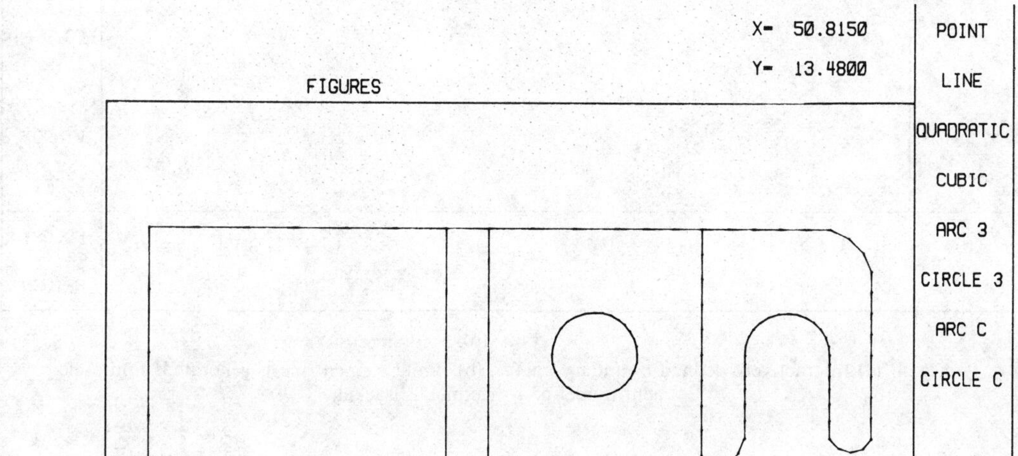

Fig. 4(a)

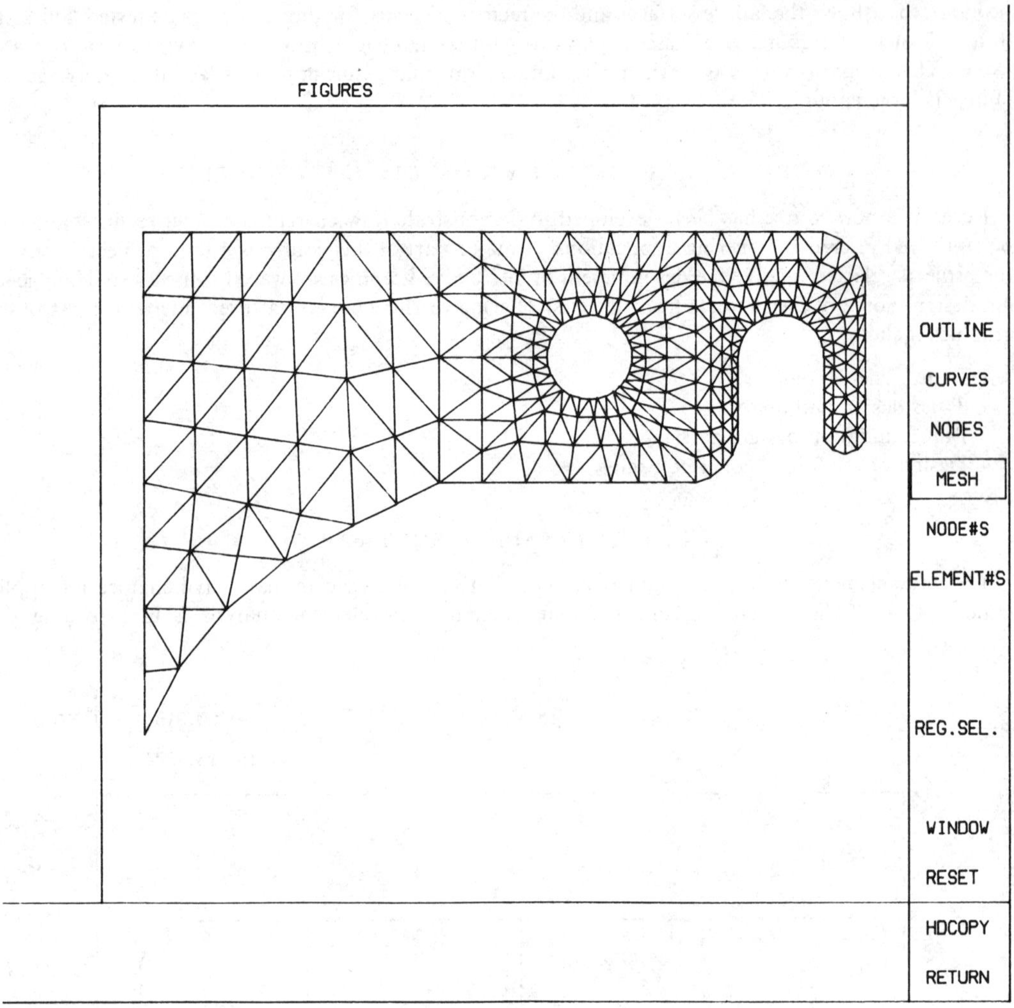

Fig. 4(b)

Fig. 4. (a) Interactively defined boundary curves. (b) Finite element mesh generated. Finite element model of a sheetmetal bracket.

students good hands-on experience, while still maintaining the major emphasis on the basic concepts underlying the analysis method. The problem is not the availability of analysis capability. For example, useful programs like SAP IV[4] and NONSAP[5] can be obtained for less than three hundred dollars each and there are several other programs of comparable capability available at similar cost. The problem is the time and effort required to generate valid problem input and to properly evaluate the analysis results.

Therefore, a finite element software system, referred to as POFES (People Oriented Finite Element Software), with an interactive graphic pre- and post-processor has been developed[6,7]. The purpose of this software is to allow the user to quickly and efficiently define finite element models, analyze them and look at the analysis results.

Unlike the interactive demonstration programs, this finite element software is not designed to demonstrate any specific theoretical or behavioral aspects, but is a general purpose software system that can be effectively employed for many types of finite element analysis problems. Therefore, to be of maximum utility in educational applications one has to specifically design the problems to be solved using such software so that the specific aspects that are to be demonstrated to the students are brought out.

As an example of how this software can be used, Fig. 4(a) shows the boundary curves interactively input by the user for the definition of a sheet metal bracket. The bracket has a circular hole in it and a hook to the right. The added lines are used to facilitate the generation of the finite element mesh shown in Fig. 4(b). The loads, material properties and boundary conditions are then interactively applied and the finite element analysis is run. After the analysis, the postprocessor can be entered and the results can be interactively viewed. In Fig. 5(a) the user has interactively obtained the peak displacements by viewing the displaced mesh and interactively obtaining the displacements at the point of maximum movement. Figure 5(b) shows the contour plot of the maximum principle stresses which can be effectively used to determine the location and values of stress concentrations. The process of defining, analyzing and looking at the results of this problem took less than 1 h.

As a demonstration of the effectiveness of such software for educational use, consider the following. The first time the author taught a finite element course he assigned a simple stress concentration problem as homework. The students were told in advance that the correct value of the stress concentration was between 2.5 and 3.0. The students were asked to generate a mesh of approx. 25 elements without the aid of an interactive preprocessor. The results were students complaining about how much work the assignment was and the resulting stress concentration values they obtained were between 0.8 and 10.0.

The next time the course was taught, the students were given a similar assignment and were asked to use a mesh of about 100 elements. The difference this time is that they were not given the answer in advance, but they were able to use the interactive graphic preprocessor to generate their models. This time all the students obtained results within 15% of the correct answer. Also, since it took only a few minutes to define and analyze a different mesh, most students analyzed at least two different meshes and compared results to be sure that they were using an adequate finite element model.

CONCLUDING REMARKS

Interactive computer graphics makes it possible to teach today's advanced analysis techniques while still being able to give the students the physical insight into problem behavior that was gained

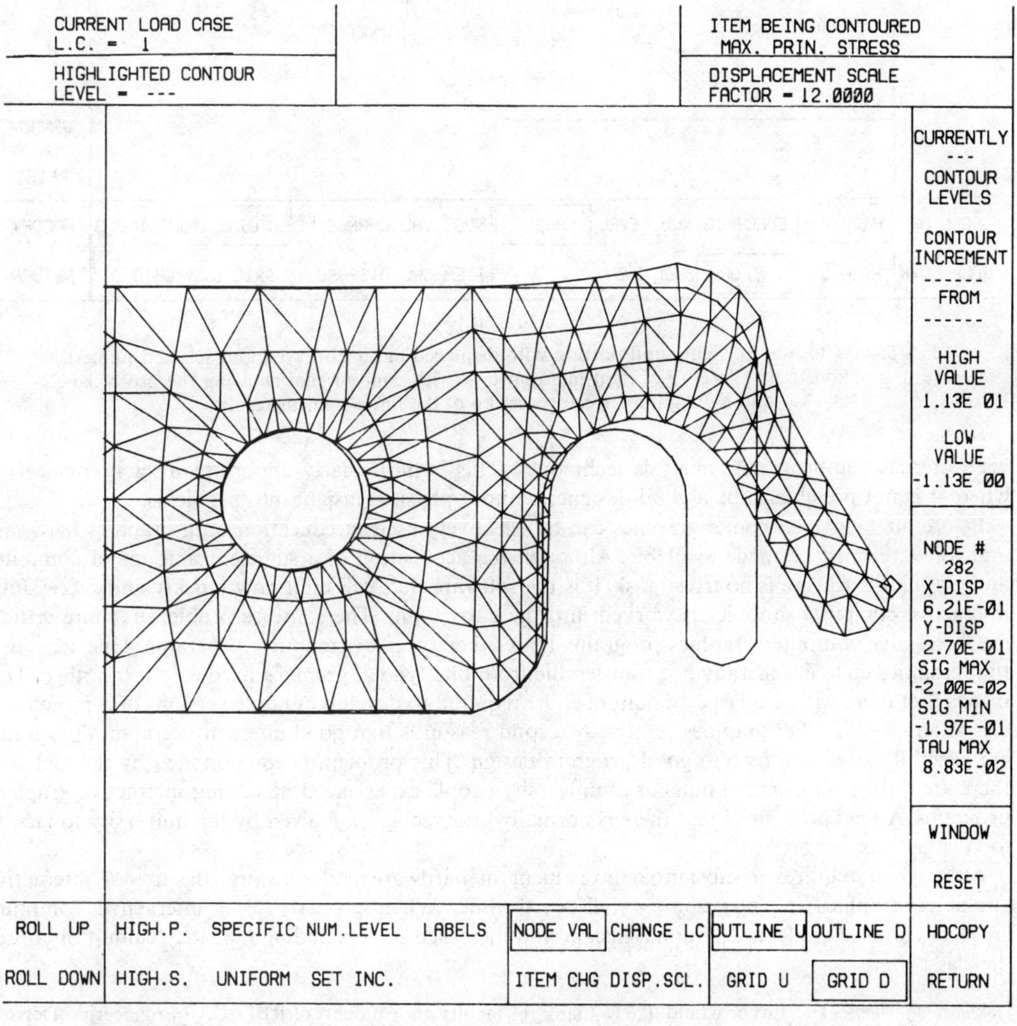

Fig. 5(a)

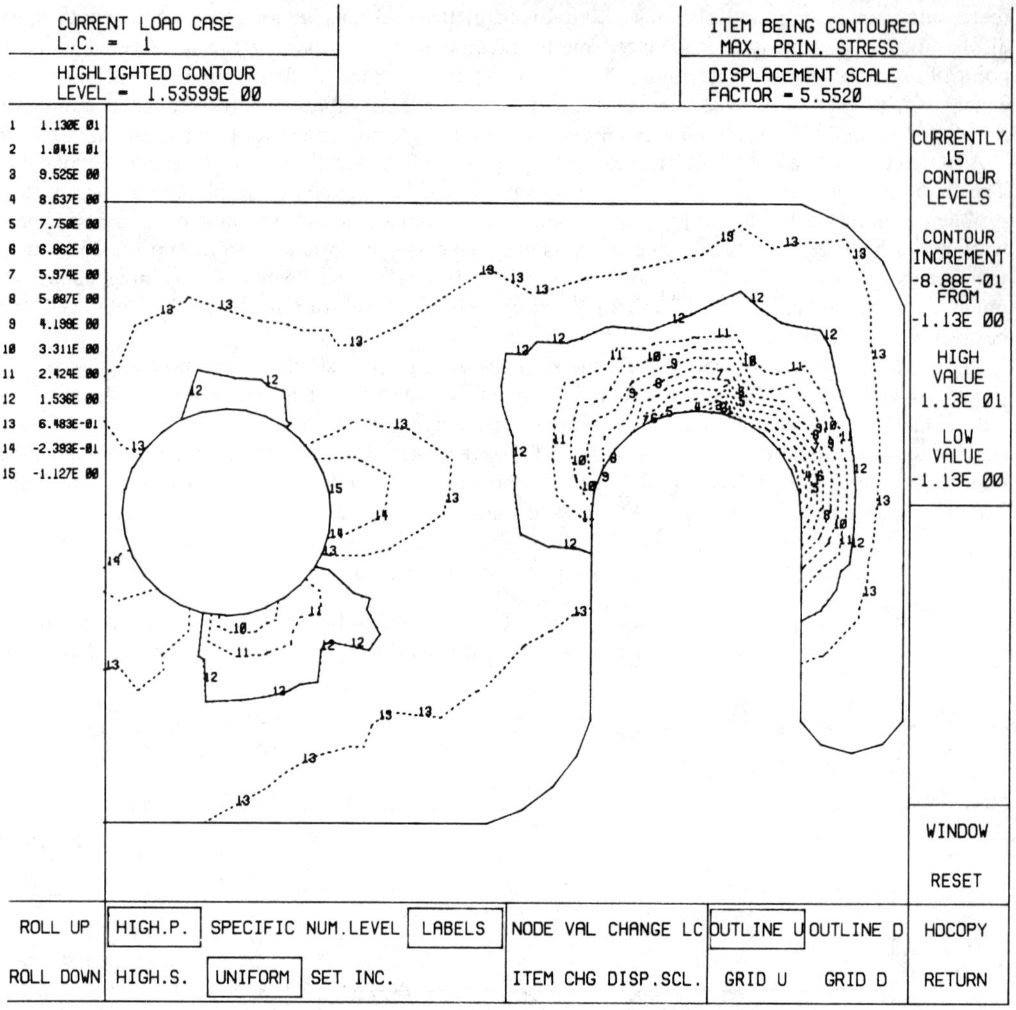

Fig. 5(b)

Fig. 5. (a) Close-up of right-hand portion with displaced mesh displayed and selected numerical results obtained. (b) Close-up of right-hand portion with contour plot showing the use of labels and highlighting. Postprocessing of the finite element results.

via yesterday's approximate analysis techniques. This is particularly important in civil engineering where it is not possible to be a good designer without physical insight into problems.

Before interactive computer graphics can be effectively used in education both graphics hardware and software must be made available. Although the acquisition of a sufficient amount of computer and graphics hardware is no trivial task, it is the software that will limit how quickly and successfully interactive computer graphics is worked into the curriculum. The software problem is more critical for interactive computer graphics programs than other types of computer programs. One reason is that graphics code is generally not transferable from one type of graphics hardware to another. This means that there will be a large amount of effort required to develop multiple versions of a program if it is to be used in other graphics centers. A second reason is that good interactive graphics programs are generally large and require good program design. This problem is compounded by the fact that there are only a very limited number of university people experienced in writing interactive graphics programs. A final problem is that there is normally little recognition given by the university to faculty for such efforts.

Although it requires a substantial investment in hardware and software, the use of interactive computer graphics in education is well worthwhile. When properly used interactive computer graphics can give students additional insight and increased understanding that they cannot obtain in the classroom.

Acknowledgement—The author would like to thank the faculty and students of RPI's Civil Engineering Department that have contributed in making interactive computer graphics part of our curriculum.

REFERENCES

1. Wozny M. J., *Comput. Educ.* **5,** 183 (1981).
2. Musgrave B., *Datamation* 195 (1980).
3. O'Rourke M. J., Johnson R. U. and Feeser L. J., *Second Conference on Computing in Civil Engineering, ASCE*, pp. 458–460 (1980).
4. Bathe K. J., Wilson E. L. and Petterson F. E., SAP IV—A structural analysis program for static and dynamic response of linear systems. Report No. EERC 73-11 (1974).
5. Bathe K. J., Wilson E. L. and Iding R. H., NONSAP—A structural analysis program for static and dynamic response of nonlinear systems. Report No. UC SME 74-3 (1974).
6. Shephard M. S. and Feeser L. J., *Proceedings of First Chautauqua on Finite Element Modeling*, pp. 99–117 (1980).
7. Haber R. B., Shephard M. S., Abel J. F., Gallagher R. H. and Greenberg D. P., *Int. J. Num. Meth. Engng* (1981).

Comput. & Educ. Vol. 5, pp. 229 to 243, 1981
Printed in Great Britain

0360-1315/81/040229-15$02.00/0
Pergamon Press Ltd

COMPUTER GRAPHICS AND COMPUTER AIDED DESIGN IN MECHANICAL ENGINEERING AT THE UNIVERSITY OF MINNESOTA

DONALD R. RILEY and ARTHUR G. ERDMAN
Department of Mechanical Engineering, University of Minnesota, Minneapolis, MN 55455, U.S.A.

Abstract—Engineering design in industry is changing as a result of the application of the new tools provided by the digital computer and interactive computer graphics. This shift is placing new demands on engineering curricula. The engineering graduate today must be trained in the use of the computer and computer graphics as a design tool—in much the same way that engineers in the past used the slide rule and today use the hand-held calculator.

This paper summarizes the efforts to integrate computer graphics and computer aided design into the design curriculum in the Mechanical Engineering Department at the University of Minnesota. Specific software packages have been developed for use in teaching engineering graphics and mechanism synthesis and analysis. These packages are discussed in detail, including the hardware used.

INTRODUCTION

The literature is full of papers and articles describing the application of computers in engineering design, documentation, manufacturing, and process planning. More and more companies are investing large sums of money in computer graphics and computer aided design and drafting systems to increase their overall productivity. This trend is placing new demands upon the educational institutions to train students in this new technology to take their place in industry. However, educational institutions typically do not have the financial resources required to acquire the necessary equipment.

This paper describes the effort undertaken at the University of Minnesota to introduce low-cost computer graphics into the mechanical engineering curriculum. Two types of graphics systems are utilized: Tektronix 4010–series storage tube displays using the University's instructional timesharing system, and Terak microcomputer-based raster graphics systems. Computer graphics, numerical methods, and computer aided design techniques are being integrated into the entire mechanical engineering curriculum, starting at the freshman level in engineering graphics, continuing through the upper division design courses, and including the introduction of upper division/graduate level courses in computer aided design and computer graphics. This paper will describe two areas of application: the engineering graphics courses and computer aided design and analysis of mechanisms.

ENGINEERING GRAPHICS

Engineering graphics at the University of Minnesota is taught in Mechanical Engineering as a sequence of three one-quarter courses, only the first of which is required of engineering students. The first course (EG 1025) is designed to provide an introduction to graphical communication as practiced in industry. In the past, this meant a concentration only on the drafting board skills: lettering, layout, dimensioning conventions, geometric constructions, graphical calculus, and so on. While these skills still receive heavy emphasis in the classroom, the course material is being updated to reflect the changes taking place in industry. Perhaps the most fundamental change that is presently occurring is the shift to computer aided drafting and computer aided design techniques.

In 1976, we began looking at the basic engineering graphics course to determine the best way to introduce computer graphics into the course content. This was motivated by several factors.

1. The last of our few remaining engineering graphics faculty were nearing retirement. As there are no Ph.D. programs and no 'leading edge' research being done in this area, it was impossible to hire new faculty to replace them.
2. Industry is moving toward increased use of computer graphics and computer aided drafting systems.
3. Engineering graphics has traditionally been "boring", and we hoped computer graphics would increase student interest (especially in their first engineering course).

In 1977, with the help of a grant from the University of Minnesota Educational Development Program and support from the University Computer Services, a pilot project was started. That pilot

Fig. 1. TERAK graphics system.

project resulted in the selection of the Terak microcomputer-based graphics display system and led to the development of the program described in this paper.

The TERAK

In 1977, as part of the pilot project, a survey was made of available computer graphics displays. The result of that survey was the selection of the TERAK graphics system.

The TERAK (Fig. 1) is based on the Digital Equipment Corporation's LSI-11 16-bit microprocessor and comes with 28K words of 16-bit memory, floating point hardware, a floppy disk controller and one drive (three more drives can be added), one serial interface (with two connectors), a video display and driver, and an audio tone generator. Two operating systems are available: DEC's RT11 operating system, supporting BASIC, FORTRAN, and assembly languages; and the UCSD Pascal operating system. The video screen allows text and graphics to be mixed and controlled independently; i.e. text may be scrolled over the graphics and the two can be turned on or off, or only certain "zones" of the screen turned on or off, independently. The resolution of the screen is 40 raster units 1/in., providing 320 × 240 screen raster units on the 8 × 6-in. display. While relatively low resolution, this has proved to be quite adequate as can be seen from the figures presented later in this paper.

The TERAK was chosen for this project for a number of reasons:

1. Compatibility with DEC's PDP-11 series of minicomputers. (There is a lot of PDP-11 software available.)
2. Availability of "standard" FORTRAN.
3. High degree of interactivity (compared to timesharing at 30 characters/s).
4. Flexibility of display format (characters and graphics can be mixed and controlled independently) and "animation" possibilities.
5. Low cost: approx. $7500 for dual disk system, $5500 for single disk system.

Graphics package

The TERAK, as purchased, had very little software for supporting computer graphics applications in FORTRAN. To provide the graphics support software for the programs to be developed, a package of FORTRAN graphics subroutines was designed and implemented called TERPAK. This package is essentially a Calcomp-compatible package, with a number of routines added to perform the required bit-mapping and to support a number of other special features, such as screen format control and "double-buffered" plotting (necessary for animation). A list of the subroutines and their arguments appears as an appendix for the reader's inspection. The TERPAK subroutine package has subsequently been licensed for distribution by TERAK with their systems.

Several variations of this software package have also been developed at the University of Minnesota which allow the TERAK to drive Tektronix CRT's and plotters, Houston Instruments plotters, and a Calcomp plotter, under RT11. In addition, any picture on the screen can be copied to a Printronix printer/plotter by calling another subroutine which copies the TERAK bit-map to the Printronix.

Use of the TERAK as a teaching aid

The course content of the graphics class has been modified to include work with the TERAK microcomputer. Of the four lecture hours per week, 1 h is now devoted to computer graphics instruction. The student is required to buy a floppy disk, onto which is copied the operating system to run the computer and DRAW, the canned program intended for his use. The DRAW program, using the graphics package developed at Minnesota for the TERAK, allows the user to define a simple three-dimensional object in terms of points and lines and display the result. Once the object has been defined by the user, there are various operations available to allow the object to be viewed from different angles or to be manipulated in various ways. This program (which will be described in greater detail later) was constructed with two principal objectives in mind: first, to serve as a teaching aid for the standard graphics curricula; and second, to serve as an introduction to more sophisticated computer graphics systems and their capabilities.

As a teaching aid, the TERAK system is used to enhance the material being learned in lecture. The programs the student uses were developed to reduce the drudgery but not displace the need to understand the basic concepts of projective geometry. For example, the computer could very easily perform computations for true length of a desired line, but the student is required to go through the same series of "fold" operations or projections on the TERAK that he would have to perform on paper. The TERAK just makes it easier and faster.

As a teaching aid, the TERAK graphics system helps the student learn to work in three-dimensions as readily as he works in two-dimensions. To date, the freshman engineering student has worked and thought in terms of two-dimensions. His mathematical background has been in planar geometry and trigonometry, and algebra within the Cartesian (X–Y) coordinate system. Later courses in mathematics will teach him to manipulate variables representing three or more dimensions, but it is particularly important for the engineer to be able to think and visualize in three-dimensions. The DRAW program requires the student to describe an object in algebraic terms he or she is already familiar with; that is, to assign X, Y, and Z coordinates to every vertex of the object. The graphics program helps the student go from this mathematical representation of an object to a pictorial one. Any errors in mathematical description become apparent when viewed three-dimensionally, thus providing the student with immediate feedback. Now, once the object has been successfully described, it may then be "rotated" to any desired view or projection. An experienced engineer is able to look at a standard three angle projection—top, front, and side views—and construct in his imagination a picture of what that object looks like in three-dimensions. This ability is fundamental to reading blueprints. By allowing the student to rotate an object from front to top, or from top to side, this process of visualization is made much easier. A three-dimensional object may be rotated through each of the standard projections typically seen on an engineering drawing, and the connection between the three-dimensional object and two-dimensional representation is strengthened.

The TERAK graphics system also serves as an introduction to the capabilities of the computer as a tool for drafting. Working on the TERAK allows the student to explore the concept of using the computer to create and manipulate objects. While it isn't possible to duplicate industrial quality drafting stations on the TERAK, it is possible, using DRAW and similar programs, to teach a student the capabilities of the computer in this area. For example, an industrial station might have an associated microprocessor controlling a menu of possible input selections. Although the DRAW program does not possess such a sophisticated system of creating an object, it does incorporate a much simplified and more elementary means of input (i.e. typing in points and lines). The manner of input might differ, but the concept remains the same—that an object must first somehow be described to the computer before any further work may be done. Use of the DRAW program teaches some of these fundamental concepts of any computer aided design and drafting system without resorting to expensive hardware.

DRAW program description

The DRAW program does not attempt to duplicate a turnkey computer aided drafting system. Rather, it is a graphics program that will draw simple three-dimensional wire-frame objects from any angle. Objects are constructed out of only two basic primitives—points and lines. Input is simply a matter of typing in X, Y, and Z coordinates for each corner of the object to be drawn. Lines are defined by specifying the point number where the line begins, followed by the point number of the

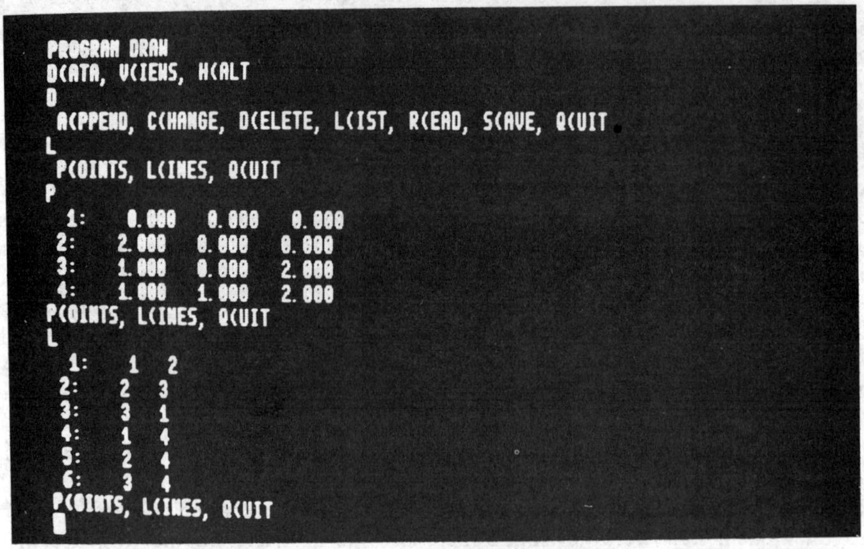

Fig. 2. DRAW program—DATA options and simple object.

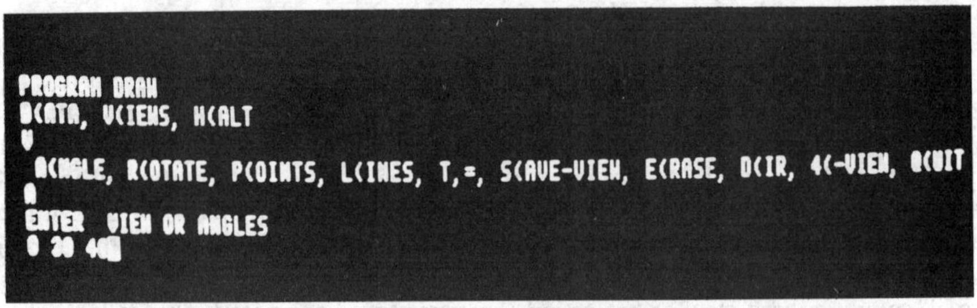

Fig. 3. DRAW program—VIEWS options.

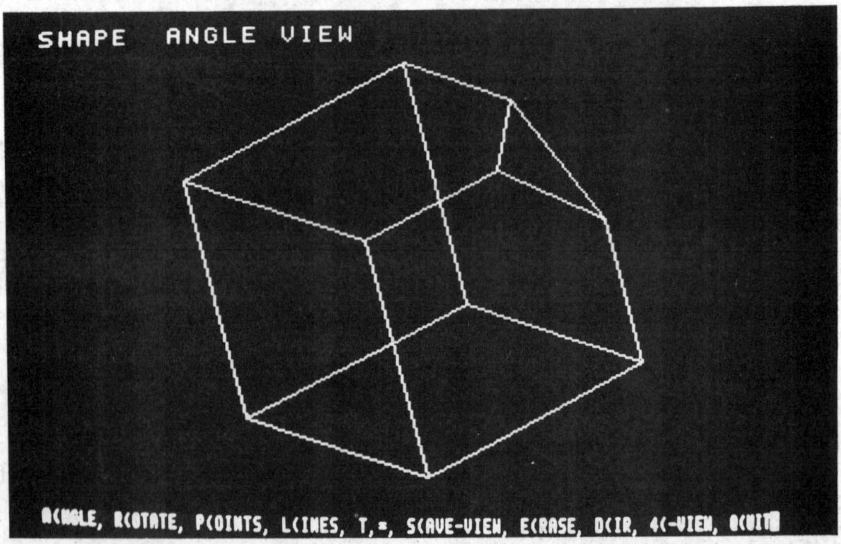

Fig. 4. DRAW program—ANGLE view.

line's end point. The input process is guided by a series of very explicit prompts, with forgiving error messages for any typing errors that might occur.

Program structure is of pyramid form. There are two main options in the program—DATA and VIEWS. Selecting the DATA option erases the screen and presents the user with a menu of different input options to choose from. This DATA section of DRAW allows objects to be entered, changed, inspected, appended to, or saved away on floppy disk. Figure 2 shows the command format and the point and line definitions for a simple object. Also in this menu of options is the QUIT option. When all input operations have been completed and the student is ready to continue, selecting the QUIT option returns the user to the top of the pyramid where he or she is again presented with the main choice, DATA or VIEWS. Selecting the VIEWS option this time erases the screen and presents the user with a menu of different output operations, as shown in Fig. 3. These options govern how the object is to be viewed on the screen. For example, the ANGLE option allows the student to specify the orientation of the object when it is viewed in terms of rotations about a right-handed coordinate system. This coordinate system is defined in terms of the screen where the X–Y plane is the plane of the screen (X = horizontal) and the Z-axis comes out of the screen. Specifying an angle of 0, 30, 40 indicates the user would like a view of the object after it has been rotated 0° about the X-axis, 30° about the Y-axis and then 40° about the Z-axis. Figure 4 shows such a view. A particular view may be given a name for later reference by the SAVE-VIEW option. For example, this 0, 30, 40 view may be named VIEW1. In other commands where a view must be specified, this particular view may then be referenced either as 0, 30, 40, or as VIEW1. The program automatically defines the three standard orthographic projections, and the student can ask for views FRONT, TOP, or SIDE in addition to any views he may have defined with the SAVE-VIEW command. Figure 5 shows a sample directory of defined views obtained by using the directory (DIR) option.

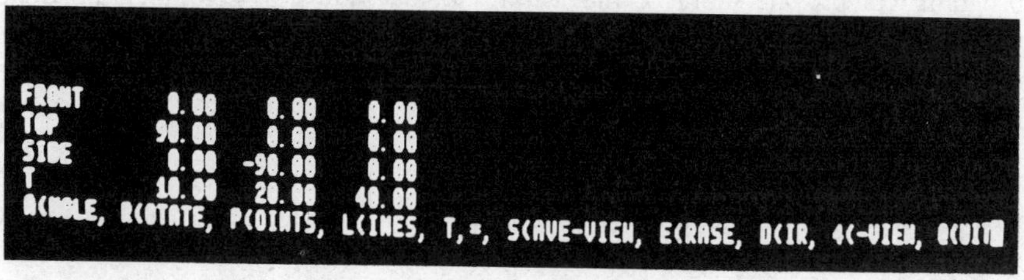

Fig. 5. DRAW program—view directory.

The ROTATE command allows the student to see the object rotated incrementally in a 'dynamic' fashion between any two views. The student specifies the starting angles or view, the ending angles or view, and the number of steps to be taken. The system then shows the object "rotating" from one position to the next in a series of steps, allowing the student to better visualize the projection process.

The 4-VIEW option allows the student to see four views of the object on the screen simultaneously. This allows the student to generate the equivalent of a standard engineering drawing—front, top, side, and one auxiliary view—as shown in Fig. 6.

The DRAW program will also allow the student to perform the equivalent of a "fold" operation either parallel or perpendicular to any line of the object (the "T" and "=" options)—necessary for generating true length and true shape projections. Another option then causes the program to compute the 'apparent' length of a selected line, as illustrated in Fig. 7. This apparent length (the projection of the line onto the plane of the screen) will be the true length of the line if the student has done his homework properly. Other options within VIEWS are largely of a bookkeeping nature. As mentioned previously, specific views of an object may be named and saved within a catalogue. That catalogue can also be accessed and updated from within VIEWS. This option also proves useful because a student will solve his assignment, then store away the view of the assignment's solution under a standard name and turn in his floppy disk. The instructor can then access his catalogue of answers and grade accordingly.

The DRAW program provides an excellent introduction to computer aided design and drafting. Using a minicomputer to define and manipulate simple objects is a good first introduction to the more sophisticated tasks of an industrial CAD/CAM system. Because of the simplicity in the method of input and the command structure, students have had to invest very little time learning how the system works; the majority of the time spent on the TERAK is freed for graphics work. Student reaction to this program has been very encouraging. The program has generated a lot of interest and excitement in the novelty of creating a three-dimensional object with the computer. Class assignments

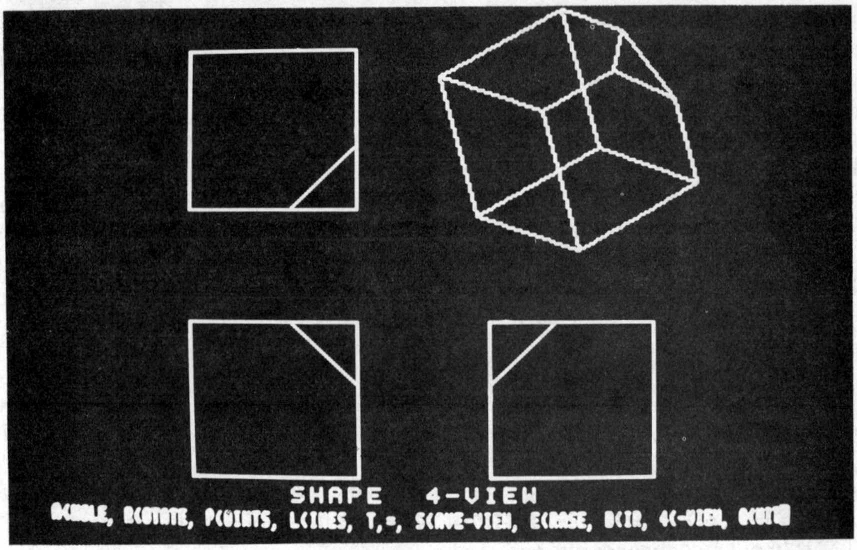

Fig. 6. DRAW program—4 view option.

are approached more in the spirit of fun than of work. In this type of learning environment, experience with the computer on this level is very easily acquired. With continued development work, the DRAW program will provide more of the features of an industrial computer aided design and drafting station. Inexpensive three-dimensional design and drafting using this approach provides a new and exciting possibility for undergraduate educational institutions.

Further development work

Continued software development is being done in several related areas that should greatly enhance the TERAK's potential as an educational tool. One asset of the TERAK is its capability of supporting two peripheral devices through its serial input/output ports. By introducing a digitizer tablet into the system, it is possible to begin actually simulating an industrial drafting station. Using a menu to select the type of input (points, lines, circles, arcs, etc.) will remove the limitation of constructing objects only from points and lines. Much more complicated objects may be constructed and more versatility obtained in manipulating that object, allowing the TERAK to perform actual drafting functions. Such

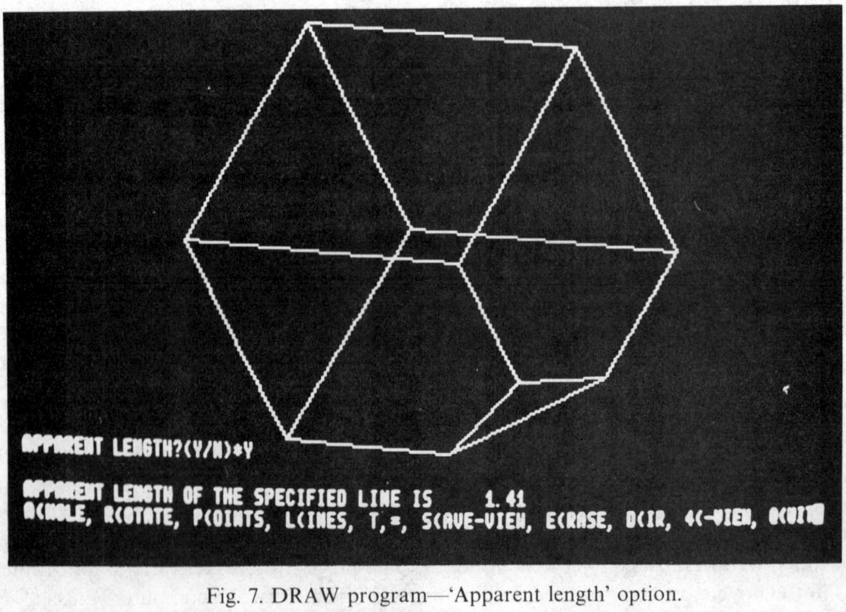

Fig. 7. DRAW program—'Apparent length' option.

Fig. 8. TERAK drafting system configuration.

an expansion of DRAW is well within the hardware limitations of the TERAK. 3-D drafting software is currently under development and will be available for classroom use by the Fall of 1981.

As part of this development, a Houston Instruments HI-PAD digitizer tablet has been interfaced to the TERAK for coordinate input and command menu selection, and the plotting package has been modified to drive a Houston Instruments HI-PLOT plotter. Once an object has been created on the TERAK screen, it can be plotted on the HI-PLOT for higher resolution hardcopy. This system configuration is shown in Fig. 8.

COMPUTER GRAPHICS AND COMPUTER AIDED DESIGN

Two new courses called "Computer Aided Design" and "Computer Graphics in Design" have been introduced at the dual senior/graduate elective level to introduce students to the basic tools of computer aided design. The first course, "Computer Aided Design", acquaints them with the basic computational tools of approximating function and curve fitting, numerical integration, and numerical differentiation. The second course, "Computer Graphics in Design" introduces the student to the hardware and the software algorithms used in computer graphics. Both courses are project-oriented courses. Students write their own programs rather than use "canned" programs or software packages.

The tools taught in these two courses have effectively been put to use in developing programs for use in the synthesis and analysis of mechanism systems. The efforts in this area will now be described in detail.

KINEMATICS AND MECHANISMS

Kinematics and dynamics of mechanisms and machines have traditionally been taught based on graphical construction. Displacement, velocity, and acceleration analyses, as well as static and inertia force analyses of mechanisms were accomplished on the drafting board. In fact, in many cases the accuracy of the graphical construction was emphasized more than learning the function of linkages and mechanisms. A glance at the introductory mechanisms textbooks of the 1950s and 1960s will confirm that little or no kinematic synthesis was covered in undergraduate instruction. As we begin the 1980s, many schools still do not offer any instruction in synthesis of mechanisms, but the trend towards computer aided design of mechanisms has begun.

Kinematic synthesis deals with the systematic design of mechanisms for a given performance. The areas of synthesis may be grouped into two categories:

Type Synthesis: Given the required performance, what type of mechanism will be suitable? (Gear trains? Linkages? Cam mechanisms?) Also, how many links should the mechanism have? How many degrees of freedom are required? What configuration is desirable? Deliberations involving a number of links and degrees of freedom are often referred to as the objectives of a sub-category of type synthesis called "*number synthesis*".

Dimensional Synthesis: The second major category of kinematic synthesis is best defined by way of its objective: to determine the significant dimensions and the starting position of a mechanism of pre-conceived type for a specified task and prescribed performance. In other words, once a specific task is defined (e.g. design a linkage to guide the opening of an automobile hood from the closed to the open position), find the specific dimensions of a mechanism which will accomplish this task.

Graphical kinematic synthesis techniques have been known for quite some time, but little emphasis was placed on these techniques in teaching since they are not powerful, they are time consuming, and they can be inaccurae.

The availability of the computer has changed the way mechanical systems are designed and analyzed. The nature of kinematic synthesis is that if a small number of prescribed positions are specified (2, 3, or 4) for planar motion, then there are numerous possible solutions available. For two prescribed positions of a four bar linkage, we can think of three "infinities" of solutions, e.g. the designer has three free choices to make. Three positions yield two "infinities" of solutions and four positions yield one "infinity" of solutions. With so many possibilities, the computer is a handy tool to use for finding the "best" one based on other unprescribed constraints, such as locations of ground pivots, size of linkage members, mechanical advantage, forces in the mechanism, and required input torque. Access to a computational aid which can solve equations of kinematic synthesis is only half the basis of the new approach to mechanism design. Computer graphics used in an interactive mode allows the comparison of numerous solutions at the same time to optimally choose a final mechanism.

At the University of Minnesota, two courses are offered on mechanism analysis and synthesis for planar motion. The required junior level course has included about 2 weeks of kinematic synthesis plus a mechanism design project for the past 10 years. Each year, more emphasis is placed on computer aided design of mechanisms and linkages. Emphasis is placed on synthesis for two and three prescribed positions since both the graphical and analytical techniques are straightforward. Kinematic synthesis for three positions results in linear equations and relatively short computer programs for the students to write. Some computer graphics is introduced in this junior level course but due to the lack of sufficient graphics terminals at this time, most students survey alphanumeric printouts to identify "best" results. Two typical student design projects from this course are found below.

Three precision point example

Completion of an assembly line requires the synthesis of a motion generator linkage to transfer boxes from one conveyor belt to another as depicted in Fig. 10(a). The pickup and release positions plus an intermediate location are specified. A four bar is picked for this task. Figure 9 shows a four bar linkage with the left side (a dyad made up of vectors **W** and **Z**) shown in two positions. The

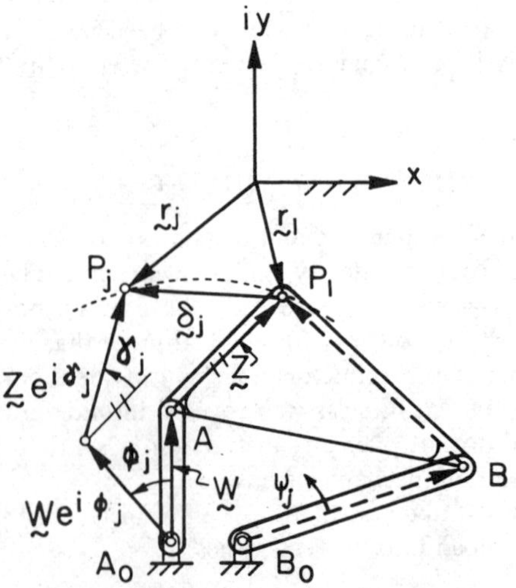

Fig. 9. Four bar linkage with left side (dyad) shown in two positions.

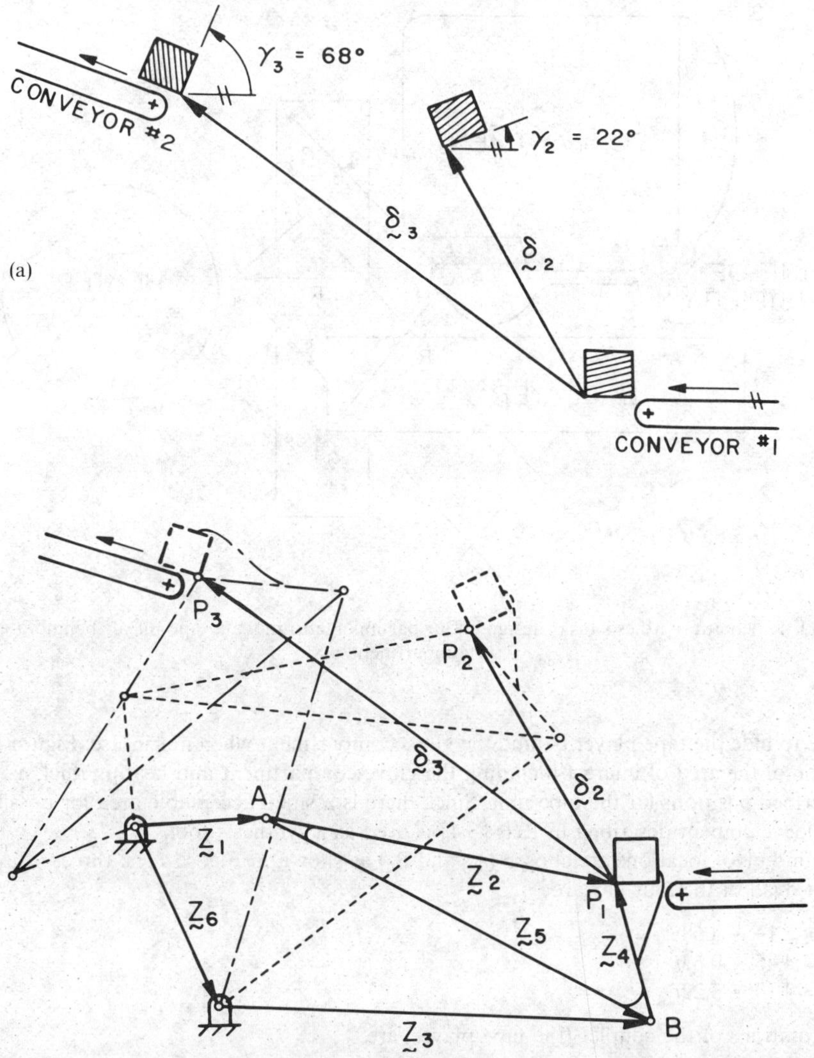

Fig. 10(a) Kinematic synthesis task: three position motion generation. (b) Synthesized four bar linkage for task shown in (a) Designed by complex number solution (1–3).

design equations are derived from this model (1–3). The prescribed quantities for the analytical solution, based on complex numbers, are:

Displacement vectors:	Rotation angles:
$\delta_2 = -6 + 11i$	$\gamma_2 = 22°$
$\delta_3 = -17 + 13i$	$\gamma_3 = 68°$.

The free choices of the relative rotations of input and output links of the four bar are:

Input:	Output:
$\phi_2 = 90°$	$\psi_2 = 40°$
$\phi_3 = 198°$	$\psi_3 = 73°$.

The input link rotations are chosen as large to try to obtain a crank rocker solution. Figure 10(b) shows the resulting four bar synthesis for this task. Note that each side (or dyad) of the linkage has two infinities of possibilities so that the computer is very helpful for this problem.

Ground pivot specification example

An engineering student who had recently purchased a tape recorder unit for his sports car was concerned with possible theft of his investment. Therefore, the student envisioned synthesis of a four

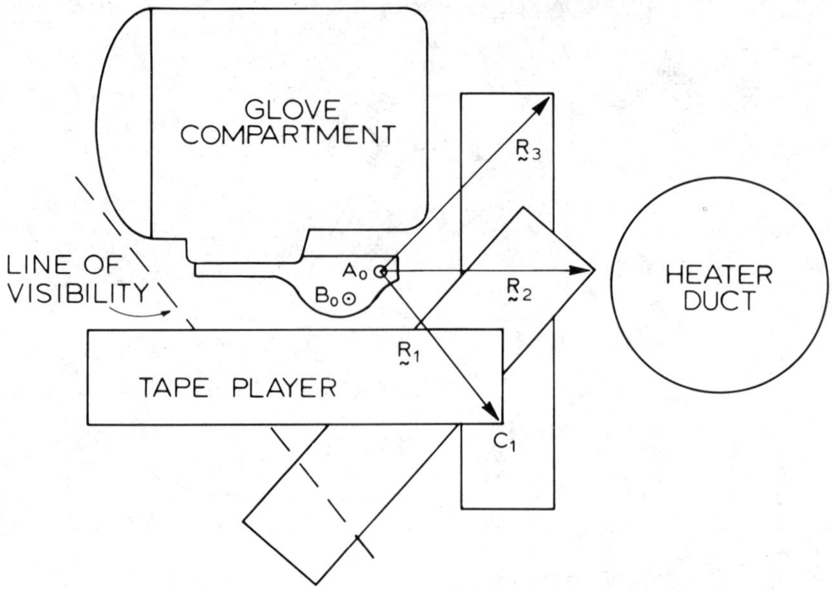

Fig. 11. Kinematic synthesis task: design a four bar linkage to move a tape player behind a glove compartment.

bar linkage to hide the tape player behind the glove compartment when not in use. Figure 11 shows a cross-section of the area of interest including the glove compartment and heating duct, as well as the three prescribed positions for the tape unit. Since there is a small acceptable area for possible ground pivots, the development described in Refs [3,4] is used as a synthesis tool.

Two ground pivot locations are chosen (A_0 and B_0) as shown in Fig. 11. The three position vectors for the first dyad of the four bar are:

$$\mathbf{R}_1 = 2.14 - 3.68i$$
$$\mathbf{R}_2 = 4.46 - 0.63i$$
$$\mathbf{R}_3 = 4.10 - 3.22i$$

while the rotations of the coupler (the tape player) are:

$$\gamma_2 = 50.7^\circ$$
$$\gamma_3 = 91.9^\circ$$

The analytical method yields the solution shown in Fig. 12. Each different choice of variables will yield a new solution.

Four prescribed positions of kinematic synthesis

The second course in mechanisms (a senior/graduate level elective) emphasizes kinematic synthesis of linkages for four and five prescribed positions. Non-linear equations result, requiring the computer for solution. From 1971 to 1975, only a batch program was used in this course. This still left the student the task of finding a best solution. Computer graphics is an ideal tool to use for kinematic synthesis, especially in the four precision point case where there is an infinity of solutions to pick from. In 1976, we began using the Tektronix terminal to strategically display parameters that allowed us to visualize many solutions at a time. For example, the infinity of solutions may be represented as an array of ground pivots and an array of moving pivots in the plane that represent all possible solutions to the specified problem (e.g. see Fig. 14). Since 1976, a computer package called LINCAGES has been developed at the University of Minnesota for the design of planar linkages (4,5). This package was inspired by the need to improve the user interface to the computer for this class of problems.

LINCAGES (Linkage INteractive Computer Analysis and Graphically Enhanced Synthesis Package)

The following briefly describes an interactive computer package which uses graphics output to help synthesize and analyze planar linkages. This program is available by contacting the second author at the Department of Mechanical Engineering, University of Minnesota.

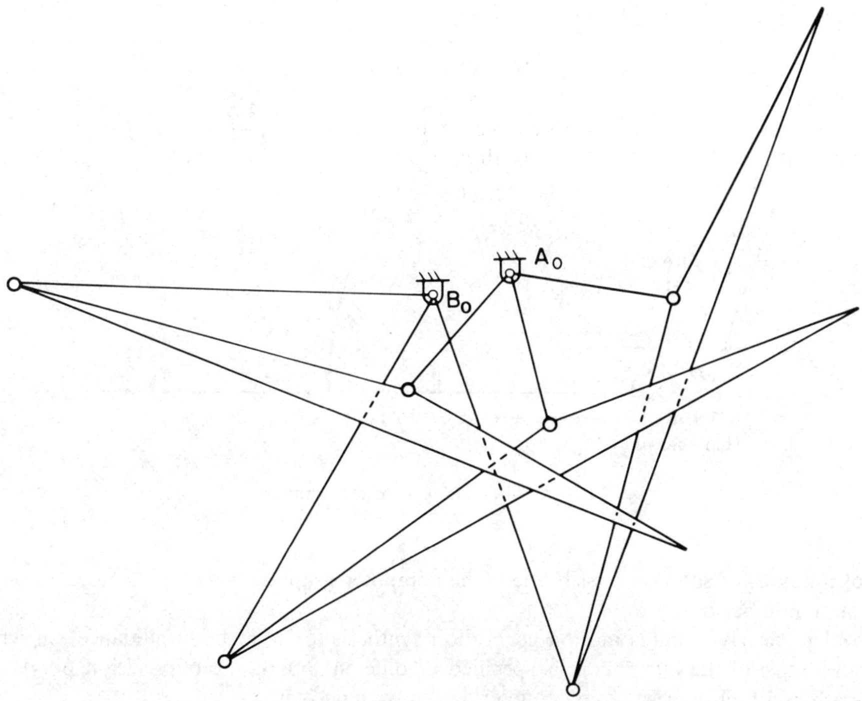

Fig. 12. Synthesized four bar linkage for task shown in Fig. 11 using the ground pivot specification method [3,4].

The LINCAGES Package is the first such program to be generally available over telephone lines in a time-sharing mode and to be designed to make optimal use of graphical output from either a teletype, graphics CRT, or a microcomputer. The computer, the designer, and graphics output are used strategically to maximize the utility of each. Synthesis programs may be applied for either 3, 4, or 5 finitely spaced precision points for combinations of motion, function, and path generation with prescribed timing.

LINCAGES example: motion generation for four precision points

The assembly of a particular filter product begins by forming the filtration material into what is known as a filter blank. Next, the filter blank is placed by hand onto a mandrel. This mandrel is part of a machine that completes the assembly of the filter. The objective of this problem is to design a four bar linkage for removing the filter blanks from the hopper and transferring them to the mandrel.

Figure 13 diagrams the kinematic synthesis objective. A gravity feed hopper holds the semi-cylindrical filter blanks with the diametral plane surface initially at a 27° angle from vertical. The blank rotates around until this plane surface is horizontal on the mandrel. The position of the hopper can be moved about within the area indicated, although the angle must remain at 27°.

At the beginning of the "pick and place" cycle, it is desirable to pull the blank in a direction approximately perpendicular to the face of the hopper. To prevent folding the filter blank on the mandrel, it is necessary to have the rotation of the blank completed at a position of approx. 5 cm above the mandrel and then translate without rotation onto the mandrel. The motion of the linkage should then reverse to remove the completed filter from the mandrel and eject it onto a conveyor belt. After this, the linkage should return to the hopper and pick another blank. Due to the requirement of reversibility, a double-crank or crank-rocker would have no real advantage over a double rocker.

An acceptable linkage solution must have ground pivots and linkage motions within areas that do not interfere with the hopper or assembler. Also, since the resulting linkage may be driven by a dyad (to provide a crank-rocker input), the total angular travel of the input link of the four bar synthesized here should be minimized so as to obtain acceptable transmission angles for the entire mechanism, including its driving crank and connecting link which actuates the input of the motion generator four bar linkage.

This example is a typical challenging problem that faces linkage designers many times. Some of the constraints are firm while others can vary within some specified range. This means mathematically a

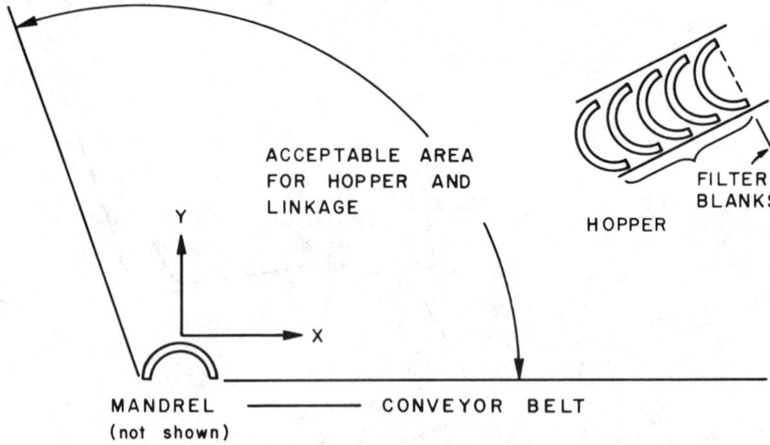

Fig. 13. Filter blank transfer example.

number of infinities of solution possibilities. The computer graphics screen is an ideal tool to help survey a large number of solutions.

The problem clearly requires motion generation synthesis (or rigid body guidance), in which the position and angle of the filter blank is specified at different points. Four precision points along a specified path and four corresponding coupler angles were chosen.

The first set of precision points chosen are shown in Table 1. The mandrel was designated position one, and the second position was picked above the mandrel with no rotation (to prevent folding the filter blank). The third position was chosen to be halfway between the second and fourth positions

Table 1. First attempt, four precision points

Position	X-coordinate (cm)	Y-coordinate (cm)	Rotation (Deg.)
1	0	0	0
2	1	7	0
3	17	18	60
4	38	21	117

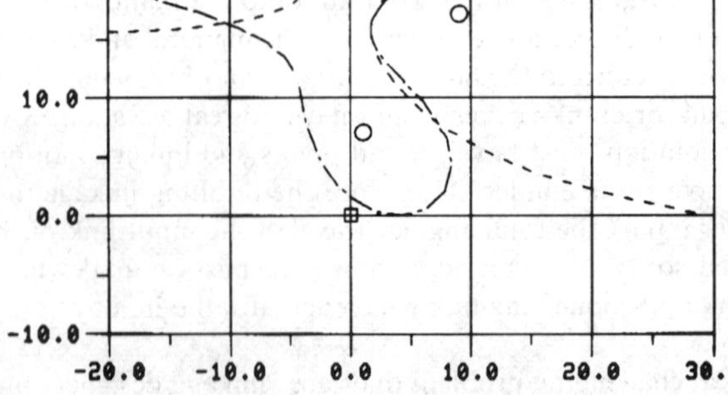

Fig. 14. Center and circle point curves for four prescribed positions (Table 1) for task in Fig. 13.

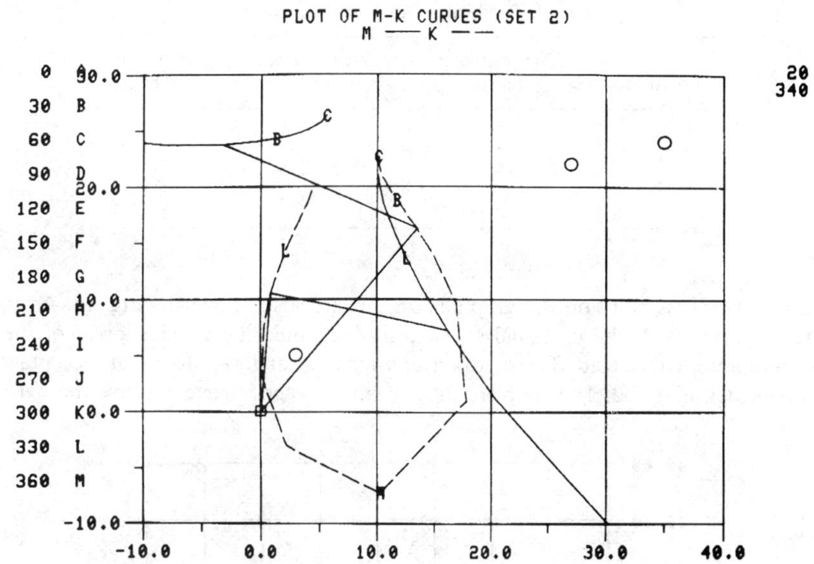

Fig. 15. Interactive graphics used to locate specific ground and moving Pivot locations.

with about half the required rotation. The fourth position corresponded to the angle and position of the hopper.

The infinity of solutions can be displayed as center and circle point curves (curves that contain ground pivots and moving pivot possibilities) for this set of precision points as is shown in Fig. 14. The solid and short dashed lines represent the portions of the center point curve, while the long dash and dash-dot lines are the circle point curve. Figure 15 shows an option where the independent variable values are correlated to their positions on the curves by letters corresponding to the table along the left hand side of the figure. The results of interactively locating ground pivots and moving

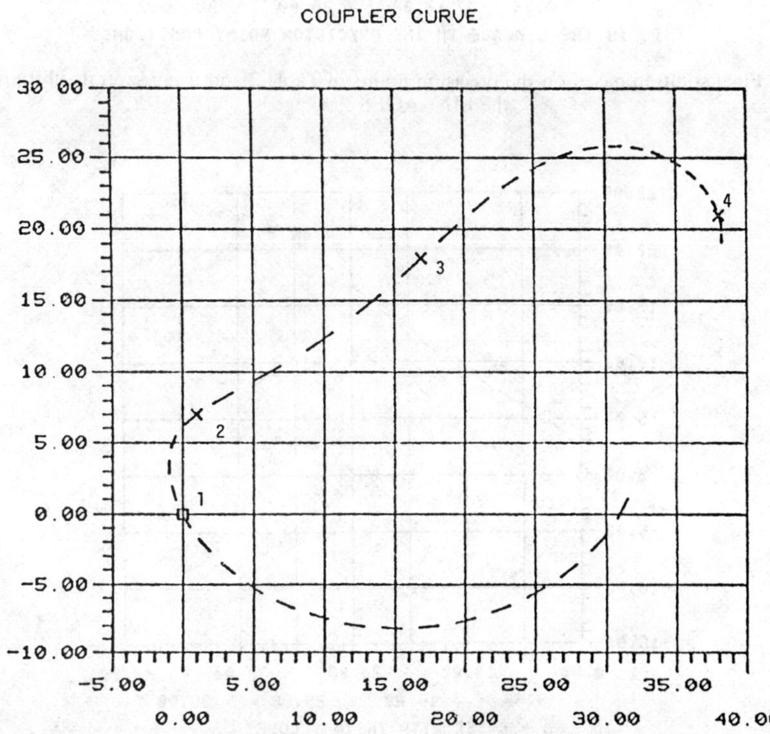

Fig. 16. Coupler curve for linkage chosen interactively in Fig. 15.

Table 2. Third set of precision points

Position	X-coordinate (cm)	Y-Coordinate (cm)	Rotation (Deg.)
1	0	0	0
2	3	5	5
3	27	22	90
4	35	24	117

pivots (by using the cross-hairs on the graphics screen) are also shown in Fig. 15. As the designer locates a ground pivot with the cross-hairs, the computer finds the moving pivot of the dyad and draws lines to represent the dyad. These two dyads form what looks to be an acceptable four-bar solution to be further analyzed. The coupler curve of this linkage is generated by another subroutine.

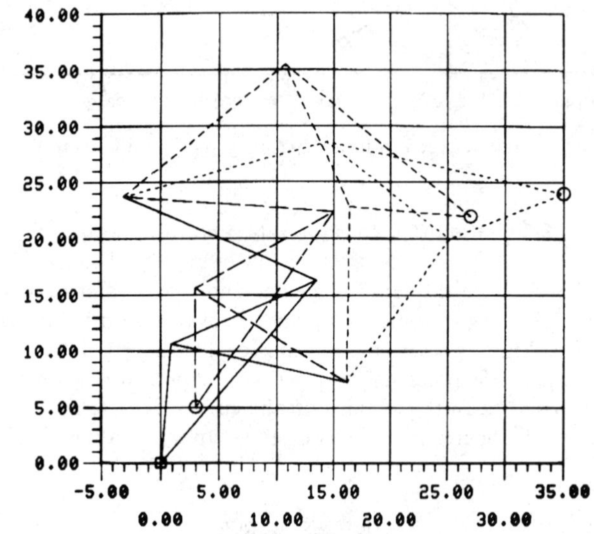

Fig. 17. Final solution based on the precision points of Table 2 and using several subroutines of the LINCAGES Package.

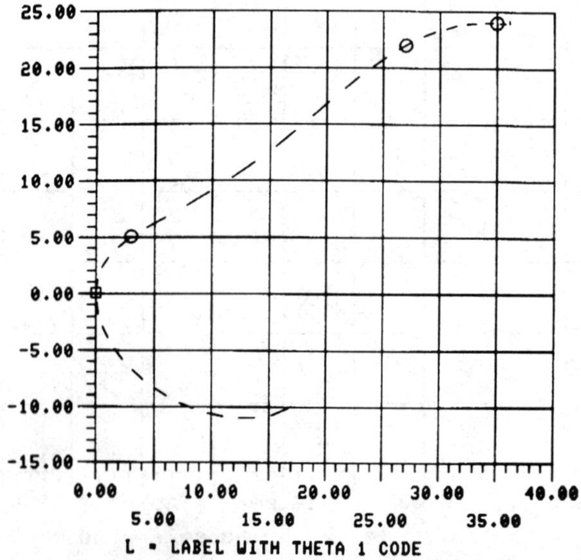

Fig. 18. Coupler curve of final solution shown in Fig. 17.

Figure 16 shows that the coupler curve shifts to the left between points one and two, and also approaches point 4 vertically. Both of these are unacceptable characteristics. Although this linkage is not acceptable, there are others which also satisfy the prescribed precision points in Table 1 as new choices for the middle two precision points.

Making a long story short, the precision points in Table 1 were changed (see Table 2), and a number of the options on the LINCAGES Package were used to optimize for the final solution. The final linkage is shown in several positions in Fig. 17 while its coupler curve is shown in Fig. 18. Many other options of the LINCAGES Package are not shown here.

SUMMARY

This paper has attempted to summarize the ways in which interactive computer graphics and computer aided design have been integrated into the curriculum in the University of Minnesota Mechanical Engineering Department. Specific software packages have been developed for use in the engineering graphics courses and the mechanisms courses, and were described in some detail. Courses teaching basic numerical methods and computer graphics, applied to mechanical engineering design, have also been introduced at the senior/graduate elective level, but were not described in detail in this paper.

The approach taken, utilizing low cost computer graphics equipment, has proven to be quite effective. Students are receiving good exposure to the new tools provided by the computer and computer graphics. Student response has been very positive. The feedback from industries who have hired graduates who have taken this sequence has been very enthusiastic. The authors feel this experience is one which can be transported to any mechanical engineering department.

Acknowledgements—The authors would like to express thanks to the gracious support of the University of Minnesota for support of this development. In particular, the Educational Development Program, the Graduate School, the Institute of Technology, the Department of Mechanical Engineering, and the University Computer Center have aided our effort.

REFERENCES

1. Erdman A. G., Three position synthesis by complex numbers. One section of *Monograph on Mechanical Design*, McGraw–Hill, New York. NSF Report No. GK-36624, Paper No. 49. To be published.
2. Erdman A. G. and Gustafson J., LINCAGES—A Linkage INteractive Computer Analysis and Graphically Enhanced Synthesis Package. ASME Paper No. 77-DTES.
3. Erdman A. G. and Sandor G. N., *Mechanism Design: Analysis and Synthesis*, Prentice-Hall, N.J. To be published.
4. Loerch R., Erdman A. G., Sandor G. N. and Midha A., Synthesis of four bar linkages with specified ground pivots. *Proceedings of the Fourth Applied Mechanisms Conference*, November (1975).

APPENDIX A:

TERPAK Subroutine Summary

AXIS (X, Y, STRING, NS, SIZE, ANGLE, AMIN, ADEL, LROT)
BELL
BLANK
DELAY(SECS)
ERASE
FACTOR (SF)
KEYBRD (KEY)-function-
LINE (X, Y, N, K, J, L)
MARK
NUMBER (X, Y, HEIGHT, VALUE, ANGLE, FORMAT)
PLOT (X, Y, IPEN)
PLOTS
RESET
SCALE (ARRAY, SIZE, N, K)
SETUP (IBUF(1))
STRING (STG, NS)
SYMBOL(X, Y, HEIGHT, STRONG, ANGLE, NS)
UNBLNK
VMODE (MODE)
WHERE (X, Y, FACTOR)
WINDOW(IXLL, IYLL, IXUR, IYUR)
ZONE (IZONE)

In each subroutine, the type of argument is indicated by the normal FORTRAN naming convention unless explicitly stated otherwise.

Comput. & Educ. Vol. 5, pp. 245 to 264, 1981
Printed in Great Britain
0360-1315/81/040245-20$02.00/0
Pergamon Press Ltd

KINEMATICS WITH COMPUTER GRAPHICS

J. ALAN ADAMS

Department of Mechanical Engineering, U.S. Naval Academy Annapolis, MD 21402, U.S.A.

Abstract—The impact which computer graphics can have on engineering education is illustrated in this paper by considering the subject area of kinematics. Details of the mathematical modeling needed to support the generation of motion curves and computer graphics simulation for kinematic analysis are given, and a comparison is made with the current popular methods of analysis. Several results of computer graphic displays are given to illustrate the wide variety of situations where computer graphics can add to the teaching and understanding of kinematics.

When computers first became available to educators they were used to reinforce the accepted manner of presenting the subject material. To be sure computational speed allowed more problems to be analyzed, and parametric studies added new insight into the behavior of mathematical models. However, the fundamental approach to mathematical model building was normally unaltered, with the exception of using finite difference or finite element techniques to represent differential equations.

Historically, the availability of new hardware and new techniques have created new approaches to problem formulation and solution, and we can expect the availability of low cost computer graphics to do the same. The subject of kinematics provides a good example. Between 1940 and 1960 the availability of drafting tables and good drawing instruments promoted the development of graphical solution techniques for obtaining the displacement, velocity, and acceleration of mechanical components. Many of these techniques are still in use today [1]. The scientific and mathematical emphasis during the past 20 years has resulted in a vector analysis approach to kinematic analysis in most engineering curricula [2]. Both the graphical and vector analysis methods lead to the determination of instantaneous kinematic values for a particular configuration of the device under study. They will continue to provide valuable design tools for the engineer.

Computer graphics makes feasible the use of complete kinematic motion curves for describing the behavior of mechanical components. This provides the option of observing the behavior of a mechanism over a complete cycle of operation, rather than at only a few instantaneous positions. The generation of motion curves may require a change in the manner in which the fundamental subject of kinematics is presented to undergraduate engineering students. The purpose of this paper is to illustrate some of the new options available to educators in engineering and physics which are feasible using low cost computer graphics.

KINEMATICS

Kinematics, the study of motion in terms of displacement, velocity, and acceleration is fundamental to understanding modern technology. All components of a device in motion are treated as rigid members, and no concern is given to the forces which cause the motion. Kinematics is the foundation for later study in dynamics, vibrations, and machine design where forces and deflections are considered. As higher speeds are encountered and energy efficient designs become more critical, a complete description of kinematic behavior will often be needed for proper analysis. This is provided by motion curves which kinematically describe every position of the device.

Motion curves can be obtained quickly and accurately with the use of computers. The equations of motion can be formulated as a set of algebraic equations containing unknown terms for displacements, velocities, or accelerations. These equations are solved either sequentially or simultaneously, depending upon the type of mechanical coupling in the device. The algebraic equations for displacement are usually non-linear equations which require numerical techniques such as Newton–Raphson iteration for their solution. On the other hand, the algebraic equations for velocities and accelerations are usually linear and solutions can be obtained using Cramer's rule or matrix inversion.

The use of computers for kinematic analysis will not necessarily reduce the importance of the graphical or vector analysis solutions being used today. These will still be used to study instantaneous behavior, to determine the mechanical advantage of mechanisms, to gain clues about how to modify a mechanism to improve its performance, and to check the validity of computer solutions. The use of computers will reduce the time and increase the accuracy associated with the generation of motion curves, help increase understanding of the kinematic behavior of mechanisms, make possible parametric studies to improve analysis and design methods, and lead to powerful techniques in computer aided design.

COMPUTER GRAPHICS

Computer graphics is finding wide application today in a variety of technological areas. It is particularly suited to kinematic analysis and simulation since it provides a way to simultaneously present a pictorial representation of geometric configurations as a function of time, along with results of kinematic analysis in the form of motion curves. This combination can also be used in producing video tapes and movies which give a realistic, animated picture of the real time motion of a device and add a new dimension to the study of kinematics. Sample video tapes are available from the author for readers who are interested in this application.

The computer graphics facilities available at the U.S. Naval Academy are described elsewhere in this issue of "*Computers & Education*." The computer graphics results given in this paper were created by use of storage tube display terminals. Once the angular and/or rectilinear displacements for each member of a mechanism are available from solutions to the governing algebraic equations as a function of the input variable, then computer graphic motion simulation can be created. If the members are represented by a series of points, then these points can be translated, scaled, rotated, reflected, etc by use of homogeneous coordinates and matrix multiplication [3].

Three advantages result from using computer graphics to display the various geometrical configurations along with its kinematic motion curves.

(a) First, the display gives a check on the numerical displacement solutions and insures that the device will actually work in all necessary positions without interference or the need for reassembly.
(b) Second, observing the relative position of various members at critical values of velocity, acceleration, torque, or mechanical advantage will suggest ways in which the geometry might be changed to improve the behavior.
(c) Third, once the members are defined as a series of points stored in a file or array, geometric properties such as center of gravity, area, and moments of inertia can easily by calculated for each member.

ANALYSIS TECHNIQUES

Perhaps the best way to illustrate the similarities and differences between the popular vector analysis approach and the closed vector loop approach is to use a simple example. Consider the pivoted collar driven by a crank (OA) and sliding link (AB) as shown in Fig. 1. The collar pivot is located at $x = 6$ cm, $y = -14$ cm relative to the crank center. The length of the crank is 4 cm, the length of AB is 20 cm, and the perpendicular distance from the collar pivot to the center of link AB is 10 cm. In the position shown, the crank angle is $\theta = 0$ and the link AB makes an angle of 36.87° with the horizontal.

Vector analysis method

A typical problem in elementary kinematics reads like this:
Given: In the position shown in Fig. 1 the crank OA has an angular velocity of $\omega_{AO} = 2.0$ rad/s counterclockwise.

Find: (a) The angular velocity of the collar ω_C.
(b) The velocity of point B at the end of link AB.

Solution:

(a) The solution can be obtained by noting the vector summation (Fig. 1b)

$$\bar{\mathbf{R}}_{A/O} + \bar{\mathbf{R}}_{D/A} = \bar{\mathbf{R}}_{C/O} + \bar{\mathbf{R}}_{D/C} \tag{1}$$

Differentiation gives

$$\bar{\mathbf{V}}_{A/O} + \bar{\mathbf{V}}_{D/A} = \bar{\mathbf{V}}_{C/O} + \bar{\mathbf{V}}_{D/C} \tag{2}$$

where in general

$$\bar{\mathbf{V}} = \dot{\mathbf{R}}\bar{\mathbf{e}}_r + \bar{\omega} \times \bar{\mathbf{R}}. \tag{3}$$

Combining Eqns (2) and (3) gives

$$\dot{\mathbf{R}}_{A/O}\bar{\mathbf{e}}_{A/O} + \bar{\omega}_{AO} \times \overline{\mathbf{R}}_{A/O} + \dot{\mathbf{R}}_{D/A}\bar{\mathbf{e}}_{D/A} + \bar{\omega}_{DA} \times \overline{\mathbf{R}}_{D/A} = \dot{\mathbf{R}}_{D/C}\bar{\mathbf{e}}_{D/C} + \bar{\omega}_{DC} \times \overline{\mathbf{R}}_{D/C}. \qquad (4)$$

Since vectors OA and CD are fixed in length, $\dot{\mathbf{R}}_{A/O} = \dot{\mathbf{R}}_{D/C} = 0$. Also $\bar{\omega}_{DA} = \bar{\omega}_{DC} = \bar{\omega}_C = \omega_C\bar{\mathbf{k}}$. The given crank angular velocity vector is $\bar{\omega}_{AO} = 2\bar{\mathbf{k}}$.

From the given geometry it can be seen that

$$\mathbf{R}_{A/O} = 4\mathbf{i}, \quad \mathbf{R}_{D/A} = 8\mathbf{i} - 6\cdot\mathbf{j}, \quad \mathbf{R}_{D/C} = 6\mathbf{i} + 8\mathbf{j}.$$

Evaluation of the angular velocity terms in eqn (3), using the rules for the vector cross-product gives

$$\bar{\omega}_{AO} \times \overline{\mathbf{R}}_{A/O} = 2\bar{\mathbf{k}} \times 4\bar{\mathbf{i}} = 8\bar{\mathbf{j}}$$
$$\bar{\omega}_{DA} \times \overline{\mathbf{R}}_{D/A} = \omega_C\bar{\mathbf{k}} \times (8\bar{\mathbf{i}} - 6\bar{\mathbf{j}}) = 8\omega_C\bar{\mathbf{j}} + 6\omega_C\bar{\mathbf{i}}$$
$$\bar{\omega}_{DC} \times \overline{\mathbf{R}}_{D/C} = \omega_C\bar{\mathbf{k}} \times (6\bar{\mathbf{i}} + 8\bar{\mathbf{j}}) = 6\omega_C\bar{\mathbf{j}} - 8\omega_C\bar{\mathbf{i}}.$$

One final observation is required. The unit vector along the link AB can be expressed as:

$$\bar{\mathbf{e}}_{D/A} = (8\bar{\mathbf{i}} - 6\bar{\mathbf{j}})/10.$$

Equation (4) can now be written

$$8\mathbf{j} + 0.8\dot{\mathbf{R}}_{D/A}\mathbf{i} - 0.6\dot{\mathbf{R}}_{D/A}\mathbf{j} + 8\omega_C\mathbf{j} + 6\omega_C\mathbf{i} = 6\omega_C\mathbf{j} - 8\omega_C\mathbf{i}. \qquad (5)$$

Taking the two components of this vector equation gives

$$0.8\dot{\mathbf{R}}_{D/A} + 14\omega_C = 0 \qquad (6)$$

$$-0.6\dot{\mathbf{R}}_{D/A} + 2\omega_C = -8. \qquad (7)$$

Solving these two equations simultaneously gives

$$\omega_C = -0.64 \text{ rad/s and } \dot{\mathbf{R}}_{D/A} = 11.2 \text{ cm/s}.$$

Thus, at the instant in question the collar is rotating clockwise at a rate of 0.64 rad/s and the length AD is increasing at a rate of 11.2 cm/s.

(b) To obtain the velocity of point B we observe that

$$\overline{\mathbf{V}}_B = \overline{\mathbf{V}}_D + \overline{\mathbf{V}}_{B/D} \qquad (8)$$

and

$$\overline{\mathbf{V}}_D = \overline{\mathbf{V}}_{D/C} = \bar{\omega}_{DC} \times \overline{\mathbf{R}}_{D/C}. \qquad (9)$$

Now,

$$\overline{\mathbf{V}}_{B/D} = \dot{\mathbf{R}}_{B/D}\bar{\mathbf{e}}_{B/D} + \omega_{BD} \times \overline{\mathbf{R}}_{B/D}. \qquad (10)$$

We observe that $\bar{\omega}_{BD} = \bar{\omega}_{DA} = \omega_C\bar{\mathbf{k}}$, and $\bar{\mathbf{e}}_{B/D} = \bar{\mathbf{e}}_{D/A}$.

Equation (8) can then be written as

$$\overline{\mathbf{V}}_B = \omega_C\bar{\mathbf{k}} \times (6\bar{\mathbf{i}} + 8\bar{\mathbf{j}}) + \dot{\mathbf{R}}_{B/D}(0.8\bar{\mathbf{i}} - 0.6\bar{\mathbf{j}}) + \omega_C\bar{\mathbf{k}} \times (8\bar{\mathbf{i}} - 6\bar{\mathbf{j}}) \qquad (11)$$

where the equality $\overline{\mathbf{R}}_{B/D} = \overline{\mathbf{R}}_{D/A}$ was used. Simplifying gives

$$\overline{\mathbf{V}}_B = (-2\omega_C + 0.8\dot{\mathbf{R}}_{B/D})\bar{\mathbf{i}} + (14\omega_C - 0.6\dot{\mathbf{R}}_{B/D})\bar{\mathbf{j}}. \qquad (12)$$

Using the results from part (a), e.g. $\omega_C = -0.64$ rad/s and $\dot{\mathbf{R}}_{B/D} = -\dot{\mathbf{R}}_{D/A} = -11.2$ cm/s gives

$$\overline{\mathbf{V}}_B = -7.67\bar{\mathbf{i}} - 2.24\bar{\mathbf{j}}. \qquad (13)$$

Thus, the magnitude of the velocity of point B is 8.0 cm/s and the direction is 196°, measured CCW from the horizontal.

It has required a fair amount of computation to determine the two instantaneous quantities of interest. These answers do not tell us what will happen next as the drive crank moves to another position. One cannot tell whether the values calculated are larger or smaller than the same velocities calculated at subsequent crank positions. The above calculations must be repeated many times for different values of crank angle θ to get a feeling for the shape of the complete velocity curves for ω_C and V_B as a function of θ. If accelerations were of interest many more computations would be required. The procedure suggested in this paper to obtain complete motion curves is *not* to program the above computational process but to obtain solutions to the algebraic equations resulting from the closed vector loop equations.

Vector loop equation method

This method was recently discussed in the textbook by Paul[4]. Using the notation shown in Fig. 1(c) we write the two component equations for the closed vector loop OADCO. Let the horizontal distance from O to C be d and the vertical distance be h. The two equations are:

$$x: \quad a\cos\theta + r\cos\phi_1 - c\cos\phi_2 - d = 0 \tag{14}$$

$$y: \quad a\sin\theta + r\sin\phi_1 - c\sin\phi_2 + h = 0. \tag{15}$$

Since the collar is always perpendicular to the link AB

$$\phi_1 = \phi_2 + 3\pi/2. \tag{16}$$

Hence, $\cos\phi_1 = \sin\phi_2$ and $\sin\phi_1 = -\cos\phi_2$. Equations (14) and (15) then become

$$a\cos\theta + r\sin\phi_2 - c\cos\phi_2 - d = 0 \tag{17}$$

$$a\sin\theta - r\cos\phi_2 - c\sin\phi_2 + h = 0. \tag{18}$$

Equations (17) and (18) are two non-linear, algebraic equations for ϕ_2 and r as a function of the crank angle θ. Solutions can be obtained by using Newton–Raphson iteration for $0 \leqslant \theta \leqslant 360°$, provided that solutions exist for the complete rotation of the crank.

Newton–Raphson iteration. Historically the popularity of the graphical and vector analysis methods are due to the fact that the methods avoid having to solve non-linear sets of algebraic equations such as eqns (17) and (18). However, a digital computer removes the drudgery of the trial and error solution procedures that are often required for coupled, non-linear equations. Most computer libraries provide programs for numerical schemes such as Newton–Raphson iteration for solving sets of non-linear algebraic equations.

The use of Newton–Raphson iteration requires an estimate of the initial unknown dependent variables at the initial value of the independent variable. For the simple example under consideration it is easily determined that $\phi_2 = 53.13°$ and $r = 10$ cm when $\theta = 0$. For more complex mechanisms it is possible to assemble the mechanism in more than one configuration and the user must take care that initial estimates yield the solution of interest.

Other precautions must also be made when specifying the geometric constants which appear in the loop equations. For many mechanisms the device will not operate for all possible values of the independent input variable. For these configurations the Newton–Raphson iteration will not converge and this fact provides valuable knowledge about the mechanism, just as surely as does convergence to a solution.

Table 1 gives the solution for r and ϕ_2 as a function of θ for the sliding collar shown in Fig. 1. These solutions, which were obtained by use of Newton–Raphson iteration, are given for every 5° of rotation of the crank. Notice that the minimum value of ϕ_2 occurs at $\theta = 45°$, and the maximum at $\theta = 270°$. The value of the variable r has a minimum at $\theta = 360°$ and a maximum near $\theta = 115°$.

Once the displacements are known, then a computer graphics display can be generated and velocity and acceleration curves can be calculated. One way to show the behavior of the device is with a schematic such as shown in Fig. 2. This type of output is more instructive when observed as it is being created on a storage tube display terminal. A more complete description is created by using a geometric construction and complete motion curves as shown in the figures which follow. These curves are shown in Figs 4–6 and 14–21.

Velocity curves. Differentiation of eqns (17) and (18) gives

$$-a\dot{\theta}\sin\theta + \dot{r}\dot{\phi}_2\cos\phi_2 + \dot{r}\sin\phi_2 + c\dot{\phi}_2\sin\phi_2 = 0 \tag{19}$$

$$a\dot{\theta}\cos\theta + \dot{r}\dot{\phi}_2\sin\phi_2 - \dot{r}\cos\phi_2 - c\dot{\phi}_2\cos\phi_2 = 0. \tag{20}$$

These two equations are a pair of linear equations in $\dot{\phi}_2$ and $\dot{r}$. In non-dimensional matrix form they are written as

$$\begin{bmatrix} (r/a)\cos\phi_2 + (c/a)\sin\phi_2 & \sin\phi_2 \\ (r/a)\sin\phi_2 - (c/a)\cos\phi_2 & -\cos\phi_2 \end{bmatrix} \begin{bmatrix} \dot{\phi}_2/\dot{\theta} \\ \dot{r}/a\dot{\theta} \end{bmatrix} = \begin{bmatrix} \sin\theta \\ -\cos\theta \end{bmatrix}. \tag{21}$$

If this matrix equation is abbreviated [B] [V] = [C], then the two unknown non-dimensional velocities $\dot{\phi}_2/\dot{\theta}$ and $\dot{r}/a\dot{\theta}$ are elements in [V] where

$$[V] = [B]^{-1}[C]. \tag{22}$$

Table 1. Displacements for rocking collar

Crank angle θ	Distance r	Angle ϕ_2	Crank angle θ	Distance r	Angle ϕ_2
0	10	0.9273	185	13.640	1.2641
5	10.485	0.9012	190	13.260	1.2877
10	10.963	0.8788	195	12.860	1.3113
15	11.429	0.8599	200	12.442	1.3348
20	11.883	0.8444	205	12.007	1.3581
25	12.322	0.8320	210	11.557	1.3811
30	12.745	0.8225	215	11.094	1.4037
35	13.150	0.8158	220	10.619	1.4259
40	13.536	0.8116	225	10.136	1.4474
45	13.902	0.8098	230	9.6466	1.4682
50	14.246	0.8104	235	9.1535	1.4879
55	14.567	0.8129	240	8.6606	1.5065
60	14.866	0.8173	245	8.1719	1.5236
65	15.140	0.8235	250	7.6923	1.5388
70	15.389	0.8314	255	7.2277	1.5517
75	15.613	0.8407	260	6.7851	1.5618
80	15.810	0.8515	265	6.3725	1.5684
85	15.981	0.8636	270	6.0014	1.5707
90	16.125	0.8769	275	5.6769	1.5683
95	16.241	0.8913	280	5.4191	1.5595
100	16.329	0.9067	285	5.2338	1.5441
105	16.389	0.9230	290	5.1320	1.5214
110	16.421	0.9402	295	5.1194	1.4913
115	16.425	0.9583	300	5.1967	1.4544
120	16.401	0.9771	305	5.3594	1.4115
125	16.349	0.9966	310	5.5990	1.3642
130	16.268	1.0166	315	5.9045	1.3141
135	16.160	1.0372	320	6.2640	1.2626
140	16.024	1.0585	325	6.6663	1.2114
145	15.861	1.0801	330	7.1014	1.1616
150	15.671	1.1021	335	7.5607	1.1140
155	15.454	1.1246	340	8.0367	1.0694
160	15.212	1.1473	345	8.5233	1.0283
165	14.945	1.1703	350	9.0155	0.9908
170	14.653	1.1935	355	9.5090	0.9571
175	14.338	1.2170	360	9.9999	0.9273
180	14.000	1.2405			

Solutions to: $a\cos\theta + r\sin\phi_2 - c\cos\phi_2 - d = 0$
$a\sin\theta + r\cos\phi_2 - c\sin\phi_2 + h = 0$
where $a = 4$, $c = 10$, $d = 6$, $h = 14$, and $0 < \theta < 360°$.

Subroutines are available in most software systems for performing the operations of matrix inversion and matrix multiplication required in eqn (22). All elements in the [B] matrix are known once the geometry is specified (a and c) and the displacement solutions (ϕ_2 and r) are found as a function of θ. Non-dimensional velocity curves are generated by calculating $\dot{\phi}_2/\dot{\theta}$ and $\dot{r}/a\dot{\theta}$ as a function of θ. The angular velocity of the input crank is assumed to be constant, $\dot{\theta} = \omega$.

Acceleration curves. Differentiating eqns (19) and (20), simplifying, normalizing, and writing in matrix form gives

$$\begin{bmatrix} (r/a)\cos\phi_2 + (c/a)\sin\phi_2 & \sin\phi_2 \\ (r/a)\sin\phi_2 - (c/a)\cos\phi_2 & -\cos\phi_2 \end{bmatrix} \begin{bmatrix} \ddot{\phi}_2/\dot{\theta}^2 \\ \ddot{r}/a\dot{\theta}^2 \end{bmatrix} = \begin{bmatrix} C_1 \\ C_2 \end{bmatrix} \tag{23}$$

where

$$C_1 = \cos\theta + (\ddot{\theta}/\dot{\theta}^2)\sin\theta + (r/a)(\dot{\phi}_2/\dot{\theta})^2\sin\phi_2 - 2(\dot{r}/a\dot{\theta})(\dot{\phi}_2/\dot{\theta})\cos\phi_2 - (c/a)(\dot{\phi}_2/\dot{\theta})^2\cos\phi_2$$

and

$$C_2 = \sin\theta + (\ddot{\theta}/\dot{\theta}^2)\cos\theta - (r/a)(\dot{\phi}_2/\dot{\theta})^2\cos\phi_2 - 2(\dot{r}/a\dot{\theta})(\dot{\phi}_2/\dot{\theta})\sin\phi_2 - (c/a)(\dot{\phi}_2/\dot{\theta})^2\sin\phi_2 .$$

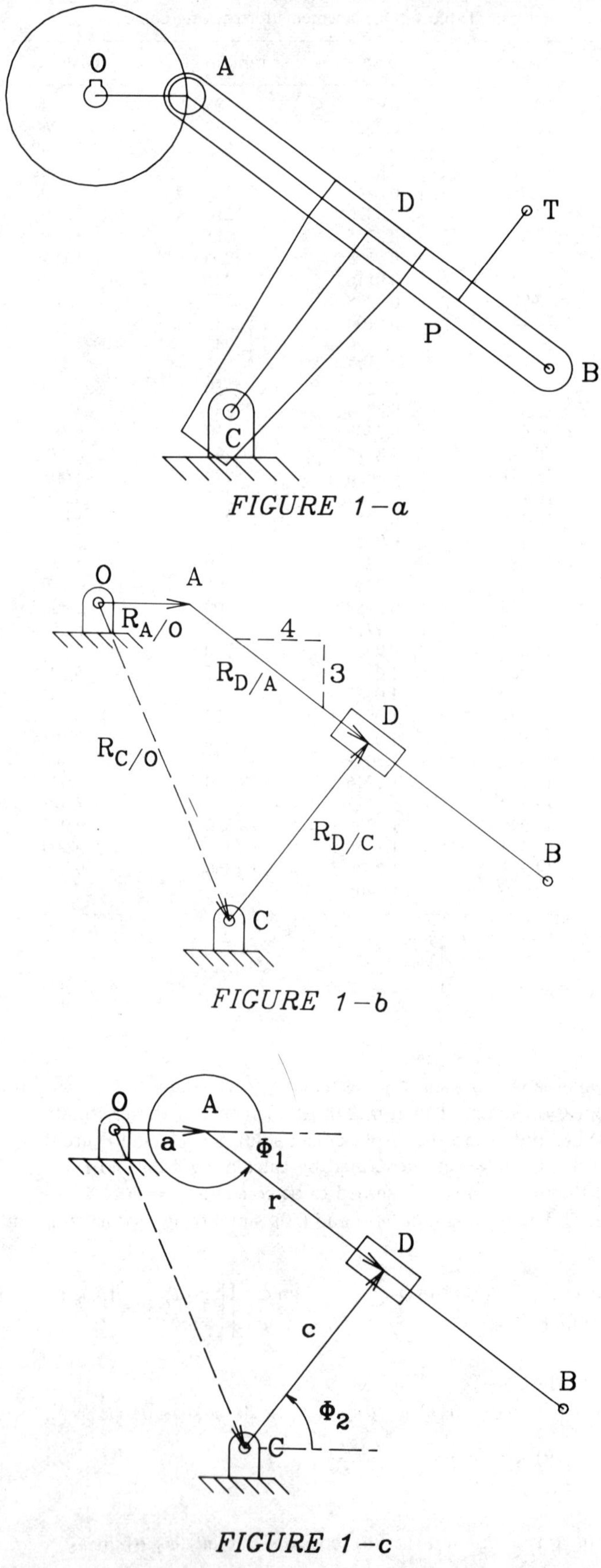

Fig. 1. Rocking collar geometry.

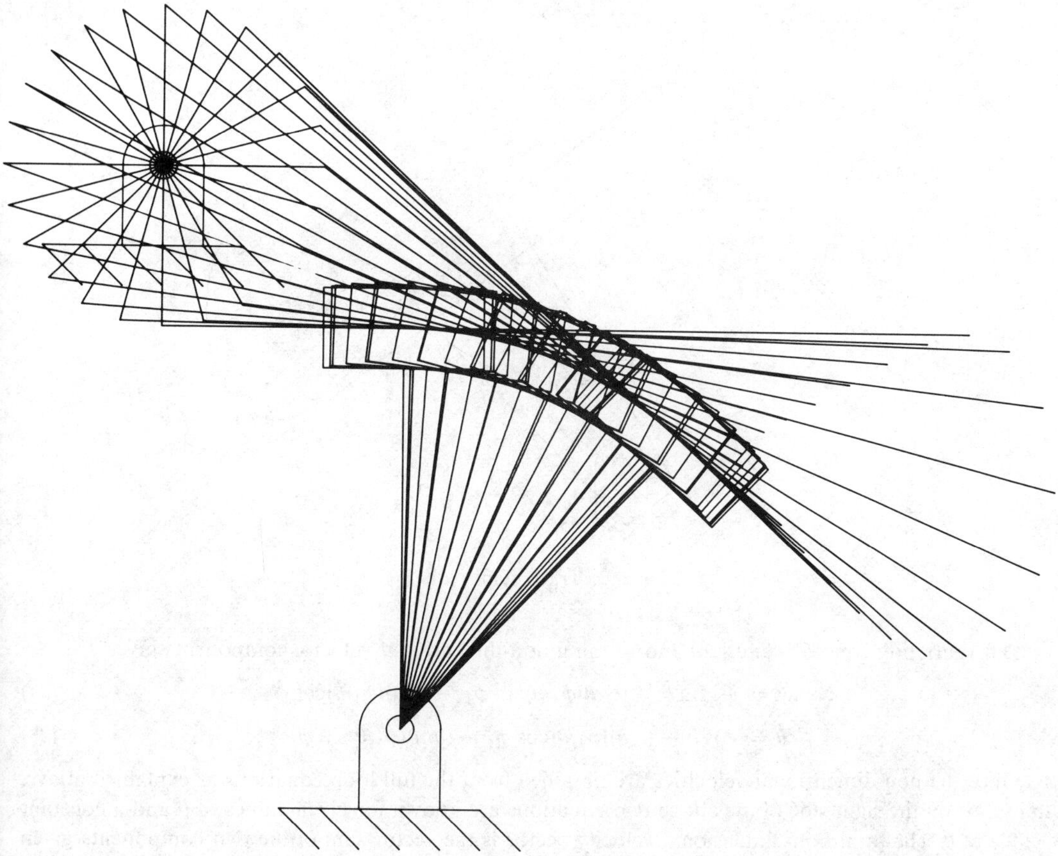

Fig. 2. Displacement schematic.

When $\dot{\theta}$ = constant, then $\ddot{\theta} = 0$. If the angular velocity of the crank is changing, then an expression for the crank acceleration $\ddot{\theta} = f(\theta)$ can be defined and used in the above equation for C_1 and C_2. All motion curves presented in this paper are based upon the assumption of $\dot{\theta}$ = constant.

Again, representing eqn (23) by [B][A] = [C], the two unknown non-dimensional accelerations $\ddot{\phi}_2/\dot{\theta}^2$ and $\ddot{r}/a\dot{\theta}^2$ can be found as a function of θ by calculating

$$[A] = [B]^{-1}[C] \tag{24}$$

for the values of interest. Notice that in eqns (22) and (24) the [B] matrices are identical, but the elements in the [C] matrices contain the terms on the right sides of eqns (21) and (23) respectively.

Trace Point Kinematics. Often one is interested in the motion of a particular point on a mechanism. This point may correspond to the center of gravity, a drive pin, the point of contact with another object, etc. A partial loop equation can be used to obtain the position, and then the complete kinematics of any trace point on a member.

Consider the point T on link AB shown in Fig. 1. Once solutions for the closed vector loop OADCO are obtained as explained above, a partial loop equation can be used to obtain the absolute position of point T as a function of the crank angle θ. The position of T, relative to a local coordinate system centered at point A and fixed to link AB is given by the coordinates AP = ζ, PT = η. The partial vector loop is chosen to be OAPTO. The components of this partial vector loop are

$$x: \quad a\cos\theta + \zeta\cos\phi_1 - \eta\sin\phi_1 - X_T = 0 \tag{25}$$

$$y: \quad a\sin\theta + \zeta\sin\phi_1 + \eta\cos\phi_1 - Y_T = 0 \tag{26}$$

where X_T, Y_T are the absolute coordinates of point T with respect to point 0. Once ϕ_1 is known for all values of θ, X_T and Y_T can be calculated directly from eqns (25) and (26). For the example shown in Fig. 1, if the motion of point B is of interest then $\zeta = 20$, $\eta = 0$. The path followed by a trace point can easily be shown by using computer graphics. The path of point B for $0 \leqslant \theta \leqslant 360$ is shown in Fig. 3.

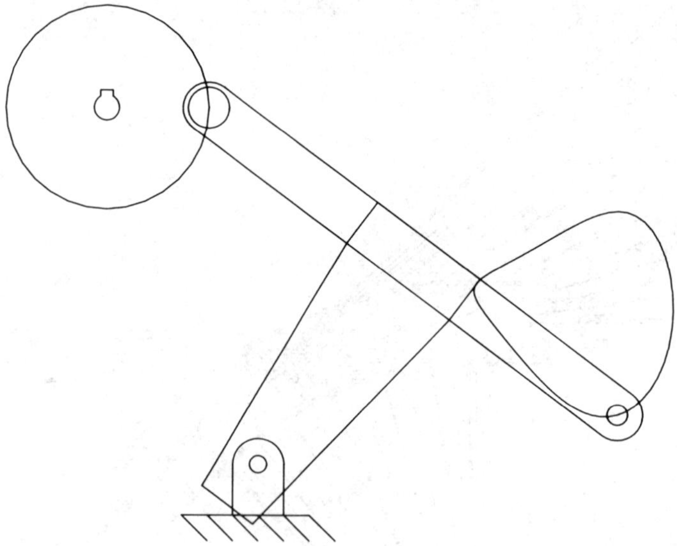

Fig. 3. Trace point path.

Differentiating eqns (25) and (26) and forming non-dimensional velocity components gives

$$\dot{\mathbf{X}}_T/a\dot{\theta} = -\sin\theta - (\zeta/a)(\dot{\phi}_1/\dot{\theta})\sin\phi_1 - (\eta/a)(\dot{\phi}_1/\dot{\theta})\cos\phi_1 \tag{27}$$

$$\dot{\mathbf{Y}}_T/a\dot{\theta} = \cos\theta + (\zeta/a)(\dot{\phi}_1/\dot{\theta})\cos\phi_1 - (\eta/a)(\dot{\phi}_1/\dot{\theta})\sin\phi_1. \tag{28}$$

Once the non-dimensional velocities are obtained from the full loop equations as explained above, all terms on the right side of the above two equations are known for given values of θ and a constant value of $\dot{\theta}$. The total non-dimensional velocity vector is the vector sum of the two components given in eqns (27) and (28), i.e.

$$|\bar{\mathbf{V}}/a\dot{\theta}| = [(\dot{\mathbf{X}}_T/a\dot{\theta})^2 + (\dot{\mathbf{Y}}_T/a\dot{\theta})^2]^{1/2} \tag{29}$$

where the velocity vector makes an angle α with the horizontal, and $\alpha = \tan^{-1}(\dot{\mathbf{Y}}_T/\dot{\mathbf{X}}_T)$. The velocity vector will be tangent to the trace point path shown in Fig. 3.

One further differentiation of the partial loop equations leads to the non-dimensional acceleration components given by

$$\begin{aligned}(\ddot{\mathbf{X}}_T/a\dot{\theta}^2) = {} & -\cos\theta - (\zeta/a)(\dot{\phi}_1/\dot{\theta})^2\cos\phi_1 - (\zeta/a)(\ddot{\phi}_1/\dot{\theta}^2)\sin\phi_1 \\ & + (\eta/a)(\dot{\phi}_1/\dot{\theta})^2\sin\phi_1 - (\eta/a)(\ddot{\phi}_1/\dot{\theta}^2)\cos\phi_1\end{aligned} \tag{30}$$

$$\begin{aligned}(\ddot{\mathbf{Y}}_T/a\dot{\theta}^2) = {} & -\sin\theta - (\zeta/a)(\dot{\phi}_1/\dot{\theta})^2\sin\phi_1 + (\zeta/a)(\ddot{\phi}_1/\dot{\theta}^2)\cos\phi_1 \\ & - (\eta/a)(\dot{\phi}_1/\dot{\theta})^2\cos\phi_1 - (\eta/a)(\ddot{\phi}_1/\dot{\theta}^2)\sin\phi_1\end{aligned} \tag{31}$$

again, the full loop equations must first be used to obtain the non-dimensional acceleration $\ddot{\phi}_1/\dot{\theta}^2$ and velocity $\dot{\phi}_1/\dot{\theta}$. Then the non-dimensional acceleration vector can be calculated as

$$|\bar{\mathbf{A}}/a\dot{\theta}^2| = [(\ddot{\mathbf{X}}_T/a\dot{\theta}^2)^2 + (\ddot{\mathbf{Y}}_T/a\dot{\theta}^2)^2]^{1/2} \tag{32}$$

where the $\bar{\mathbf{A}}$ vector makes an angle β with the horizontal, where β is given by $\beta = \tan^{-1}(\ddot{\mathbf{Y}}_T/\ddot{\mathbf{X}}_T)$.

DISCUSSION OF RESULTS

Figure 4 shows the complete set of non-dimensional motion curves for the device analyzed previously. At $\theta = 0$ the non-dimensional velocity is -0.32. Hence, for the given values of $\theta = 2$ rad/s, $\dot{\phi}_2/\dot{\theta} = -0.32$. This gives $\dot{\phi}_2 = -(0.32)(2) = -0.64$ rad/s. This answer agrees with the vector analysis results. The motion curves give a complete picture of what the collar is doing during its full cycle. Notice that when the slope of the displacement curve is zero, the velocity is zero, and when the slope of the velocity curve is zero, the acceleration is zero. When the velocity and acceleration curves are of the same sign, acceleration of the collar occurs. When the signs are opposite, deceleration occurs. Thus the collar decelerates for $0 \leqslant \theta < 45°$, accelerates for $45 \leqslant \theta < 180°$, decelerates for $180 \leqslant \theta < 270°$, accelerates for $270 \leqslant \theta < 315°$, and decelerates for $315 \leqslant \theta < 360°$.

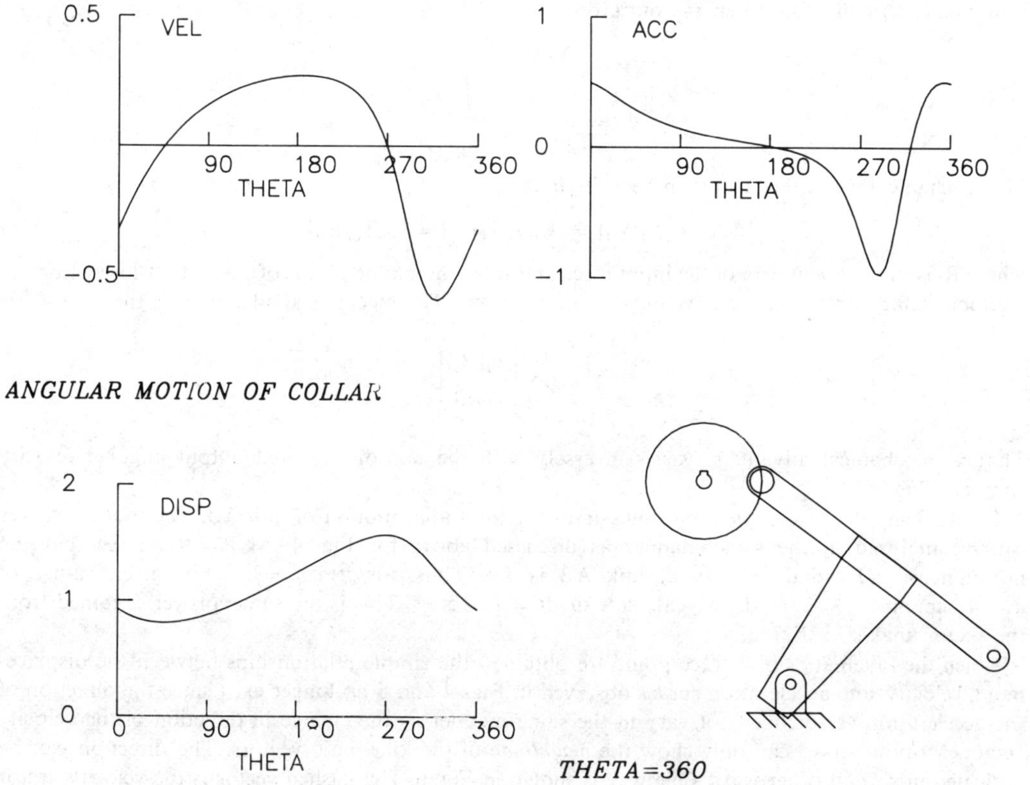

Fig. 4. Rocking collar angular motion curves.

At $\theta = 0$ the non-dimensional angular deceleration is seen to be $\ddot{\phi}_2/\dot{\theta}^2 = 0.5$. Hence, $\ddot{\phi}_2 = 2.0\ \mathrm{rad/s^2}$ (counter-clockwise). The maximum magnitude at $\theta = 270$ gives a dimensional acceleration of $\ddot{\phi}_2 = -4.0$ rad/s (clockwise). The maximum counter-clockwise angular collar velocity occurs at $\theta = 180°$, and the maximum clockwise angular velocity, which has a larger magnitude, occurs at $\theta = 315°$.

Other information is available from the motion curves. If the mass moment of inertia of the collar about its pivot is known, then the output torque $T_O = I\alpha = I\ddot{\phi}_2$. The output power is $P_O = T_O\dot{\phi}_2 = I\ddot{\phi}_2\dot{\phi}_2$. In non-dimensional terms,

$$P_O/I\dot{\theta}^3 = (\ddot{\phi}_2/\dot{\theta}^2)(\dot{\phi}_2/\dot{\theta}). \tag{33}$$

For a conservative force system (negligible friction) we use the conservation of energy principle to equate the power input, $P_i = T_i\dot{\theta}$, to the power output. This leads to

$$T_i/I\dot{\theta}^2 = (\ddot{\phi}_2/\dot{\theta}^2)(\dot{\phi}_2/\dot{\theta}). \tag{34a}$$

This equation shows that the non-dimensional input torque required is equal to the product of the non-dimensional acceleration and velocity curves. It is easy to generate a complete input torque curve once the motion curves are available. With this knowledge it is feasible to consider varying the input current to an electric drive motor to generate only the input torque required to drive the mechanism at each value of crank angle θ. If the output motion of mass m is rectilinear rather than angular, then eqn (34a) becomes

$$T_i/ma^2\dot{\theta}^2 = \left(\frac{\mathrm{d}^2x/\mathrm{d}t^2}{a\dot{\theta}^2}\right)\left(\frac{\mathrm{d}x/\mathrm{d}t}{a\dot{\theta}}\right). \tag{34b}$$

Another piece of useful information obtainable from the motion curves is the mechanical advantage of the device as a function of θ. Mechanical advantage is defined as the absolute value of the ratio of output force to input force.

$$\mathrm{M.A.} = |F_O/F_i|. \tag{35}$$

Equating energy in equal to energy out gives

$$F_iV_i = F_OV_O \tag{36}$$

or

$$T_i\omega_i = T_O\omega_O. \tag{37}$$

The mechanical advantage can then be written as

$$\text{M.A.} = |V_i/V_O| = |R_i\omega_i/R_O\omega_O| = |R_iT_O/R_OT_i| \tag{38}$$

where R_i is the moment arm of the input force and R_O is the moment arm of the output force. For the example being considered we have $\omega_i = \dot{\theta}$ and $\omega_O = \dot{\phi}_2$. The mechanical advantage is then

$$\text{M.A.} = \left|\frac{R_i/R_O}{\dot{\phi}_2/\dot{\theta}}\right|. \tag{39}$$

That is, mechanical advantage varies inversely with the non-dimensional output angular velocity shown in Fig. 4.

Figure 5 shows the complete motion curves for the radial motion of link AB. The motion curves can be analyzed in the same manner as discussed above for Fig. 4. At $\theta = 0$ we see that the non-dimensional radial velocity of link AB is 1.4. Thus, $(dr/dt)/a\omega = 1.4$. For given values of $a = 4.0$ cm and $\omega = 2.0$ rad/s we calculate $dr/dt = 11.2$ cm/s. This is the same answer obtained from the vector analysis solution.

When the kinematics of a trace point are obtained the simple relationships between the displacement, velocity, and acceleration curves observed in Figs 4 and 5 no longer exist since the direction of the acceleration vector does not vary in the same manner as the change in direction of the velocity vector. Motion curves can only show the *magnitude* of the kinematic vectors. The direction can be indicated in several other ways. One way is shown in Fig. 6. The dashed vector is the velocity vector and the solid vector is the acceleration vector. The proper non-dimensional *magnitude* of these vectors

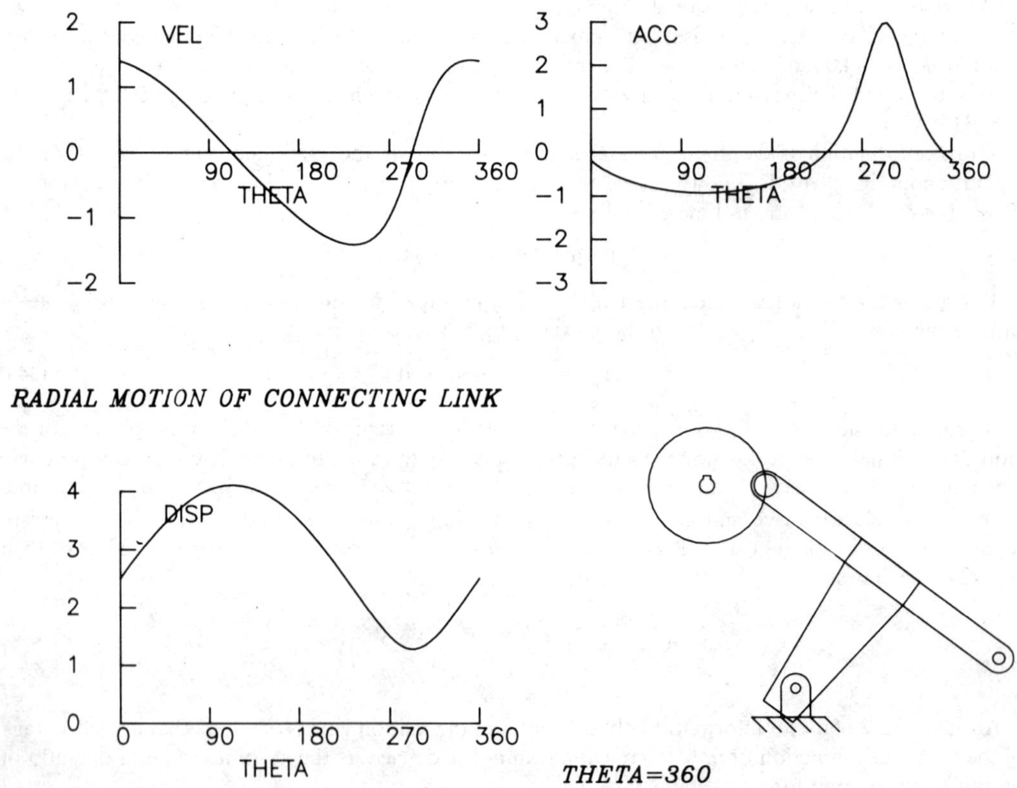

Fig. 5. Connecting link radial motion curves.

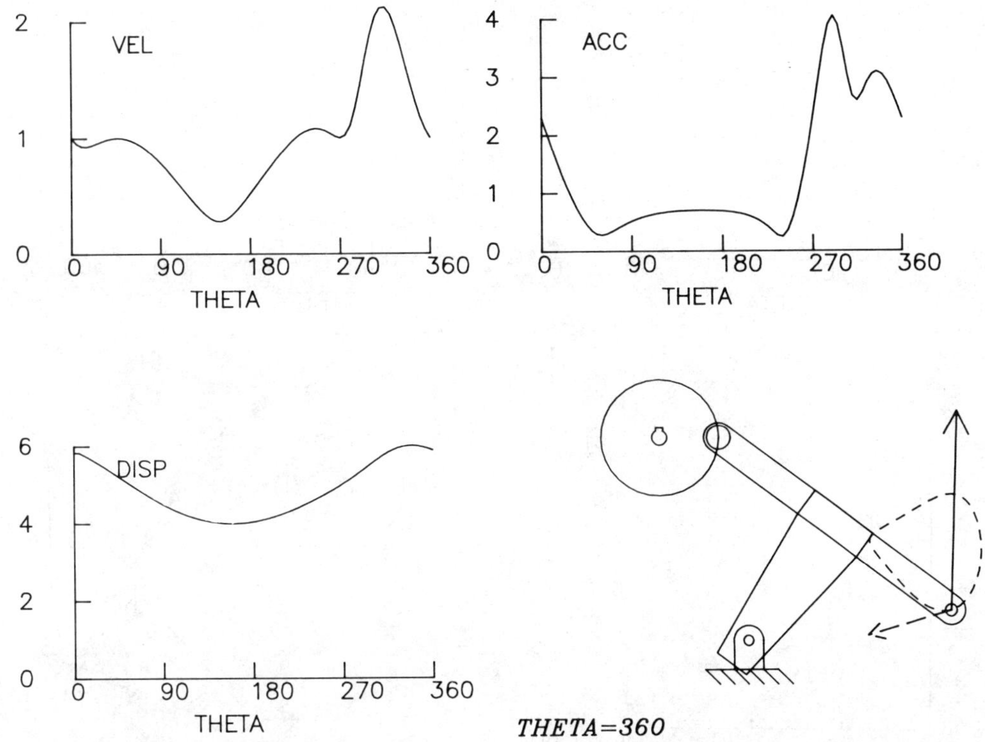

Fig. 6. Trace point motion curves.

can be read from the motion curves. At $\theta = 0$ the non-dimensional velocity is 1.0. Hence, $|V/a\dot{\theta}| = 1.0$. For $a = 4.0$ cm and $\omega = 2.0$ rad/s this given $|V| = 8$ cm/s. The direction of the velocity vector α is equal to 196°. These two answers agree with those obtained by using the vector analysis approach.

Figures 7–13 show both the magnitudes of velocity and acceleration (by the motion curves) and directions (by the vectors) for point B at various positions of the crank angle. A more exciting presentation can be made by creating dynamic animation on a film or video tape. The kinematic history for a complete cycle is shown by the motion curves in Fig. 6, as far as the *magnitude* of the kinematic variables are concerned. Notice that the velocity is never zero since point B never stops moving. The acceleration is always positive because only the absolute magnitude is shown. The displacement shown in the motion curves is the variable distance between point O and point B as the trace point path is followed. Once the computer graphics programs are available one can of course vary the geometry of the device and rapidly obtain many sets of motion curves similar to those shown in the previous figures.

Additional figures are presented to illustrate the generality of the closed vector loop method for planar mechanisms. The motion curves shown provide the starting point for computer aided design and analysis.

Figure 14 shows the motion curves for $|\phi|$, $[d\phi/dt]/\omega$, and the absolute values of $[d^2\phi/dt^2]/\omega^2$ for a 4-slot external Geneva driven by a crank, where ϕ is the angular displacement of the Geneva wheel. The angular velocity is a maximum when $\theta = 0$ but the maximum acceleration for a 4-slot wheel occurs near $\theta = 12°$. The initial step change in acceleration at $\theta = 45°$ causes a jerk that may cause problems in some applications. The maximum output torque occurs where the angular acceleration is a maximum. However, the maximum input torque occurs near $\theta = 8°$, as can be seen by creating the product of the non-dimensional velocity and acceleration curves. For a 4-slot external Geneva the maximum input torque is greater than the maximum output torque. The reverse is true for a 6-slot external Geneva due to the effective gearing between the crank and wheel.

Figure 15 shows ϕ, $[d\phi/dt]/\omega$ and $[d^2\phi/dt]/\omega^2$ for a crank slot mechanism. For the configuration shown the driven arm completes a full 360° rotation about its pivot point. If the shaft separation distance is greater than the crank radius, the driven pivoted arm will oscillate. Notice the rapid changes in acceleration which occur between $160 \leqslant \theta \leqslant 200°$. Again, the input and output torque curves can be easily constructed from the motion curves shown.

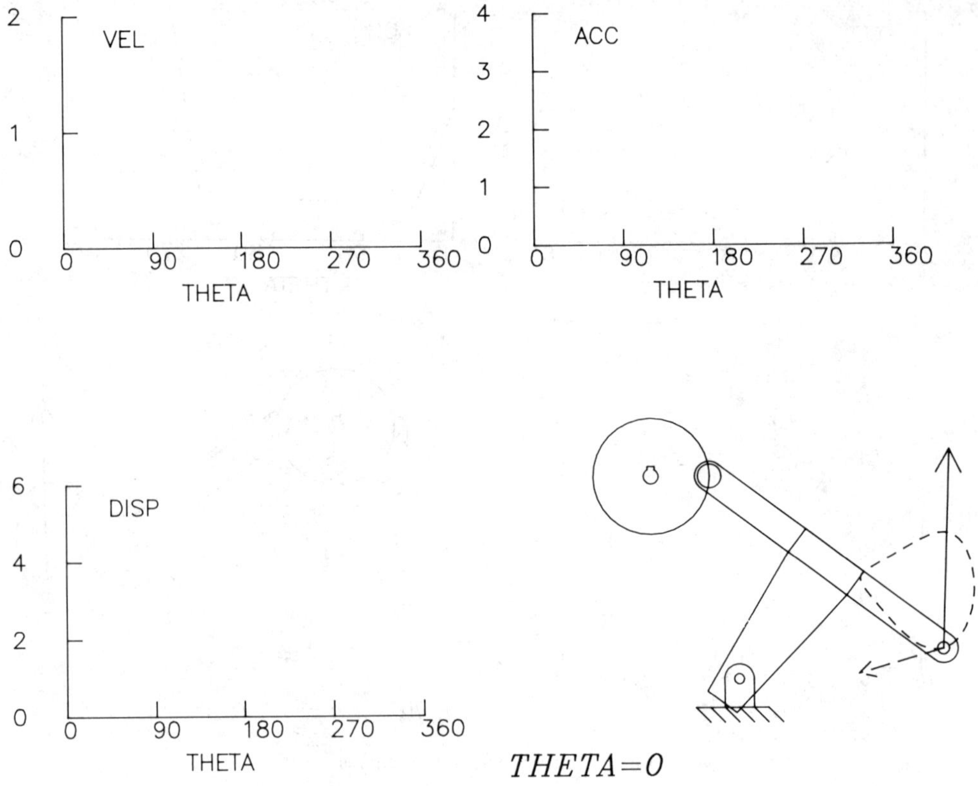

Fig. 7. Trace point kinematics at $\theta = 0$.

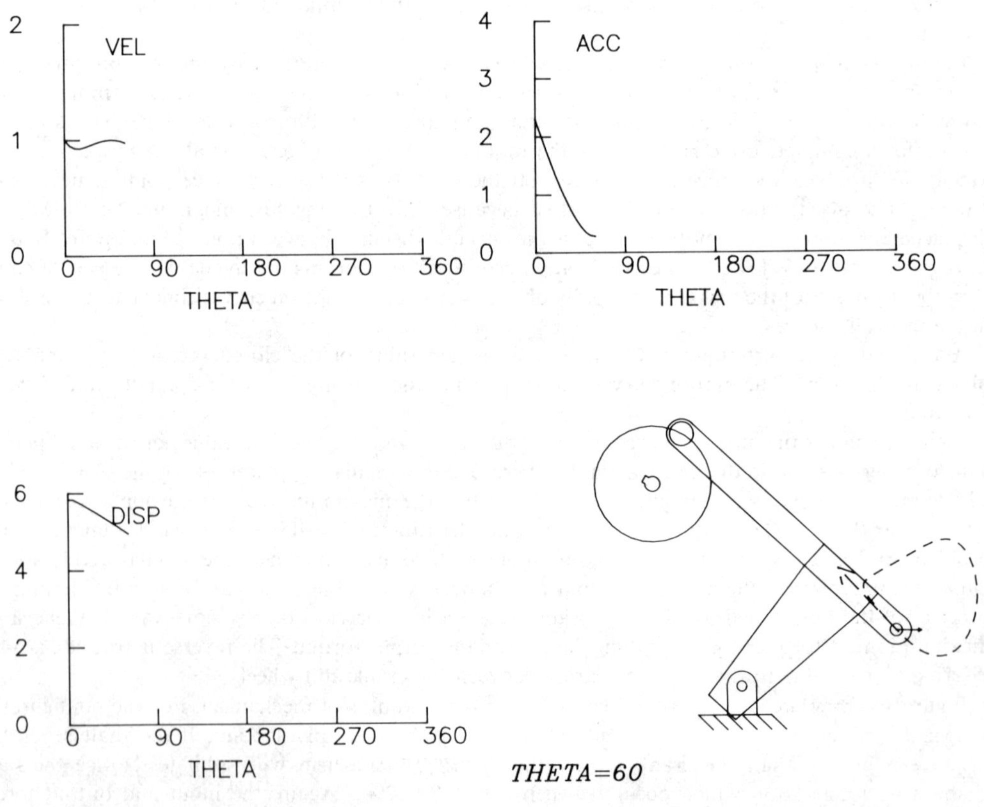

Fig. 8. Trace point kinematics at $\theta = 60$.

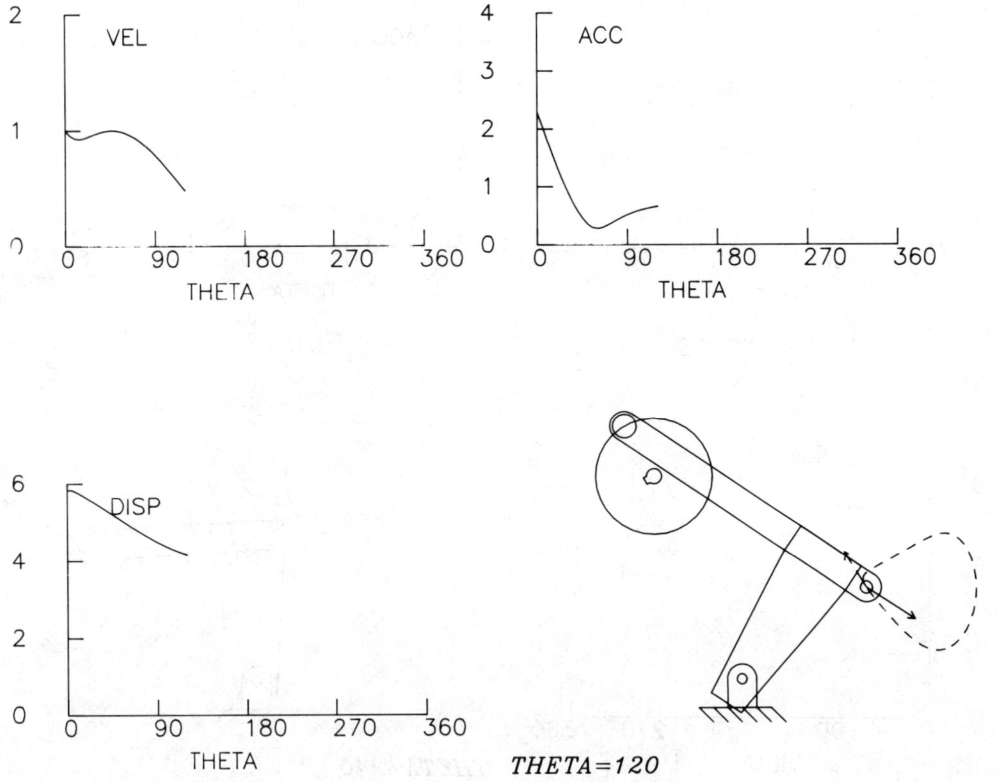

Fig. 9. Trace point kinematics at $\theta = 120$.

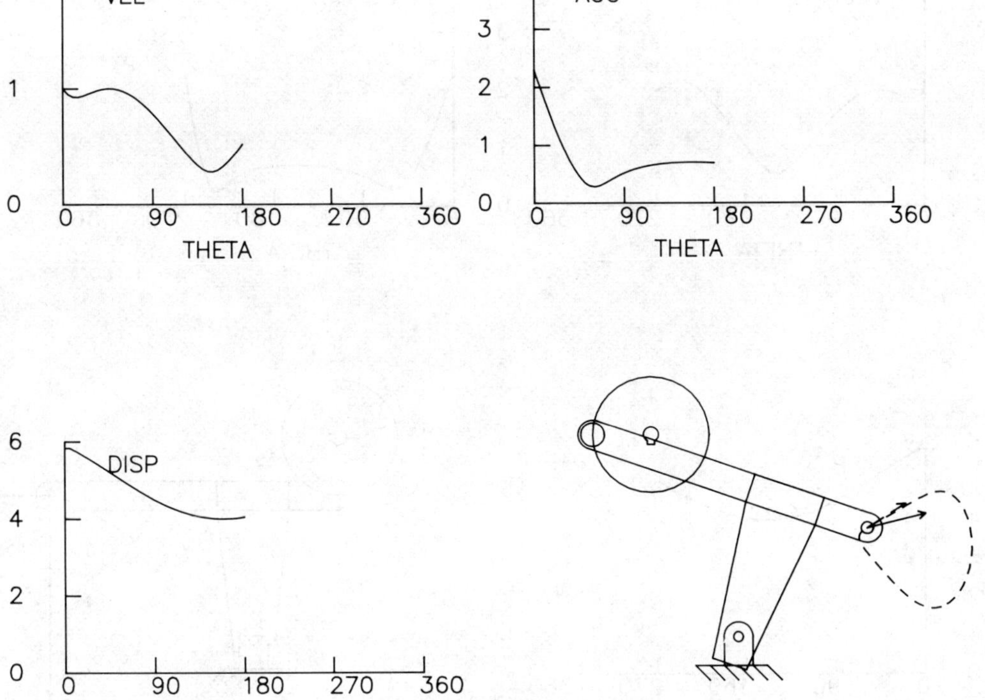

Fig. 10. Trace point kinematics at $\theta = 180$.

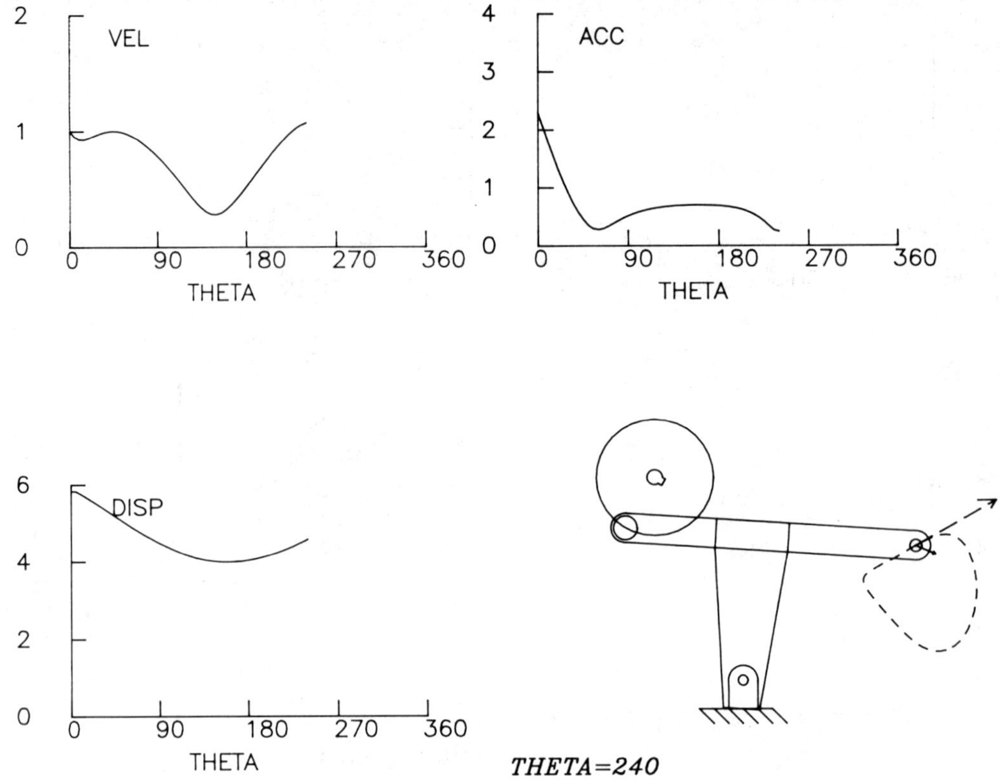

Fig. 11. Trace point kinematics at $\theta = 240$.

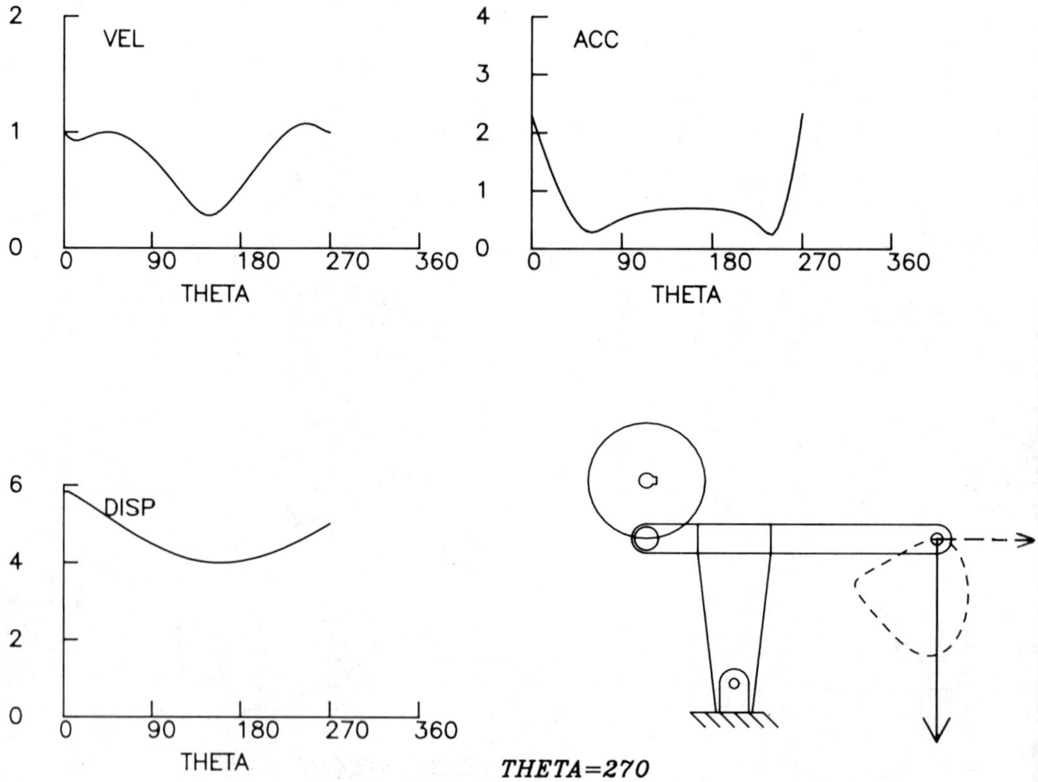

Fig. 12. Trace point kinematics at $\theta = 270$.

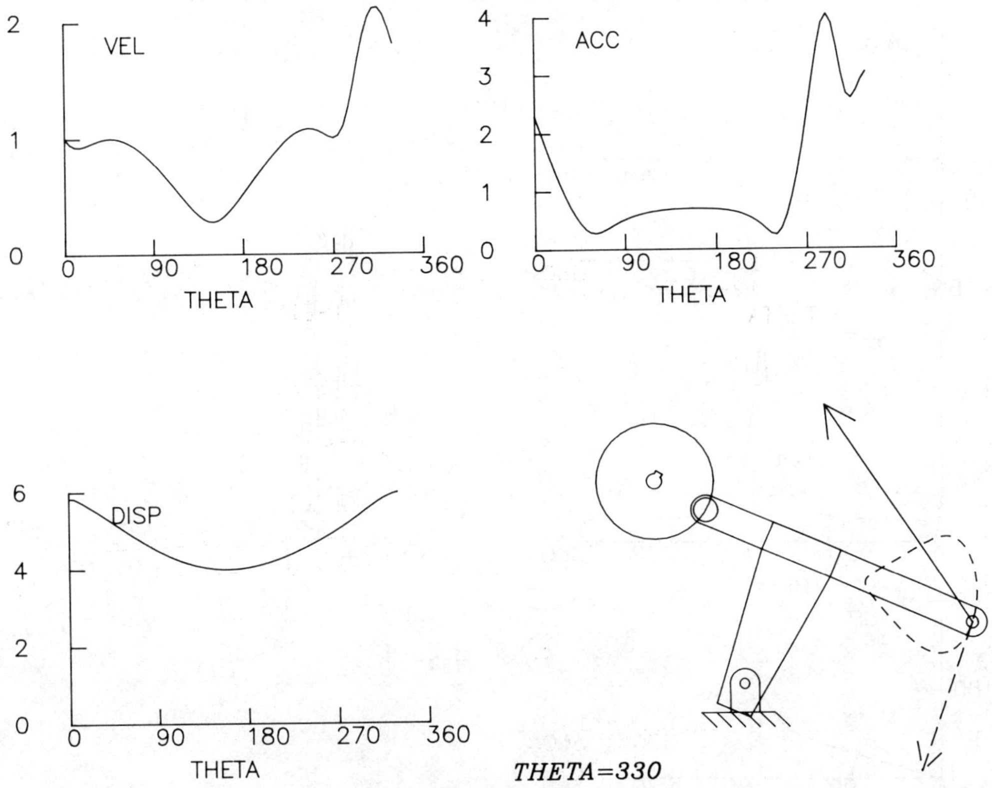

Fig. 13. Trace point kinematics at $\theta = 330$.

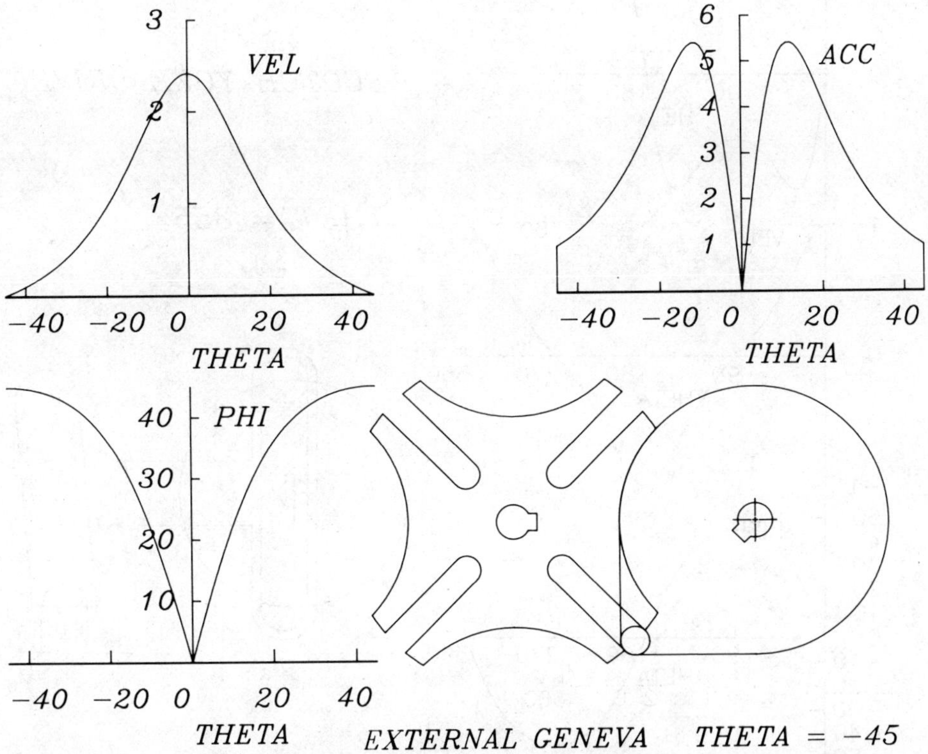

Fig. 14. External Geneva wheel.

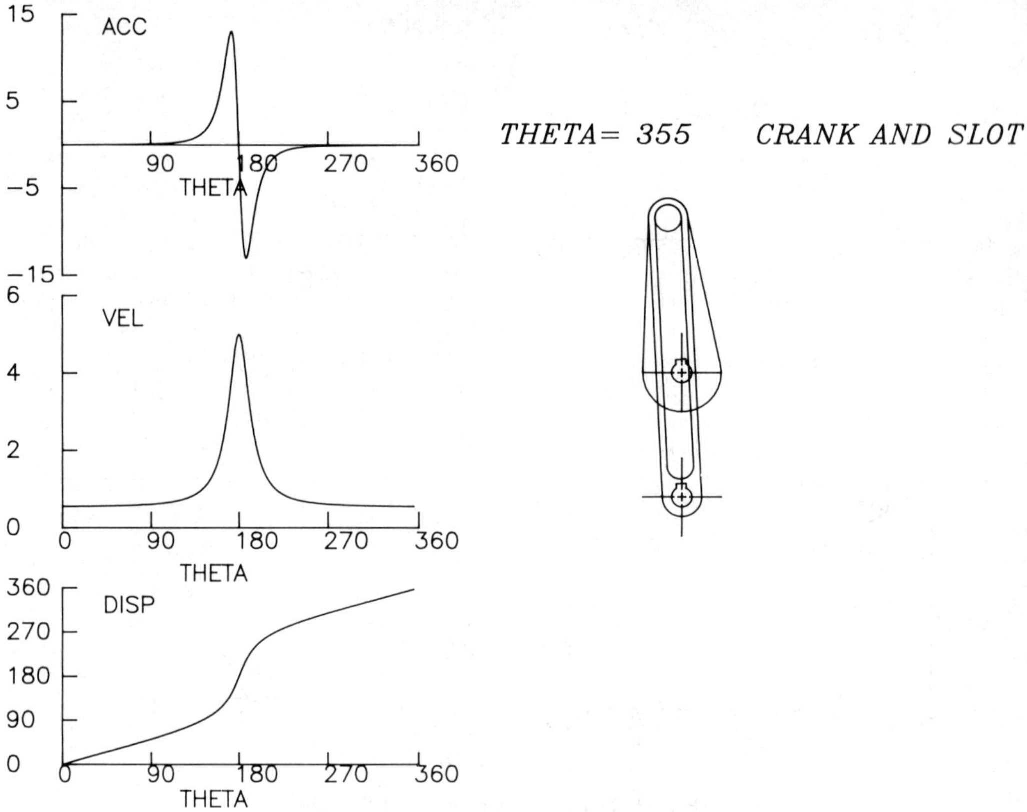

Fig. 15. Crank-slot mechanism.

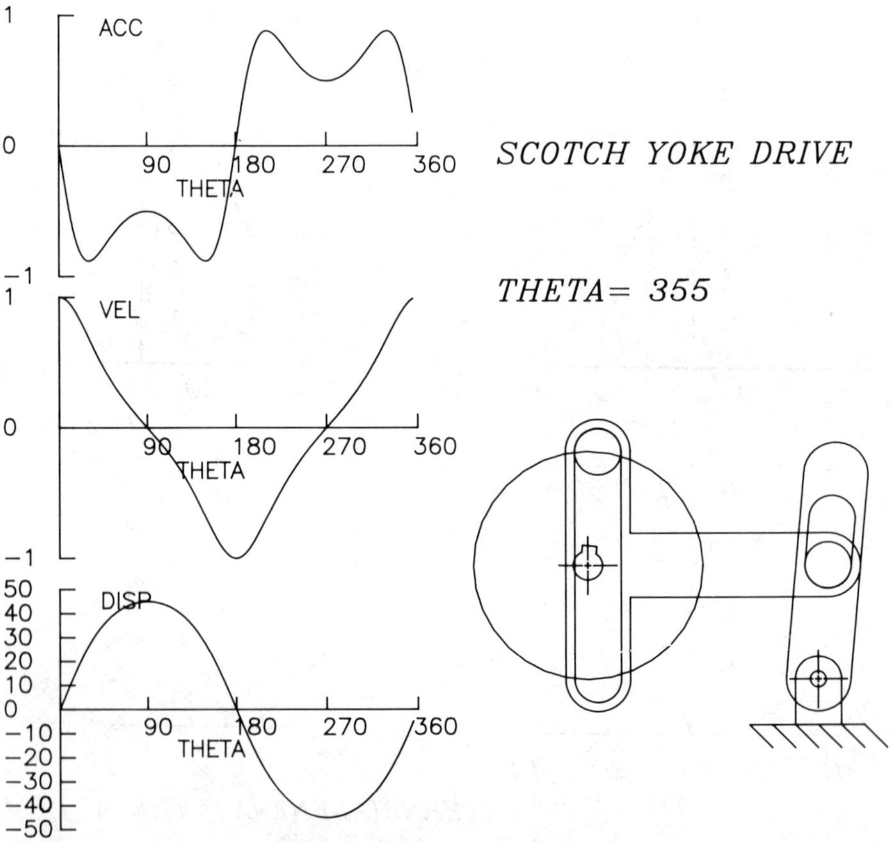

Fig. 16. Scotch yoke drive.

Figure 16 shows the angular displacement and non-dimensional angular velocity and acceleration for the pivoted arm driven by a Scotch yoke. Notice that the displacement curve looks like pure sinusiodal motion but the velocity and acceleration curves show that it is not. The driven arm is accelerating when the acceleration and velocity are both positive or both negative. Otherwise it is decelerating.

Figure 17 gives the non-dimensional motion curves x/a, $[\mathrm{d}x/\mathrm{d}t]/a\omega$, and $[\mathrm{d}^2x/\mathrm{d}t^2]/a\omega^2$ for the device shown, where x is the vertical distance traveled by the driven slider, and the fixed crank length is a. Notice the nearly linear variation in the displacement curve between $100 \leqslant \theta \leqslant 260°$. This produces constant velocity and near zero acceleration during this part of the cycle.

Figure 18 gives the non-dimensional rectilinear motion curves for the driven slider in a Whitworth quick-return mechanism. The motion curves show the non-dimensional displacement, rectilinear velocity, rectilinear acceleration of the horizontal slider. This slider is often a cutting tool in machinery. The quick return action causes sudden changes in velocity and acceleration near $\theta = 180°$.

Figure 19 shows the kinematic behavior of the driven output link in a simple 4-bar linkage. The geometry is such that a complete rotation of the input crank is possible while the pivoted output arm rocks back and forth. This crank-rocker behavior is only one type of 4-bar linkage behavior. The analysis technique can easily be extended to more complex linkages.

Figure 20 shows the horizontal, rectilinear motion of the upper slider for another quick return device. The quick return behavior is indicated in each of the three motion curves which show the behavior of the slider moving in a horizontal direction. This device produces a quick return motion between $300 \leqslant \theta \leqslant 340°$.

As a final example Fig. 21 shows the angular motion for a pivoted arm being driven by an epicycloidal gear train of gear ratio 4:1. Four distinct dwell periods can be seen in the arm motion.

The complete kinematic behavior of any planar mechanism can be presented in a similar fashion. The approach given in this paper extends directly to more complex linkages consisting of many individually moving parts. The author is currently writing a text "*Applied Kinematics with Computer Graphics*," which will document the mathematical and numerical analyses required to generate motion curves such as those given in this paper.

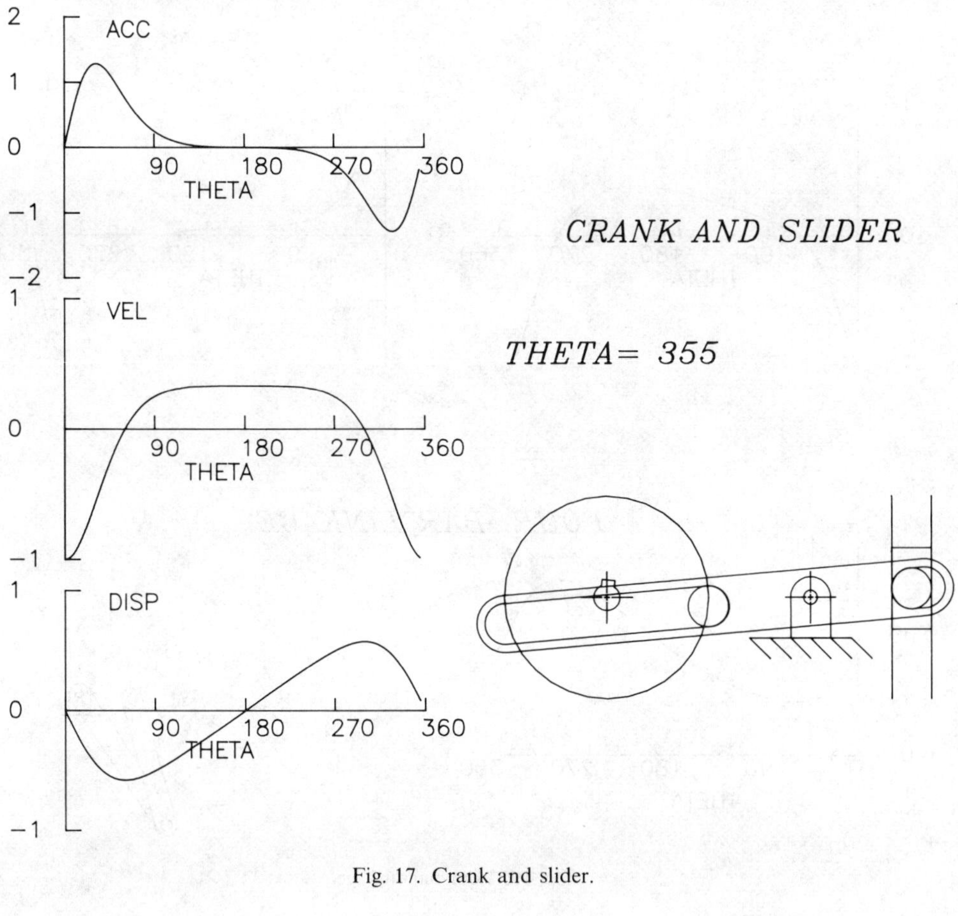

Fig. 17. Crank and slider.

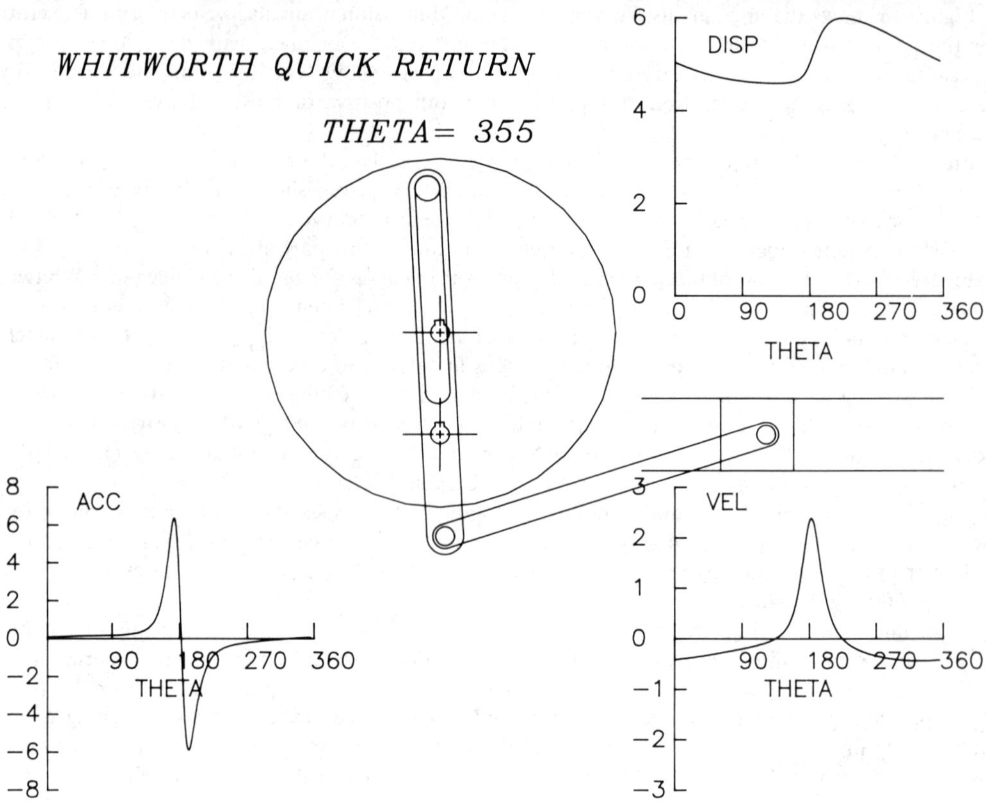

Fig. 18. Whitworth quick return mechanism.

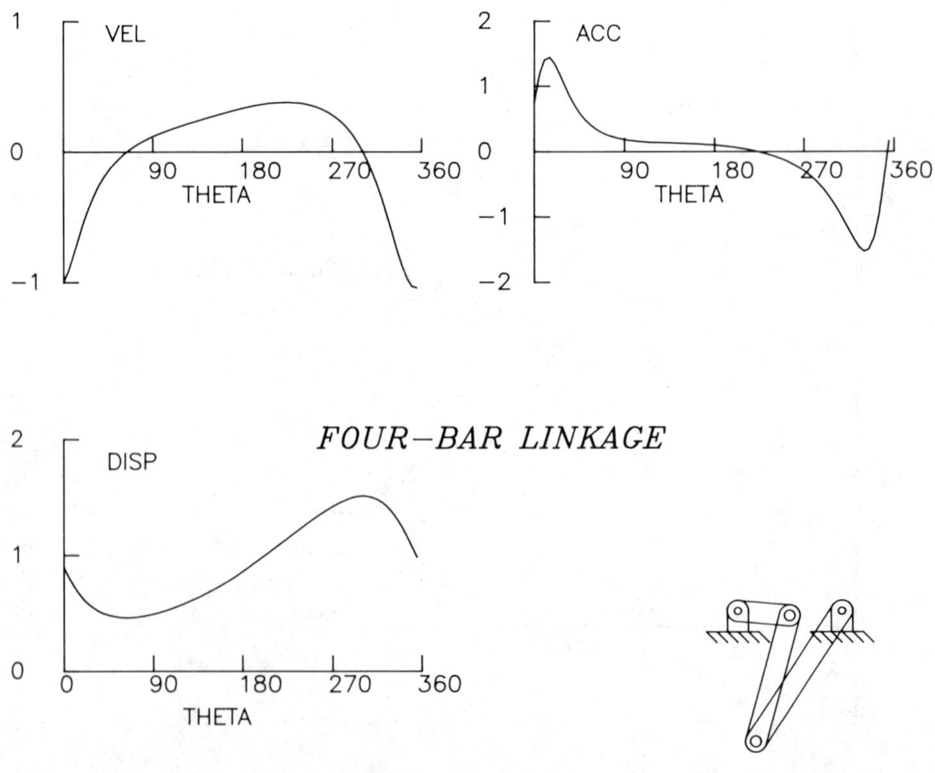

Fig. 19. Four-bar linkage.

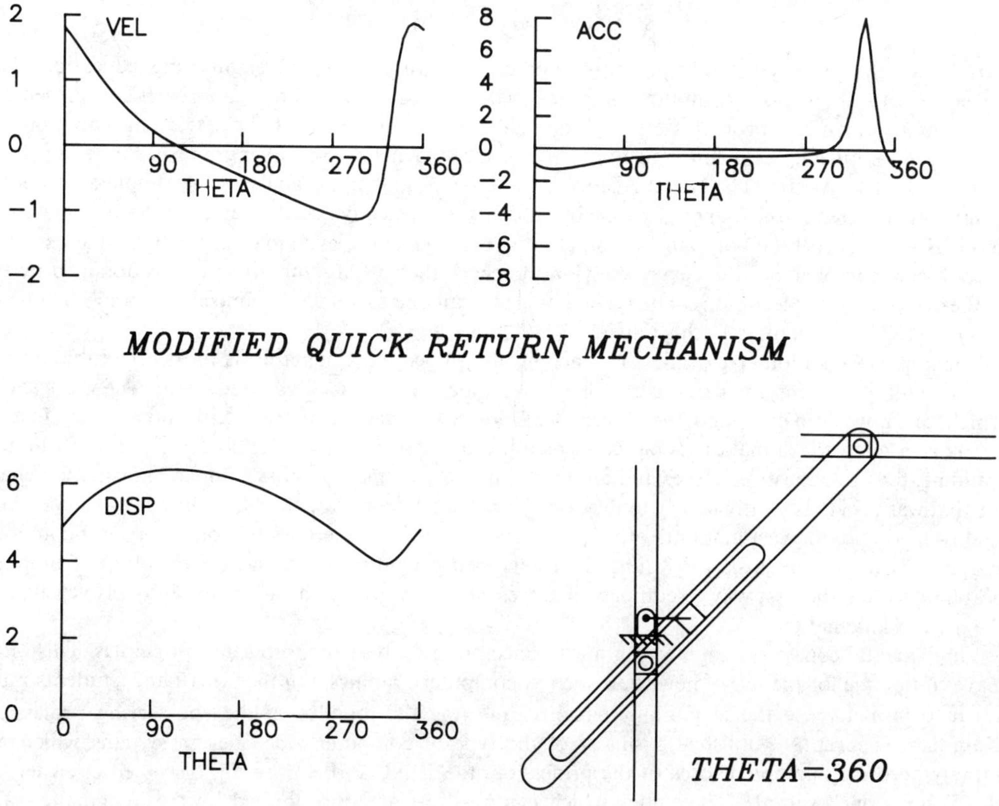

Fig. 20. Modified quick return mechanism.

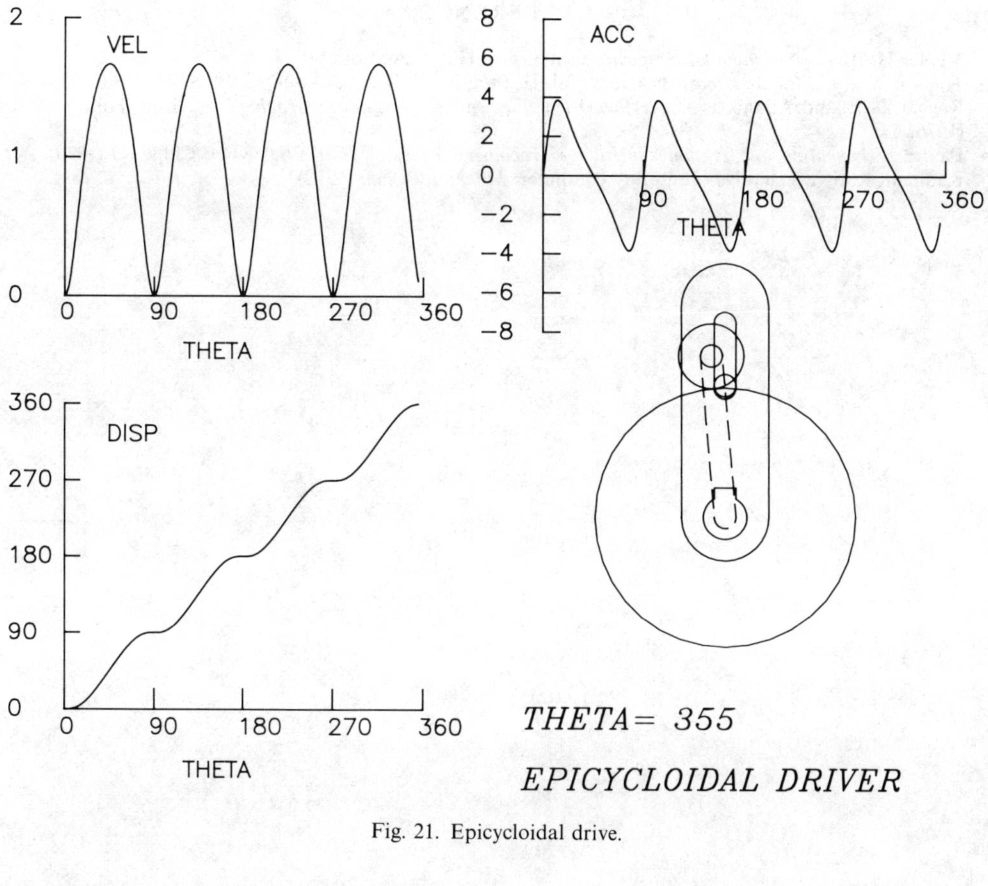

Fig. 21. Epicycloidal drive.

EDUCATIONAL IMPACT

It is not the purpose of this paper to predict the future trends in engineering education. The purpose is to show how computer graphics makes possible a different approach for presenting solutions to kinematic problems, as well as a different formulation of the governing equations of motion. Since kinematics is fundamental to many subsequent courses, changes in pedagogy must be made with care. At the U.S. Naval Academy the type of kinematic analyses and applied computer graphics illustrated in this paper are done by students in an elective course taught at the junior/senior level. However, working computer graphics programs are made available to underclassmen so they can observe complete motion curve behavior and check their instantaneous solutions obtained by use of the vector analysis technique. The type of output available to students in mechanics and kinematics is illustrated by the figures in this paper.

The impact of computer graphics on teaching the subject of kinematics is most noticeable on the understanding and insight demonstrated by the students. This is illustrated by the new questions which can now be asked, and the design decisions which can be more intelligently made. Just as surely as a microscope makes visible patterns of behavior which affect the observer's physical understanding, the use of motion curves and animated simulations make visible complete kinematic behavior that was previously only faintly understood, if at all, by many students. Learning how to deal with and properly use the vast amounts of new information readily generated by computers and computer graphics is a suitable task for young engineers being readied for today's technology. Computer graphics is often the best way to compact and present this information. It has certainly proven true in the area of kinematics.

Fundamental courses in engineering must concentrate on basic concepts and principles. This often leaves little time for the use of new tools such as computer graphics. On the other hand, students must learn to properly use the technology which is affecting the practice of the engineering profession. Kaufman[5] recently published a survey of the type of computer aided design systems which are rapidly becoming accepted tools of the profession, the LINCAGES program discussed elsewhere in this issue is one example. The things which can be done are only limited by the imagination and (unfortunately) the resources available to an institution. Computer graphics offers the potential for many exciting changes.

REFERENCES

1. Kepler H. B., *Basic Graphical Kinematics*. McGraw–Hill, New York (1973).
2. Higdon A. *et al.*, *Engineering Mechanics* Vol. II. Prentice Hall, Englewood Cliffs, NJ (1976).
3. Rogers D. F. and Adams J. A., *Mathematical Elements for Computer Graphics*. McGraw–Hill, New York (1976).
4. Paul B., *Kinematics and Dynamics of Planar Machinery*. Prentice Hall, Englewood Cliffs, NJ (1979).
5. Kaufman R. S., Mechanism design by computer. *Machine Design* (1978).

Comput. & Educ. Vol. 5, pp. 265 to 274, 1981
Printed in Great Britain
0360-1315/81/040265-10$02.00/0
Pergamon Press Ltd

COMPUTER GRAPHICS IN NUCLEAR ENGINEERING EDUCATION AT QUEEN MARY COLLEGE

P. R. SMITH
Department of Nuclear Engineering, Queen Mary College, Mile End Road, London E1 4NS, England

Abstract—Computer graphical display has been used in teaching nuclear engineering at Queen Mary College since 1971 and has assumed an increasingly important role in the modelling and simulation of engineering systems, not least nuclear engineering systems, for teaching purposes. The role of computer graphics is illustrated by means of examples selected from a suite of nuclear engineering programs in current use, indicating the highly flexible interaction and enhanced presentation of information which can be achieved. The facilities provided at Queen Mary College for the implementation of graphics-based teaching programs are described and the associated laboratory organisation indicated.

COMPUTERS IN NUCLEAR ENGINEERING EDUCATION

The digital computer has played an important role in the development of the Nuclear Engineering Industry, which relies heavily upon extensive suites of computer programs in most aspects of nuclear reactor design and development, as well as in the monitoring and control of many of the operational procedures associated with nuclear reactor plant. Equally the Nuclear Engineering Industry has played an important rôle in the development of the digital computer, through the industry's growing requirements for increased computer power and versatility which have been a major stimulus to the development of digital computer techniques and capabilities.

It is a natural consequence of this close interrelationship between nuclear engineering and computation, dating back to the infancy of the industry over 20 years ago, that many of the problems which are central to a proper understanding of nuclear engineering can be solved only by computer. It is a further natural consequence that the computer should play a prominent part in the presentation of these problems to undergraduate students of nuclear engineering.

Engineers need to put numbers into calculations in order to get a feel for the sizes of components and the responses of systems, nuclear engineers no less than others. The complexity of the modelling involved in nuclear engineering means that students are unable, in most cases, to develop their own computer programs, since even if it were desirable to divert so much effort to programming, there would be insufficient time available to treat more than a small fraction of the problems encountered in the syllabus of a typical undergraduate course. The alternative is the preparation by staff of special programs for student use.

Once the decision has been taken to provide computer based learning programs, there is much to be gained educationally if they are interactive, both in the immediacy of the response and in the exploratory progression in understanding which becomes possible [1].

It should perhaps be stressed that there is no implication of a "black box" philosophy in these procedures. Before being allowed access to the programs, the student receives a full explanation in lectures of the mathematical basis of the model used and of any special numerical techniques adopted in the computer solution.

Computer assisted learning in nuclear engineering was introduced at Queen Mary College in 1967 as part of a new first degree course, and has assumed a steadily increasing importance in both undergraduate and postgraduate studies since that date, as evidenced by the number of programs available, the number of courses in which they are used and the number of student hours devoted to this activity.

The computer system used for the implementation of the programs has increased correspondingly in its capability, from a small PDP-9 single user system with a necessarily severely limited capacity in terms of student hours, to the present PDP-11/40 system with 16 terminals, which is barely adequate to meet the current demand.

A Tektronix 611 graphics terminal was added to the PDP-9 system in 1971 and the then existing programs suitably converted to make use of it. Graphical display has been widely used in almost all the programs developed since then and half the terminals on the present system have high definition graphical display capability.

The organisation of the computer assisted teaching unit laboratory at Queen Mary College will be described in more detail below, but first an attempt will be made to extract some of the salient features from 10 years' experience of the use of computer graphics in a teaching rôle, drawing from programs in nuclear engineering by way of illustration.

These programs offer to the student the opportunity to examine in some depth a selected topic, usually associated with a multivariate model of a nuclear engineering system or process, giving access to parameters of the model in a highly flexible interaction through "menus" or option lists. This is in the "discovery learning" mode of computer based learning[2] in which control of the procedures is exercised, predominantly, by the learner, with guidance from a student text and often with supervisory assistance.

The student is allocated a session in the computer laboratory, usually of 2–3 h duration, for each of the programs associated with the courses he has selected, and is expected to write an account of his experience as he would for any other engineering laboratory experiment. For most of the computer experiments the information supplied by the program is supplemented by a laboratory sheet (or student guide) which suggests objectives and a procedure to attain them.

THE RÔLE OF GRAPHICAL DISPLAY

High definition graphical display terminals are considerably more expensive than other visual display units and in most educational establishments it will be necessary to examine carefully the advantages which accrue before their purchase can be justified.

Engineers are accustomed to assimilating information presented in the form of graphs and diagrams, and in many instances they would need to convert other forms of computer output into graphs and diagrams in order to extract the information they require. Whilst it may be argued that the plotting of graphs by hand is an essential part of an engineer's education, the plotting of large numbers of graphs by hand is time-consuming, boring and destructive of student interest. Computer graphics can be used to display information rapidly and effectively in the appropriate forms, increasing the amount which the student can assimilate and the range of studies which he can complete in a given time at the terminal, and at the same time stimulating his interest.

Computer aided design techniques are becoming widely used in industry and, although the nuclear engineering industry has been cautious in its adoption of these methods, there is little doubt that they will assume increasing importance in the future. The experience which the student gains when using graphics oriented computer based learning programs is highly relevant to these interactive design processes and provides a valuable basis for and understanding of the procedures which he will meet in industry after graduation.

The impact of the use of graphical output in highly interactive computer based learning routines is perhaps best illustrated by specific examples. The examples which follow have been selected from a suite of programs in regular use at Queen Mary College[3], an indication of the nuclear engineering context has been given in each case to the extent necessary to appreciate the flexibility and versatility of the graphical display routines.

REACTOR PHYSICS

The first examples are taken from programs concerned with topics in reactor physics. In the QMC undergraduate nuclear engineering curriculum three course units contribute to this subject area; part of an introductory first year course, a second year half unit and an advanced course comprising a half unit in the third year.

The operation of a nuclear reactor depends upon neutron multiplication in a fission chain reaction; the critical size of nuclear reactor core which is able to sustain a steady fission rate with a corresponding steady thermal power output is dependent upon the relative proportions of fuel (in which the fissions occur) and moderator (which reduces the kinetic energy of fission neutrons to increase the probability of fission). The multiplying properties of a homogeneous mixture of fuel and moderator are examined in the *first year course*; a diagram from the associated computer program is shown as Fig. 1. In this, as in all display examples, the ranges of variables for which results are shown will have been selected by the user, unless otherwise stated.

In this instance the calculations relate to natural uranium fuel and graphite moderator. The graph, which shows the variation in neutron multiplication with the ratio of moderator atoms to fuel atoms, is seen to exhibit a maximum, indicating that there is an optimum ratio for these ingredients. It also

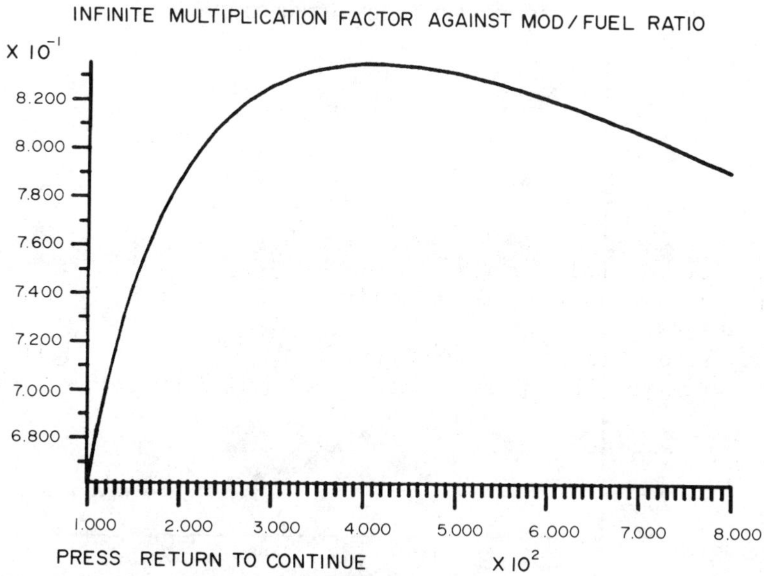

Fig. 1. Display showing the variation of neutron multiplication with moderator/fuel ratio for a homogeneous mixture of natural uranium and graphite.

shows that the greatest possible value of neutron multiplication factor is less than unity, indicating that a chain reaction cannot be sustained by such a mixture, which is therefore not a possible reactor medium. Whilst this information could be obtained from a computer tabulation of the numerical values, it has much greater impact when presented in the form of a graph and is more readily assimilated.

The program can be used similarly to examine the neutron multiplying properties of other moderating media in combination with natural uranium and also to investigate the effect of using uranium in differing enrichments. Graphs showing the variation of thermal utilisation and resonance capture (which indicate respectively the rates of absorption of slow and resonance neutrons in the fuel) can also be displayed; these give insight into the physical processes involved in neutron multiplication.

In all of these computations the student is required to select in order to display—to select ranges of moderator to fuel ratio or moderator material or fuel enrichment— so exploring the processes of neutron multiplication and building up, by discovery, a library of information which will be used elsewhere in his courses.

In the *second year reactor physics course*, which is obligatory for all nuclear engineering students as a prerequisite for many third year courses, students are offered four computer experiments. An example from one of these is shown in Fig. 2.

A nuclear reactor comprises a core region which contains fissile material and a reflected region which does not. The function of the reflector is to reduce the loss of neutrons from the core, thus reducing its size, and to flatten the radial neutron density distribution in order to increase the reactor power output. The criticality condition (in a two neutron energy group approximation) can be written

$$\Delta = 0$$

where Δ is a 4×4 determinant whose elements involve both the materials properties and the geometry of the core and reflector regions; the critical core radius is the lowest value of radius which satisfies the criticality condition.

Figure 2 displays the results of a computation of some complexity. To obtain it the student has first selected or specified some dozen or more parameters which define the material content of the core and reflector; he has then indicated that he wishes to perform a sequence of criticality calculations for different values of reflector thickness, in each case to obtain the critical core radius. It is immediately apparent from the graph that, as might be expected, the critical core radius decreases as the reflector thickness is increased. It is also evident that, as the reflector thickness is further increased, there is a diminishing return in the corresponding reduction in critical size until a point is reached where no further sensible reduction can be obtained. The reflector is then "effectively infinite", a concept of some importance in reactor physics.

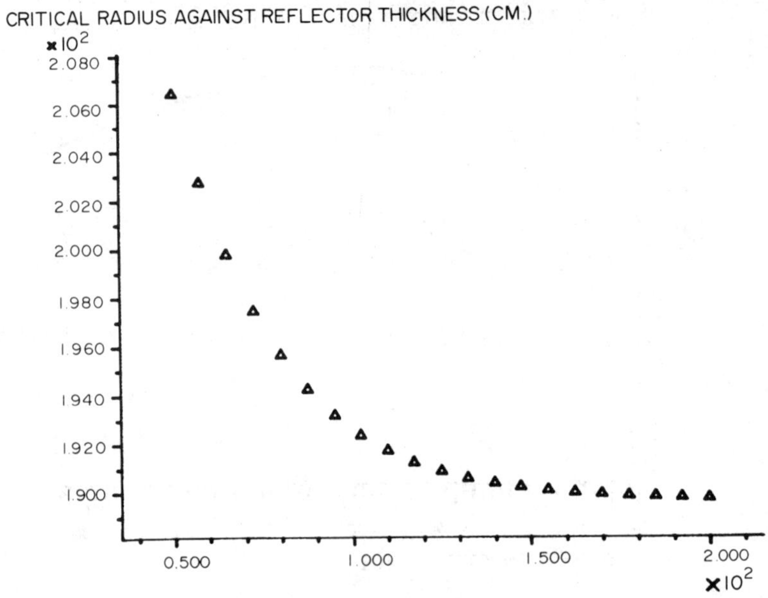

Fig. 2. Display showing the variation in critical core radius with reflector thickness from a program which examines the criticality of a reflected system in the two neutron energy group approximation.

This program can also be used for many other investigations. At a fundamental level the value of Δ can be plotted against core radius to demonstrate the existence and significance of higher order solutions to the critical equation. Dissimilar systems can be compared, for instance, to show the marked difference in size between water moderated and graphite moderated reactor cores. The change in critical radius with materials parameters can also be examined, to consolidate understanding of the physical processes involved. All of these features involve calculations which can only be attempted by computer, and the effective presentation of the information which results demands the availability of computer graphics.

One of the topics which is examined in depth in the *third year reactor physics course* is that of resonance capture. One of the isotopes of uranium, ^{238}U, which is present in most reactor fuels, has pronounced neutron absorption resonances; that is, it preferentially absorbs neutrons of particular kinetic energies. Since the absorption of a neutron in ^{238}U results in the formation of a plutonium isotope, ^{239}Pu and since this plutonium isotope can be fissioned and so contribute to the reactor thermal power, it is necessary, though difficult, to calculate the effects of neutron resonance capture. One of the two computer programs available for this advanced course in reactor physics deals with the topic of resonance capture. Figure 3 shows a display from the program.

Resonance absorption is a complex physical phenomenon and its accurate evaluation is crucial for the efficient design of a nuclear reactor. Although it is possible to find simple semi-empirical formulae for this evaluation, these give little insight into the many processes which are occurring, and it is essential for students to perform calculations on realistic models.

The program gives access to many parameters of the models, in particular allowing the specification of a selected absorption resonance, and includes calculations for both homogeneous and heterogeneous arrangements of fuel and moderator. There are two models available, known respectively as the "wide resonances" and "narrow resonances" approximations. Figure 3, which is one of many possible graphical outputs, shows a direct comparison of the neutron energy spectrum in the vicinity of a selected resonance for both homogeneous and heterogeneous arrangements in both approximations. The exercises undertaken using this program include an examination of the effect of changes in temperature upon resonance capture.

Other topics in reactor physics for which computer based learning programs have been developed are:

statistics of counting, in which experimental data can be analysed and displayed

cell neutron flux distributions, for which both diffusion theory and collision probability theory models are avilable to examine a fuel-moderator cell

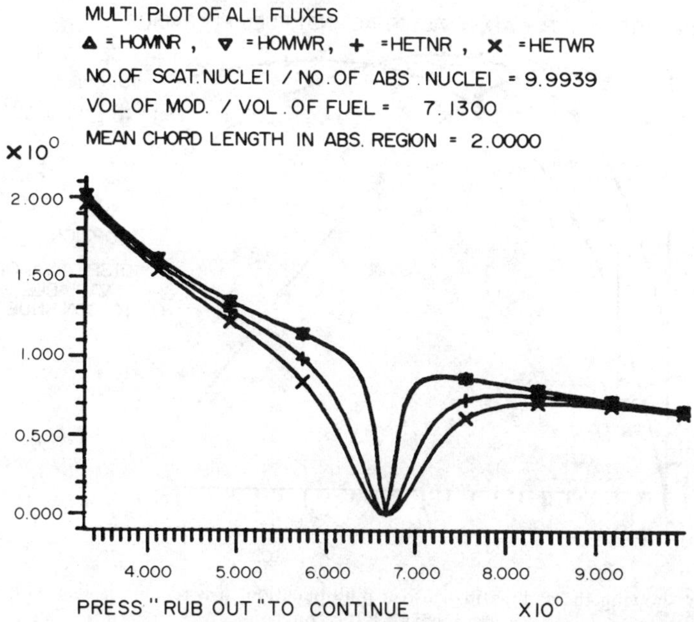

Fig. 3. Display showing the neutron energy spectrum in the vicinity of an absorption resonance, calculated for homogeneous and heterogeneous arrangements of fuel and moderator in both wide and narrow resonance approximations.

reactor kinetic response, which investigates variations of neutron flux following a step change in reactivity [4]

xenon transient response, in which the effect of an important fission product poison is studied.

NUCLEAR SYSTEMS DESIGN

A third year course unit in nuclear systems design includes a substantial section concerned with computational design methods in nuclear engineering. This section has evolved in association with three teaching programs, in a carefully integrated combination of lectures and computer coursework. The *first* of these programs illustrates some of the techniques of computer aided design and the structure of the program is discussed at some length in lectures. It is concerned with the design of a fuel-moderator lattice typical of a large well-moderated reactor system such as the UK Magnox reactor or the Canadian CANDU. The lattice is optimised for maximum neutron multiplication (with a corresponding minimum critical reactor size) and once the material properties of fuel, cladding and moderator have been set, this can be reduced to a two-parameter optimisation with variables fuel pin radius and lattice pitch. A display from the program is shown as Fig. 4.

The point in the design process represented by this display will have been reached by the average student in about an hour, during which time he will have viewed and discarded many similar displays. He is free to choose one of several procedures to achieve this; here he has decided to examine the variation of neutron multiplication with fuel pin size at a particular pitch and, after a number of trials, has found that there is a best pin size for that pitch. The program has a retain/discard routine which allows a result to be held for later comparison, if so desired; he will have made use of this and proceeded to examine the effect of variation of pin size at another pitch, again retaining the display showing the best pin size. In this way he has built up a multiple display, as shown in Fig. 4, which indicates the overall optimum lattice. Graphical display is an essential requirement for this procedure.

The program has other features of interest and can be used to examine a variety of nuclear reactor lattices with different material properties, or to look more closely at the physics of neutron multiplication. It differs in detail from a computer aided design program in such respects and in that the latter might well use a more elegant optimisation routine which would not, however, be susceptible to such detailed examination.

The *second* program used in this course examines in detail an application of the method of finite differences to determine a neutron flux distribution. Its purpose is to indicate the errors which can be introduced in such computational procedures as a result of the approximations inherent in the

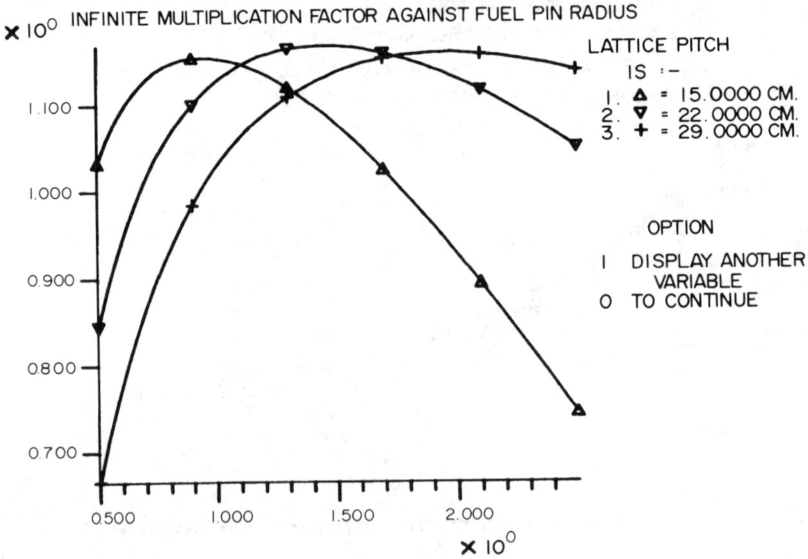

Fig. 4. Display showing the change in neutron multiplication in a reactor lattice with fuel pin radius and lattice pitch.

numerical method and to distinguish between errors of this kind and errors due to approximations in the formulation of the model of the physical process to which the numerical solution technique is applied. Finite difference approximations are used widely in the determination of neutron flux distributions. The example selected in the program is a two neutron energy group representation of a three region cylindrical reactor; the required solutions are neutron multiplication factor and radial form factor, the latter being a measure of the shape of the distribution. An example of a display from the program is shown in Fig. 5. A converged solution is achieved by an iterative procedure in which successive flux profiles are generated, and the display shows an intermediate stage in this process. The student is able to observe the development of this procedure and the eventual convergence when the shape of the neutron distribution becomes stable. Whilst this is a striking example of the use of graphical display, the main purpose of the program is to investigate the effect of changing key parameters in the numerical procedure (e.g. the spatial mesh or the point convergence criterion) upon the speed and accuracy of computation.

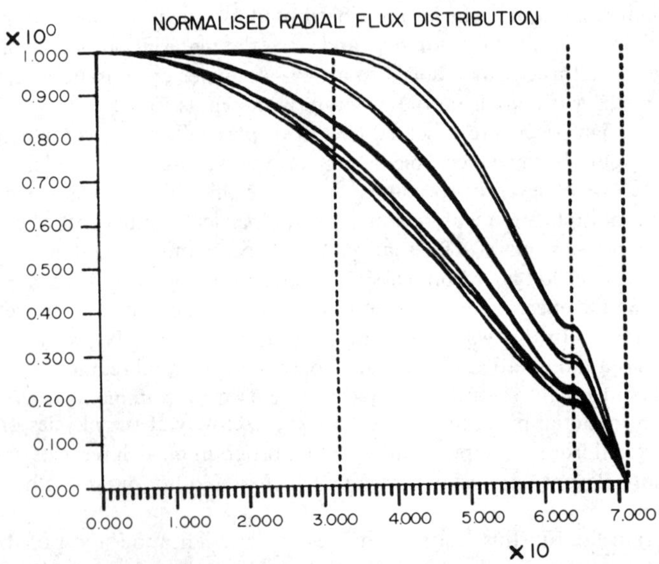

Fig. 5. Display showing successive iterations in the convergence of a neutron distribution, in a finite difference solution of a two group three region diffusion theory representation.

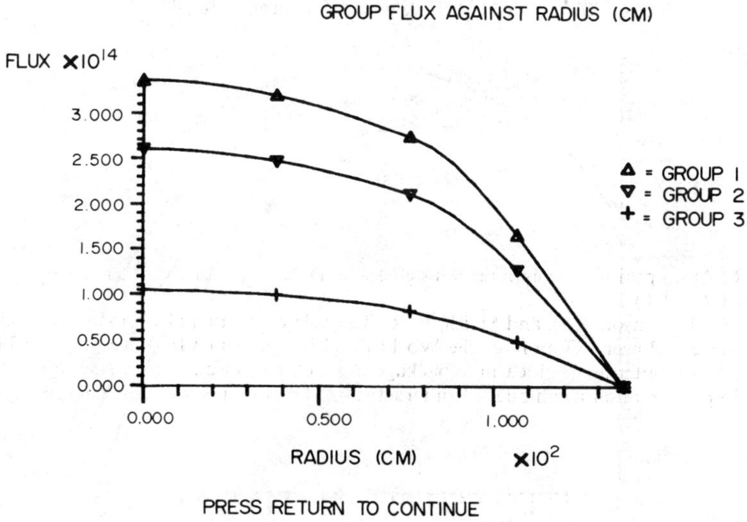

Fig. 6. Display of neutron distribution from a three group criticality program.

The *third* program in this group is a few group criticality program which is typical of those in use in the nuclear engineering industry for water reactor calculations, although suitably simplified for educational use. It features the usual multiplication factor and neutron distribution calculations, but also allows for the control of excess multiplication by the addition of a soluble neutron absorber, calculating the absorber concentration required in what is known as a poison search. An example of a display from the program is shown in Fig. 6; this is a graph of comparative distributions of fast, intermediate and slow neutrons for a system incorporating a soluble poison. This program is also highly interactive, permitting the variation of nuclear, material and geometric properties.

It is used for a variety of design exercises in which the students become familar with the program procedures and with the changes in neutron multiplication and flux distribution which result when key parameters are changed. The final exercise using this program is a full design specification which is presented as a formal technical report.

REACTOR FUEL TECHNOLOGY

A further group of programs is associated with a third year course which examines various aspects of the nuclear fuel cycle, with emphasis upon in-core reactor fuel management and the techniques of uranium enrichment.

The cost of electricity produced by a nuclear power station is reduced if the amount of energy extracted from the fuel is increased. One method of achieving this improvement in costs is to add additional fissile material to the initial fuel charge, compensating for the associated excess neutron multiplication or reactivity by adding a neutron absorber known as a 'burnable poison'. One of the programs associated with this course, a display from which is shown as Fig. 7, calculates the variation of reactivity with irradiation for a reactor which has a homogeneous burnable poison added to the fuel. There is a wide range of investigations open to the student using this program, as is the case with many of the programs already described. Figure 7 is a typical result of a study of the effect of increasing the burnable poison content of the fuel to compensate for added fissile material. It shows that as the burnable poison content increases, so does the maximum value of reactivity which has to be balanced by the reactor control system; consequently for a given control capability there is a practical limit to the amount of burnable poison which can be used. As with so many of these examples, graphical display is the only effective way of presenting the complex inter-relationships, in this case between initial conditions, subsequent changes in reactivity and control capability.

Most nuclear reactors utilise fuel in which the fissile material is the uranium isotope ^{235}U, and for many systems the balance between neutron losses by absorption and leakage on the one hand and neutron production in the fission process on the other, makes it necessary to "enrich" the fuel by increasing the proportion of ^{235}U relative to the more abundant non-fissile isotope ^{238}U. The principal methods of achieving this enrichment are gaseous diffusion and gaseous centrifugation. Both of

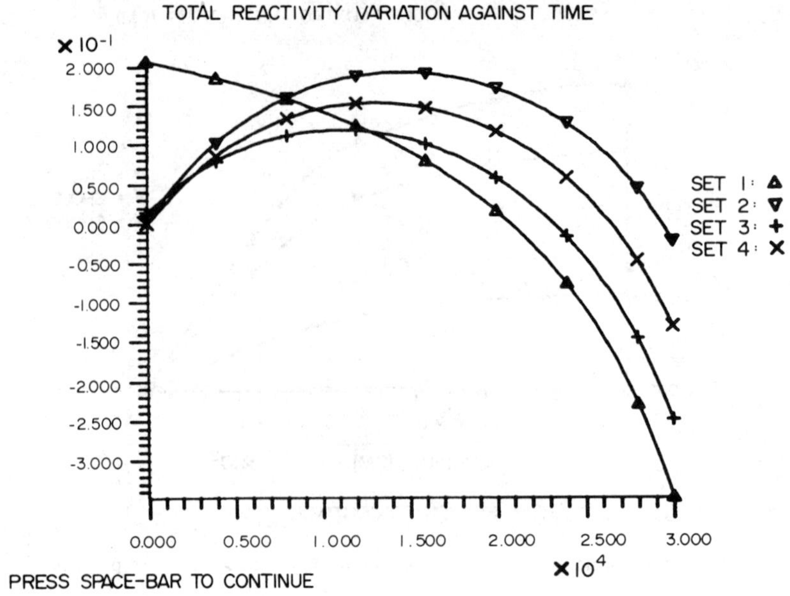

Fig. 7. Display showing reactivity profiles for different concentrations of burnable poison.

these processes involve large multi-stage cascades, and the design of such cascades is the subject of the final program to be considered.

The fractional enrichment which can be achieved by a single stage in a cascade is described by a stage separation factor; each stage is made up of a number of units in parallel, the number differing from stage to stage. The shape of a cascade to achieve a required pattern of enrichment depends upon the number of stages which, in turn, depends upon the stage separation factor. Figure 8 is a display from the program and shows how the shape of the cascade changes when the stage separation factor is varied. The student is able to use this and other graphical outputs to examine many aspects of cascade design and to compare the characteristics of diffusion and centrifugation cascades.

Other topics in this curriculum area for which programs have been developed are:

heavy element variation with irradiation, which examines the growth and depletion of trans-uranic elements in nuclear fuel and the related reactivity changes

optimisation of radial form factor, which simulates the use of flattening absorbers to improve a radial neutron flux distribution.

THE QMC COMPUTER ASSISTED TEACHING UNIT LABORATORY

The CATU laboratory provides computer based learning facilities for the six departments of the Faculty of Engineering, which has a total undergraduate student population of about 700. The computer system is a PDP-11/40 servicing 16 terminals using the RSX-11(M) operating system. Seven of the terminals are Tektronix 4010 graphics units; for many applications these are paired with seven teletypes which provide hard copy for limited data output or a record of input. Alternative forms of hard copy are available from a switched Tektronix hard copier and a spooled fast printer. One Lear–Siegler ADM-3A terminal has a lower definition graphics capability at a correspondingly lower cost, its main purpose, however, is to generate a signal for monitor replication of graphics output for lecture room display.

The availability of on-line computer graphics output in the lecture room or seminar room offers to the lecturer the possibility of illustrating the theoretical treatment of a topic with numerical evaluation using the associated program. This can be by way of demonstration or through a group interaction which involves the students in an exploration of the programmed model. Lecture room display may also be a useful pre-cursor to student use of a program in scheduled laboratory sessions, to indicate the procedures available and the purpose of the study.

The operation of the CATU laboratory has been described by Balman[5]. The Faculty has a morning lectures, afternoon laboratories timetable and CATU has, correspondingly, scheduled labor-

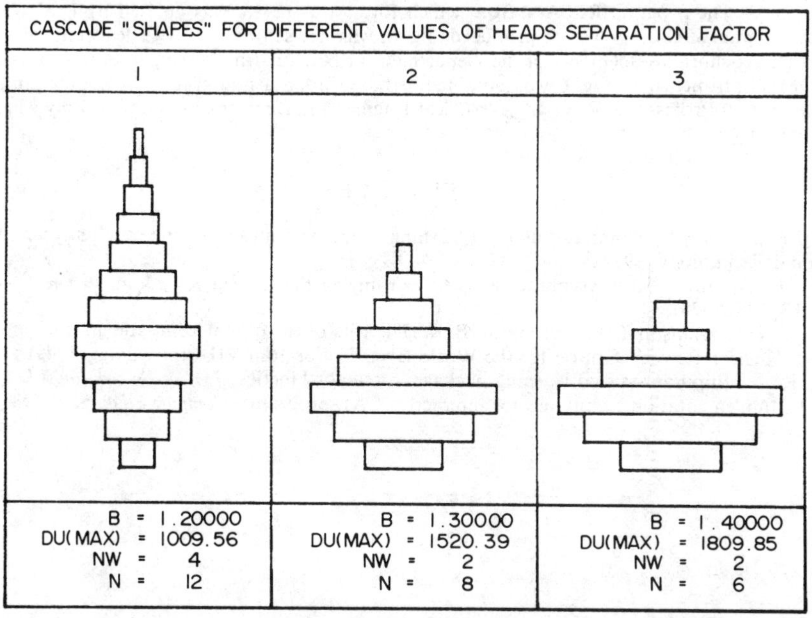

Fig. 8. Display comparing the shapes of enrichment cascade designs for different values of stage separation factor.

atory sessions in the afternoon and open-access in the mornings. In the 1979–1980 academic year a total of 21 courses made use of the facilities, 10 of which were nuclear engineering courses. The total recorded student-terminal-hours was 4765, of which 1250 was for nuclear engineering students. The total number of computer based teaching programs available was 48, and of these 18 were concerned with topics in nuclear engineering. The demand upon the facilities continues to grow and there is a continuing programme of development of new material, including new topics in nuclear engineering.

Most of the programs which are in use at QMC, including those described in this paper, are available to members of the Engineering Science Program Exchange, which is based at QMC. The programs have been written with transfer in mind; FORTRAN IV has been adopted as the standard language, apart from a few programs in BASIC, and a modular construction has been adopted with extensive internal and external documentation. The graphical display standard adopted in the later programs is GINO-F, but some earlier programs may have variants—if so, these are clearly indicated and documented. Experience indicates that, while it is unlikely that the first transfer of a graphics oriented teaching package to a different operating and terminal system will be without some program modification, the amount of effort involved can be considerably reduced by careful design and should be much reduced for subsequent transfers.

CONCLUSION

Computer based learning programs using graphical display have much to offer the engineering student, particularly in association with modelling and simulation of engineering systems. This is especially true for the student of nuclear engineering, whose studies involve numerous models of such complexity that computer evaluation is essential and graphical display desirable to aid in the assimilation and interpretation of results.

Such programs can extend the range of studies available to the student by presenting models of systems which could not otherwise be experienced. Many engineering systems are too expensive to be provided for student experimentation in the engineering laboratory; many, especially in the nuclear field, cannot be made available for reasons of safety. Computer models and computer simulations can repair these omissions, and can also be associated with the processing and interpretation of data obtained in conventional laboratory experiments.

Computer graphics can be made an attractive feature of all these interactions, in the display of system diagrams and system information, in the illustration of the application of numerical techniques, in offering insight into physical processes and in the graphical or pictorial display of results.

Acknowledgements—The program RESAN, from which Fig. 3 was taken, was devised by Professor M. M. R. Williams; the program CASCAD, which produced Fig. 8, was devised by Dr R. C. Raichura. Both Professor Williams and Dr Raichura are members of the Department of Nuclear Engineering, Queen Mary College. The program ODMUG, from which Fig. 6 was obtained, is based upon a non-graphics computer module of the same name written by Professor J. R. Thomas, Nuclear Engineering Department, Virginia Polytechnic Institute and State University.

REFERENCES

1. Technical Report No. 14, Computer assisted learning in higher education—the next ten years. Council for Educational Technology (1977).
2. Hartley J. R., An appraisal of computer assisted learning in the United Kingdom. *Progr. Learning Educ. Technol.* **15, 136** (1978).
3. Gibbs D. C. C., Parkinson T. F. and Smith, P. R., The rôle of the digital computer in nuclear engineering education. Nuclear Power—Option for the World ENC'79 Foratom VII Proceedings (1979).
4. Smith P. R., A computer assisted learning package in reactor kinetics. *J. Inst. Nuc. Educ.* **17,** 6 (1976).
5. Balman T., Implementation techniques for interactive CAL programs. *Comput. Educ.* **5,** 1 (1981).

Comput. & Educ. Vol. 5, pp. 275 to 287, 1981
Printed in Great Britain

0360-1315/81/040275-13$02.00/0
Pergamon Press Ltd

THE IMPACT OF COMPUTER GRAPHICS ON MECHANICAL ENGINEERING EDUCATION AT THE OHIO STATE UNIVERSITY

GARY L. KINZEL, JOHN A. CHARLES and JAMES E. A. JOHN
Department of Mechanical Engineering, The Ohio State University, 206 West 18th Avenue, Columbus, OH 43210, U.S.A.

Abstract—Three years ago, The Ohio State University began to incorporate computer graphics into the regular undergraduate and graduate curriculum in Mechanical Engineering. This required the establishment of a graphics facility dedicated to Mechanical Engineering and changes in course structure to use the facility. This paper describes the formulation of the graphics laboratory, changes made to integrate computer graphics and computer aided design into several courses, and the favorable impact this has had on the curriculum.

INTRODUCTION

During the last 10 years, there has been a rapid increase in the use of computer graphics in various industries in the United States, Western Europe, and Japan. The cost-effectiveness of this tool is obvious especially in the drafting and machine-design and finite-element modeling areas. Until recently, however, most universities have lagged behind industry in the computer graphics area due in part to the relatively high costs of the computer equipment involved combined with generally shrinking university budgets. Those universities which began to emphasize computer graphics when the hardware first became available did so primarily from a research standpoint although an occasional elective course was made available to undergraduate students. Much of this research was funded by the manufacturers of computer graphics equipment who provided laboratory equipment for the research. The emphasis on research uses and the elective nature of the available courses in computer graphics have prevailed in many schools until the present time.

As in most major universities, various departments, namely Electrical Engineering and Computer Science, at The Ohio State University (OSU) have been experimenting with graphics terminals essentially since they first became available. However, in Mechanical Engineering, the primary mode of operation in the computational area remained FORTRAN-IV-based batch processing until 1977. At that time, a decision was made at OSU to incorporate computer graphics and other computer aided design (CAD) tools into the regular undergraduate and graduate curriculum in Mechanical Engineering. The decision was a direct result of the influence of forward-thinking alumni and industrial advisors. Implementation of the decision not only necessitated the establishment of a computer graphics facility but also required some fundamental changes in the courses being taught. Currently, finite-element modeling, mechanism analysis, machine-element design, design optimization, dynamic analysis, and data reduction techniques are all taught with the aid of interactive programs utilizing graphics. Thus far, the use of graphics has been concentrated in the design/solid mechanics area. As a result of the changes, there has been a dramatic shift in the interest of both graduate and undergraduate students toward the area of design.

This paper describes the establishment of the graphics facility at OSU and the changes in the design courses made to integrate CAD into the curriculum and discusses several CAD projects. Experiences at OSU have shown that student interest and enthusiasm permit these changes to be introduced without significantly reducing the amount of traditional engineering material being taught.

DEVELOPMENT OF THE GRAPHICS FACILITY

Any new laboratory requires a heavy commitment of capital for equipment, operation, and maintenance. Because of a restricted budget at OSU, it was not possible to establish the graphics facility using university funding alone. Consequently, the Engineering College embarked on an aggressive capital campaign to obtain the necessary equipment and operating support for the laboratory from the industrial community who will benefit directly from the hiring of engineers with state-of-the-art knowledge in CAD. As a result of this campaign, the Advanced Design Methods Laboratory (ADML) was established.

Fig. 1. Overview of the computer graphics laboratory.

Prior to the actual establishment of the laboratory, several key faculty members interviewed knowledgeable people in industry and other universities. These people gave valuable suggestions as to what courses were relevant, what hardware and software were appropriate, and how funding for necessary hardware and software purchases might be obtained. Many of the industrial advisors believed strongly enough in the project that they helped the university obtain industrial funding support. To date, most of the budgeted funding has been industrial. OSU has provided a one-time interest-free loan of $165,000; however, it has been necessary to repay this loan from the industrial contributions. The laboratory has benefited substantially from end-of-year equipment monies from the Engineering College, but these were not budgeted. Fortunately, in 1977 when the department was soliciting funds from industry, most corporate profits were high and then (as now) there was a high demand for graduate engineers with CAD experience. Consequently, the concept of industry supporting the ADML was a salable one. In 1977 and 1978, 6 companies (General Motors, Structural Dynamics Research Corporation, TRW, Eaton, Ford, and Pittsburg Plate Glass) pledged to support the laboratory with annual contributions for a period of 5 years. In addition, equipment gifts have been received from Hewlett–Packard and Standard Oil of Indiana. To keep the sponsors informed on the progress of the ADML, at least one annual all-day meeting is held at OSU and a detailed annual report is prepared.

An overview of the ADML is shown in Fig. 1. The current ADML hardware configuration centers around a fully expanded DEC PDP-11/60 minicomputer. This computer has a parallel, high-speed floating point processor and is well suited to the FORTRAN-based calculations common to mechanical engineering problems. The PDP-11/60 acts as a host computer to nine Tektronix 4014–1 graphics display terminals and eight Infoton and one Decwriter alphanumeric terminals. The terminals are supported by a high-speed Printronix 300 printer plotter, a Tektronix hard-copy unit, and two 76-107 cm Tektronix 4954 graphics tablets with stands. Data and program storage are provided by a dual floppy disk drive and two RK06 and one RK07 cartridge disk drives.

Considerable research time was expended on the choice of minicomputer and graphics terminals. Minicomputer manufacturers considered were DEC, Hewlett–Packard, Data General, Prime, and IBM. Each system had its own advantages and disadvantages relative to this particular application at Ohio State. The computer finally chosen was a DEC VAX 11/780; however, due to limited funding and the realization that ultimately a dedicated data-acquisition, control, and specialized minicomputer would be needed, the DEC PDP-11/60 computer was purchased. This machine has proven to be a good initial choice for starting the laboratory although now the capacity of the machine is saturated. Currently, plans are underway to purchase a new DEC VAX 11/750 machine. The Tektronix 4014 terminals were chosen because of their high resolution and omnipresence in the industries supporting the laboratory. The terminals have an enhanced graphics module which was modified at OSU to provide a high quality animation feature. The alphanumeric terminals which are less expensive than the graphics terminals by more than a factor of 10 are used preliminarily for program development.

The current PDP-11/60 is capable of performing most of the calculations required for interactive-design and dynamic-analysis problems. However, for structural analysis, a larger computer is required. For this reason, a 4800 band synchronous line is connected between the PDP-11/60 and the university's Amdahl 470/V6 computer. The PDP-11/60 can then emulate a remote batch entry station through a HASP interface. This eliminates the need for a large tape drive system or for card reading and punching equipment in the ADML.

The primary analog-to-digital (A/D) converters used for data acquisition are the DEC LPA system, which can sample at up to 40 kHz and can be multiplexed up to 16 channels, and a GENRAD system, which has four channels of antialiasing filters and has a maximum sampling rate of 160 kHz on each channel.

The laboratory has an agreement with Structural Dynamics Research Corporation (SDRC) to utilize a number of its software products. These include 3-D mode-shape animation display and graphics-tablet data input routines for finite-element analyses. Also, a number of other special purpose software packages have been purchased or developed in the laboratory for student use. These include a number of programs for machine-element and kinematic analyses. All of the OSU-written graphics programs are written using Tektronix TCS Plot 10 software.

The expenses associated with the laboratory during the last 3 years have been about $730,000. Approximately $160,000 has been associated with operating costs (staff salaries and maintenance), $420,000 has been for equipment, and $150,000 for software. The staff includes a full-time lab manager and four student site monitors. None of the faculty have been directly supported by the laboratory.

INTEGRATION OF CAD INTO ENGINEERING COURSES

The first course using the ADML was introduced during Autumn Quarter of 1978. Although the laboratory was not fully operational at the time (four graphics terminals and two alphanumeric terminals had been installed), it was decided that the ADML should be fully integrated into the curriculum as soon as possible. The educational objective in the department is that every student graduating with an OSU degree in Mechanical Engineering will have a working knowledge of the following:

(1) basic modeling techniques and use of commercially available finite-element programs;
(2) the use of computer-based analytical models for experimental test data;
(3) computer-based, real-time acquisition of experimental test data;
(4) the ability to use and write programs employing graphics for interpreting analytical results;
(5) the ability to use and write interactive design programs which interrogate the user for input information;
(6) the use of computer-based, design-optimization techniques.

The courses using the ADML each quarter and the years of their introduction are shown in Table 1. As indicated, the ADML is involved in the courses for both required laboratory exercises and required and optional projects. It has also been used extensively on an individual study basis.

During its first quarter of operation, one elective course (ME 651) used the facility. This course is Kinematic Synthesis with Computer Graphics Applications and is generally taken by an equal number of seniors and MS graduate students. This course had been taught previously as a synthesis only course with all computer computations being done in the batch mode. A kinematics/mechanisms type of course is an obvious selection for the initial course using the ADML because kinematics tends to be visually oriented. The course began with simple graphics operations such as rotating a triangle across the terminal and ended with each of the students writing an interactive program for the design of a four-bar linkage using Burmester theory. This latter project requires a working knowledge of the various coordinate transformation procedures and most of the common plotting routines in addition to the kinematics associated with the theory. The overall concepts taught in the course did not differ from what had been taught in previous quarters; however, now solution procedures were based on computer graphics rather than on construction graphics.

By restricting the use of the ADML to one course during the first quarter of operation, the general faculty could effectively determine how the facility could best be integrated into other courses. At

Table 1. Timetable for integrating graphics into the mechanical engineering curriculum

Autumn Quarter 1978
(1) ME 651—Kinematic synthesis of mechanisms (L)*

Winter Quarter 1979
(1) ME 561—Principles of machine design (L)
(2) ME 510—Heat transfer (L)

Spring Quarter 1979
(1) ME 564—Design project (OP)
(2) ME 562—Design of machine elements (P)
(3) ME 693—Individual studies (P)
(4) ME 561—Principles of machine design (P)

Summer Quarter 1979
(1) ME 664—Computer aided design I (L)

Autumn Quarter 1979
(1) ME 553—Kinematic analysis of mechanisms (OP)
(2) ME 562—Design of machine elements (P)
(3) ME 650—Machine dynamics (D)
(4) ME 651—Kinematic synthesis of mechanisms (L)

Winter Quarter 1980
(1) ME 561—Principles of machine design (L)
(2) ME 664—Computer aided design I (L)
(3) ME 581—Design lab (P)
(4) ME 850—Advanced dynamics (OP)
(5) ME 564—Design project (P)

Spring Quarter 1980
(1) ME 561—Principles of machine design (L)
(2) ME 562—Design of machine elements (P)
(3) ME 694—Composite material design (P)
(4) ME 861—Stress analysis (P)
(5) ME 693—Individual studies (P)

Summer Quarter 1980
(1) ME 764—Computer aided design II (L)

Autumn Quarter 1980
(1) ME 281—System dynamics (P)
(2) ME 553—Kinematic analysis of mechanisms (OP)
(3) ME 651—Kinematic synthesis of mechanisms (L)
(4) ME 564—Design project (OP)
(5) ME 693—Individual studies (P)

Winter Quarter 1981
(1) ME 553—Kinematic analysis of mechanisms (OP)
(2) ME 561—Principles of machine design (L)
(3) ME 664—Computer aided design I (L)
(4) ME 693—Individual studies (P)

Spring Quarter 1981
(1) ME 561—Principles of machine design (L)
(2) ME 564—Computer aided design I (L)
(3) ME 694—Composite material design (P)
(4) ME 661—Design optimization (P)
(5) ME 861—Stress analysis (P)
(6) ME 693—Individual studies (P)

* Letters in parentheses refer to the following: L—required laboratories; P—requires project; OP—optional project; D—demonstration.

this time, most of the faculty members themselves had not used graphics terminals before. Also, prior to their exposure to the facility, several of the faculty were unconvinced of the need for computer graphics.

The course ME 651 was taught again in Autumn Quarter 1979 using the same format. Compared to the previous year, the enrollment increased by a factor of 2. In 1980, the course was taught again and the enrollment was 28 students, which is 4 more than in 1979.

During its second quarter of operation, the ADML was used by two required, junior-level courses, ME 510 and 561. The first is in heat transfer and is taught using the format of three 1-h lectures and one 2-h laboratory per week. One of the laboratory sessions is conducted in the ADML and uses interactive programming to solve a two-dimensional, steady-state, conduction heat transfer problem using both the method of successive overrelaxation and the Gauss–Seidel method.

The second course, ME 561, is the second course in the mechanical design sequence and is also taught using the format of three lectures and one laboratory per week. The primary subject matter for the course is a comprehensive survey of mechanical failure theories. The laboratory, which was added for the first time in Winter Quarter 1979, is composed of five computer aided design experiments and five traditional ones. Each of the CAD experiments was designed to use the ADML and to serve as an introduction to some phase of computer-aided design. Each laboratory session was limited to 16 students, which required that the students work at the graphics terminals in groups of four during class. Each student was able to work individually outside of class, however, to gain more firsthand experience.

Two basic types of CAD experiments were formulated for ME 561. The first type involved the generation and solution of a finite-element model. Two laboratory sessions were devoted to this effort: one for generating the geometry and a second for completing the required input file and analyzing the results. The final model studied was a plate with a central hole, loaded in tension. A value for the stress concentration factor for the geometry was found using the finite element method and compared with published data. The SDRC program SUPERTAB was used for data generation and SUPERB for the actual analysis. Quarter symmetry was used for the model, thereby requiring the students to learn about symmetry boundary conditions.

The second type of CAD experiment developed involved the use of short interactive programs to solve typical design problems. Using programs written by the faculty, the students analyzed a slider-crank mechanism for shaking forces and determined the deflection of a complicated, stepped shaft. These experiments introduced the students to numerical techniques other than the finite element method and illustrated their utility in solving complicated, time-consuming mechanical design problems. One of the graphic output frames from the shaft analysis program is shown in Fig. 2.

The ADML was also used in traditional experiments of ME 561 for data reduction. Data for experiments involving fatigue, fracture mechanics, and strain gages were reduced with special programs written by the faculty for each experiment. These programs made extensive use of computer graphics whenever possible.

ME 561 was also taught during Spring Quarter and a total of 140 students took the course in 1979. The reaction of the students to the ADML was overwhelmingly positive on the course evaluations at the end of each quarter. There has also been a rapidly increasing enrollment in subsequent courses which use the ADML and a clear increase in graduate study in computer aided design.

Currently, the format for ME 561 is similar except for a modification of the finite-element experiments. Rather than use a large finite-element program which cannot be executed in the ADML, a small special purpose planar program having only plate elements was written for use in the laboratory. Using this program the students are given different problems to model and analyze, and the analysis can be completed within the normal 2-h laboratory period.

During Spring Quarter 1979, the ADML was introduced into three more courses, ME 562, 564, and 593. The first of these is a sequel to ME 561 and covers the detailed design of some common machine elements such as shafts, gears, and bearings. This course was divided into two groups of students of approx. 30 students each, and only one of the sections was assigned a special project using the ADML. The students were asked to write individually an interactive, graphics-oriented computer aided design program for one of the standard machine elements found in the textbook. Many of the

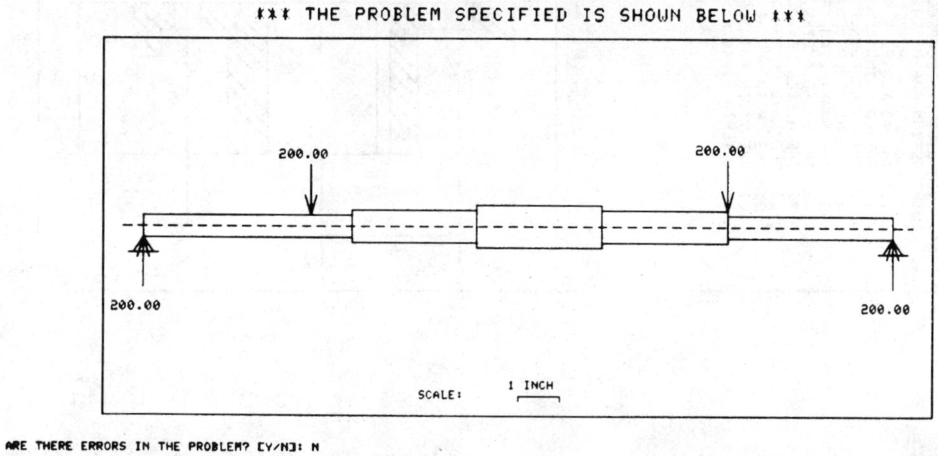

Fig. 2. Typical output from shaft analysis program used in ME 561.

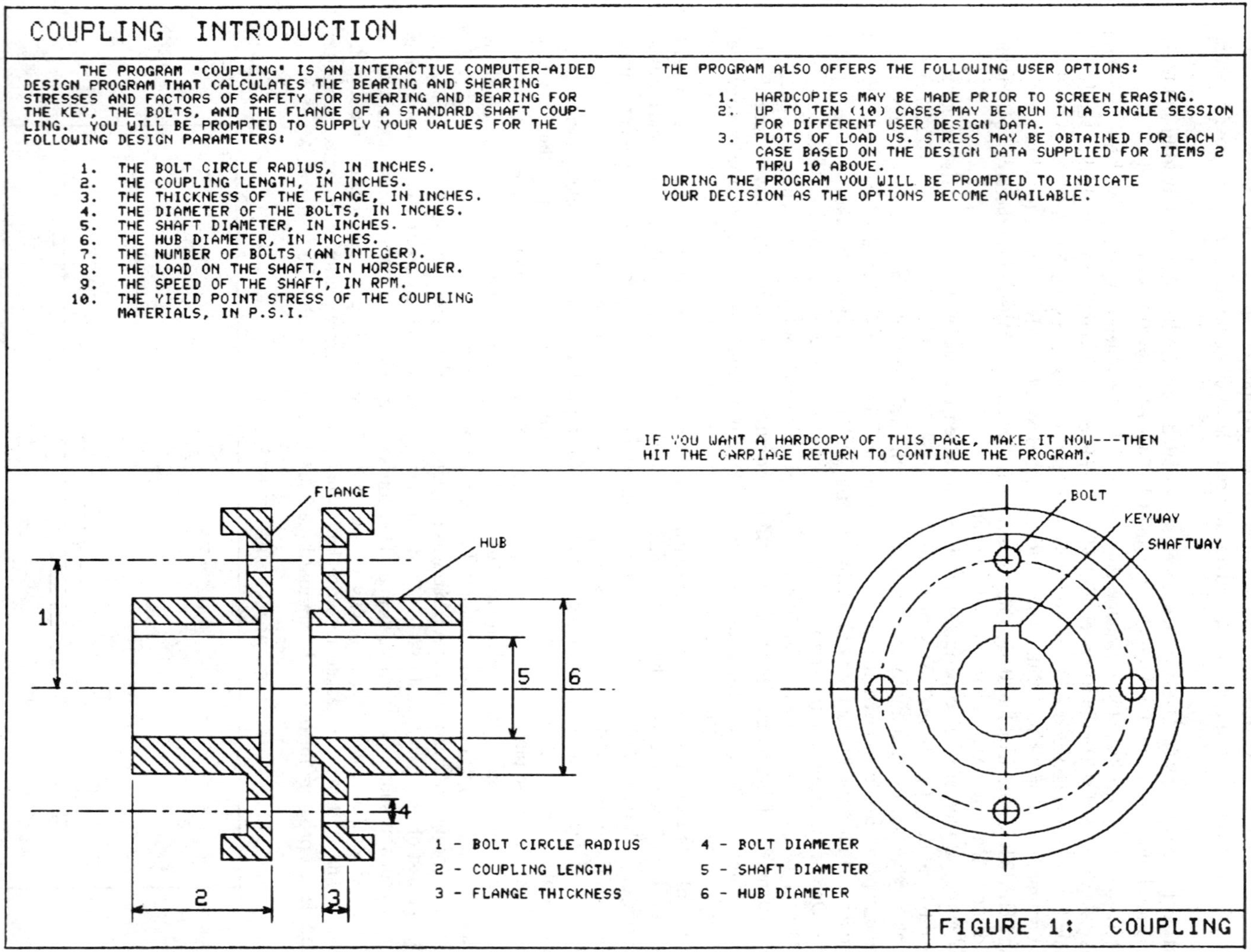

Fig. 3. First frame of a student-written coupling analysis program.

students had taken ME 561 prior to the introduction of the ADML, so this represented their first attempt at graphics-oriented, interactive programming. Nevertheless, many of the programs written were exceptionally well organized and executed. One such program is represented in Fig. 3, which shows the first frame of a five-frame sequence of an interactive coupling design program. This project was assigned as additional work for the course; and except for one lecture on the ADML, all of the lecture material was devoted to traditional design methods. The ADML project took between 10 and 50 extra hours to complete depending on the student, yet when the students were asked to evaluate the course the vast majority suggested that the project be continued as a part of the course. The same student enthusiasm has been shown in the other courses using the ADML, and in general it has been found that extra projects involving the ADML can be assigned without reducing the amount of traditional material taught. This course is continuing with the same format.

All senior mechanical engineering students at OSU are given the opportunity to design a major assembly from its conception through the blueprint stage in the required design course, ME 564. In this course, classes are divided into teams of about four members and each team is assigned a design project. The effort includes all stages of design from conception through detailed design and costing, and in some cases the designs are constructed in later classes. The ADML is made available for the projects although its use is not required.

During Spring Quarter 1979, two projects made extensive use of the ADML. One of these entailed the design of a one-man off-road vehicle to be entered in a national competition called Mini-Baja. The ADML was used to optimize the frame design for strength-to-weight ratio. Designs were analyzed using the finite element method to identify high- and low-stress points for each predicted loading condition. After four iterations, a final design was developed which was 40% lighter than the initial design. The finite-element model for this design is shown in Fig. 4. The vehicle was constructed later in the quarter and was raced over rough terrain in Milwaukee in May 1979. The vehicle was able to complete the course with no apparent structural damage, testifying to the validity of the frame design. Since that initial competition, three more teams of students in ME 564 have designed vehicles for the competition and again the ADML was used for frame optimization analyses.

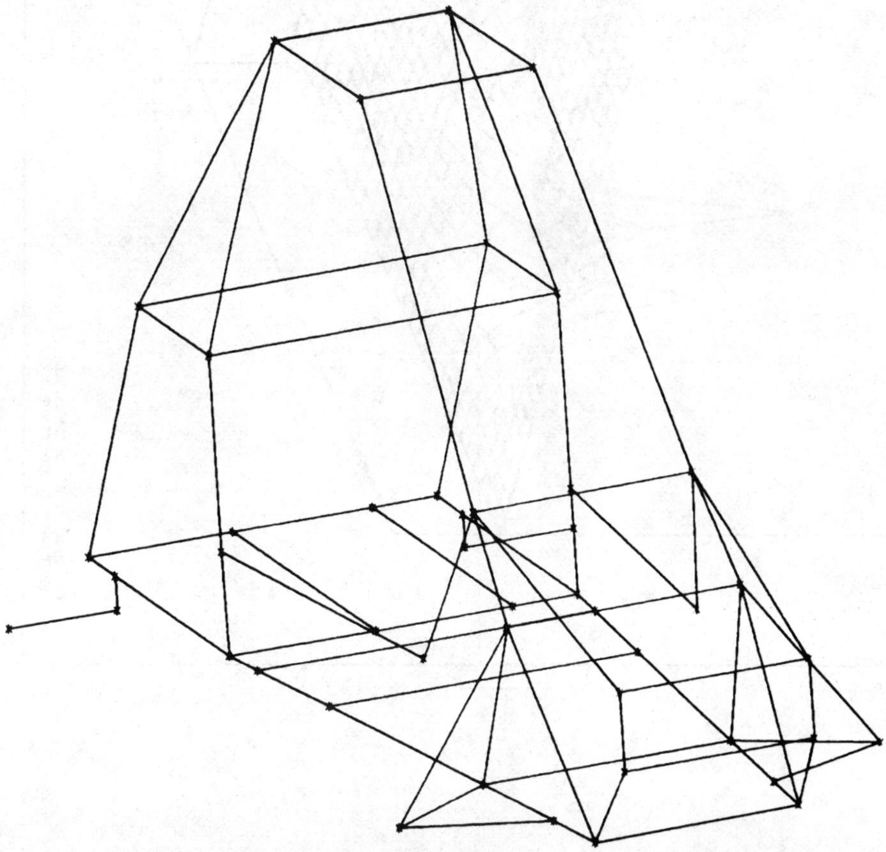

Fig. 4. Finite-element model of all-terrain vehicle developed in senior level design course.

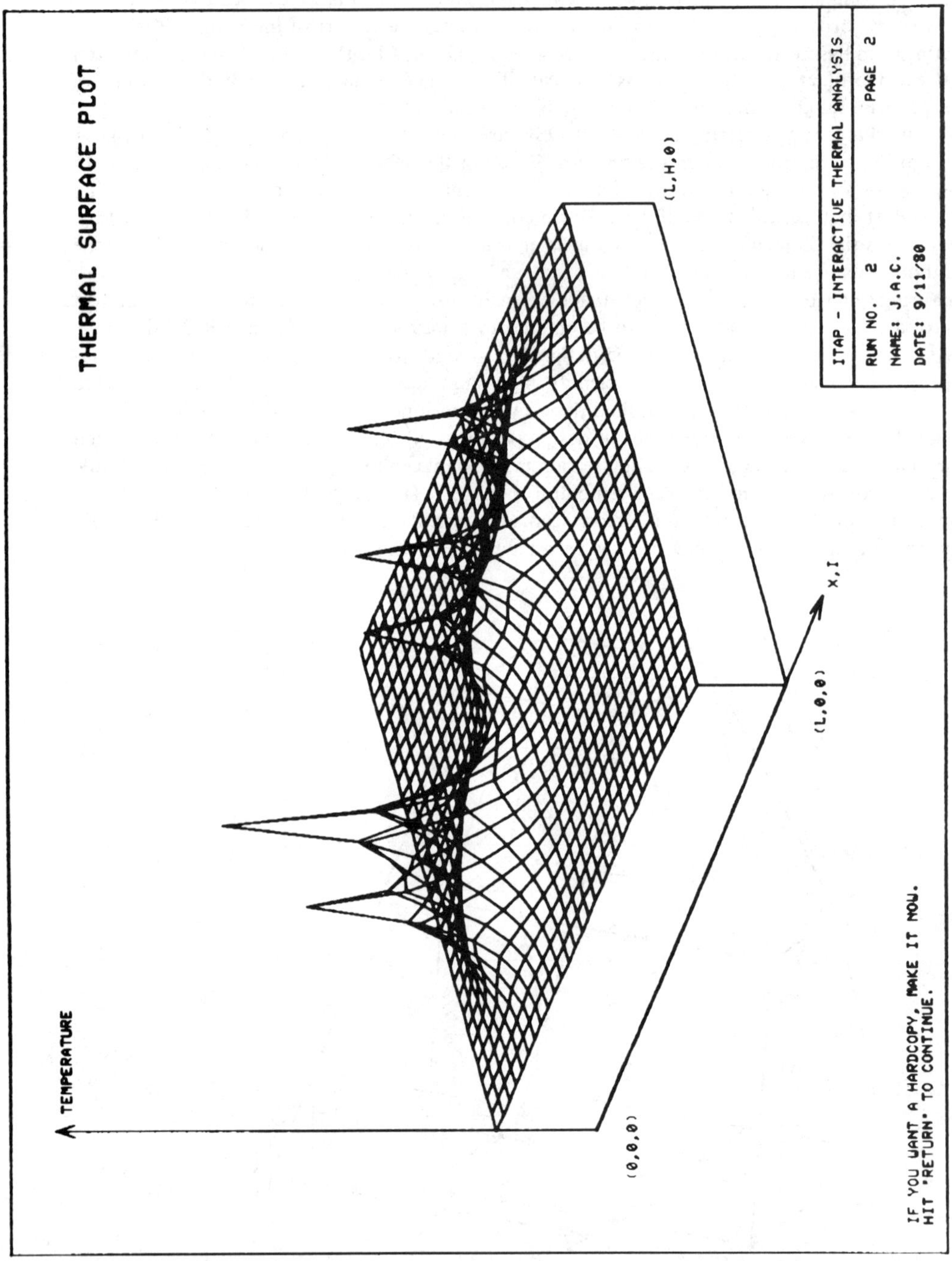

Fig. 5. Plot from finite-difference heat transfer program used in ME 664.

In a second project, a lift table for general factory work was designed by one team in ME 564. A three-dimensional mechanism used in the design was analyzed using the ADML and finite-element methods. The worst loading position for the mechanism was found, and displacements and stresses for the computer model were used to size components.

Since 1979, more than 15 teams of students have used the ADML for some aspect of their ME 564 design projects. In these projects, the ADML provides the students with the opportunity to optimize the design of a complicated part of an overall product. In the 3 months available for these projects, such an effort would be unreasonable without the aid of such computer graphics facilities.

In addition to the structured courses ME 562 and 564, several students have enrolled in individual studies courses to use the ADML. In these courses, the student works directly with a faculty member to define and complete a project on an individual basis. During Spring Quarter 1979, two students worked in the ADML on special finite-element projects on an individual basis. Since then, from 2 to 5 students per quarter have used the ADML on this basis. The projects range from the development of special purpose plotting packages to the development of detailed programs for machine-element design.

During Summer Quarter 1979, the next course to use the ADML was introduced. This elective course, ME 664, has the title Computer Aided Design and is intended to give the students a working knowledge of various numerical techniques used in computer-aided design. Prior to summer 1979, all computing for this course was done using batch processing and punched card input although the course content was essentially the same. The course is structured around two 1-h lectures and one 2-h laboratory session per week. The lectures deal with the theoretical basis for finite differences, optimization, solution to nonlinear algebraic equations, and finite-element methods. In the laboratories, the students write their own programs to solve some of the simple problems and use system routines for those which are more difficult. In most cases, a new project is assigned each week and the projects require from 2 to 6 h to complete. The results from a finite-difference heat-transfer analysis in the course is shown in Fig. 5. For the finite-element problems, the SDRC programs SUPERTAB and SUPERB are used extensively. The finite-element problems begin with a space beam frame and end with a complex journal bearing involving a steel shaft riding in a polymeric bushing which is pressed into a cast iron frame. As in the other elective courses using the ADML, this course has experienced a dramatic increase in enrollment. In the summer of 1979, it was 28, which was more than twice as large as the previous time the course was taught. During the 1979–1980 school year, the enrollment was 50, and during the current year the enrollment has climbed to 75. The course has become so popular that it is necessary to limit enrollment.

During Autumn Quarter 1979, two other courses ME 553 and 650 in addition to 651 and 562 used the ADML on a special project basis. ME 553 is a junior-level course which deals with the kinematic analysis of mechanisms, and as part of the course, all students are required to write a batch program in FORTRAN to analyze a compound linkage for position, velocities, and accelerations. For extra credit, the students were asked to write an ADML program to animate the linkage for a 360° rotation of the crank. No regular class time was devoted to the ADML part of the project although two optional lectures on the ADML were given in the evenings. Approximately half of the class attended the optional lectures and about 20% completed the extra credit part of the project. For most of the students, this was their first exposure to the ADML, since ME 553 is normally taken before 561. The project required approx. 60 lines of code and about 6 h of the student's time to complete. The mechanism model is shown in Fig. 6. Some variation of this extra credit problem has been given each quarter since 1979 with equal success.

The second course, ME 650, deals with the vibration analysis of mechanisms and is an elective course for seniors and graduate students. The course structure is three 1-h lectures and one 2-h laboratory session per week. Three of the labs are now ADML-based to familiarize the students with modal analysis and the use of the SDRC dynamic analysis programs SABBA and MTL. During Autumn Quarter 1979, 45 students were enrolled in the course. During the last two offerings, the enrollment has been limited to 50.

Two new courses using the ADML have been introduced during the last year. These are a course on design with composite materials and design optimization. Both courses require numerous programming projects where graphics is required. In the composite materials class, for example, the students write a laminate stress analysis program for a composite strip. A typical frame from such a program is shown in Fig. 7.

On the graduate level, the graphics laboratory is used on a project basis in two courses. The first, ME 850, is a sequel to ME 650 and uses modal analysis on more complicated problems. The second, ME 861, is an advanced stress analysis course. In this course, students are taught how to stress analyze complicated shapes by using closed-form stress equations in a process called formula match-

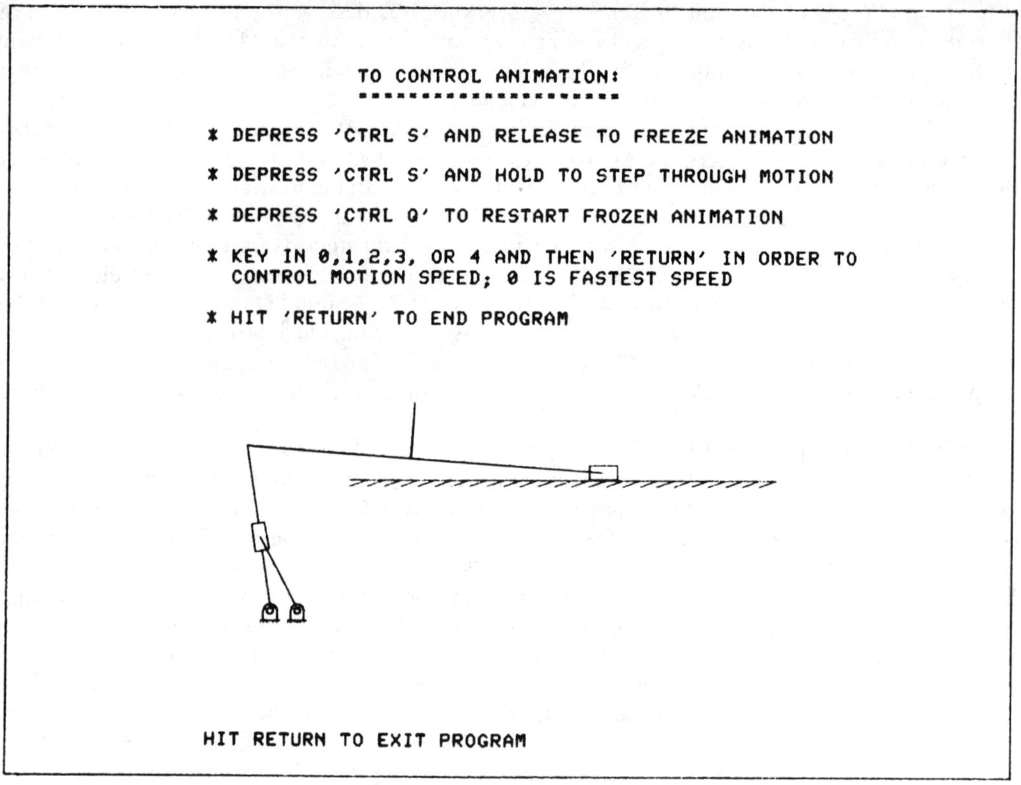

Fig. 6. Frame from animation program written in beginning kinematics course.

ing. To help the students develop confidence in the formula matching method, they are required to analyze selected problems using both formula matching and finite elements.

The ADML is available to students for approx. 60 h per week. During formal laboratory class hours, the use of the ADML is restricted to the students involved in that class, but at all other times the students are free to sign up for available terminal time up to a day ahead of when they want to use a terminal. This orderly sign-up approach permits an efficient utilization of facilities, and the terminals are used more than 95% of the time available.

GRADUATE PROGRAM

From September 1979 to March 1981, 5 students have completed theses associated with the ADML. The subjects of the theses varied from the development of a method for the interactive design of helical springs to the modal analysis of a crankshaft. Currently 25 students are working on either MS or Ph.D theses involving the ADML. This is about 25% of the active graduate students in mechanical engineering at OSU. More than half of our students who are supported by fellowships have chosen research topics which will give them the opportunity to work in the ADML.

PROBLEMS IDENTIFIED DURING INTEGRATION OF ADML

During the integration of the computer aided design procedures into the OSU design curriculum, a number of potential problems and solutions were identified. Some of these are discussed in the following.

Student–terminal ratios

During the first three quarters of operation of the ADML, formal laboratory classes were operated with 4 students per terminal. This was found to be too high for optimal education. Generally 1 or 2 of the students would assume leadership roles and the remaining students would remain in the background. The optimum ratio appears to be 2. This gives the students an opportunity to discuss problems and generally increases the confidence of both students. One student per terminal seems to

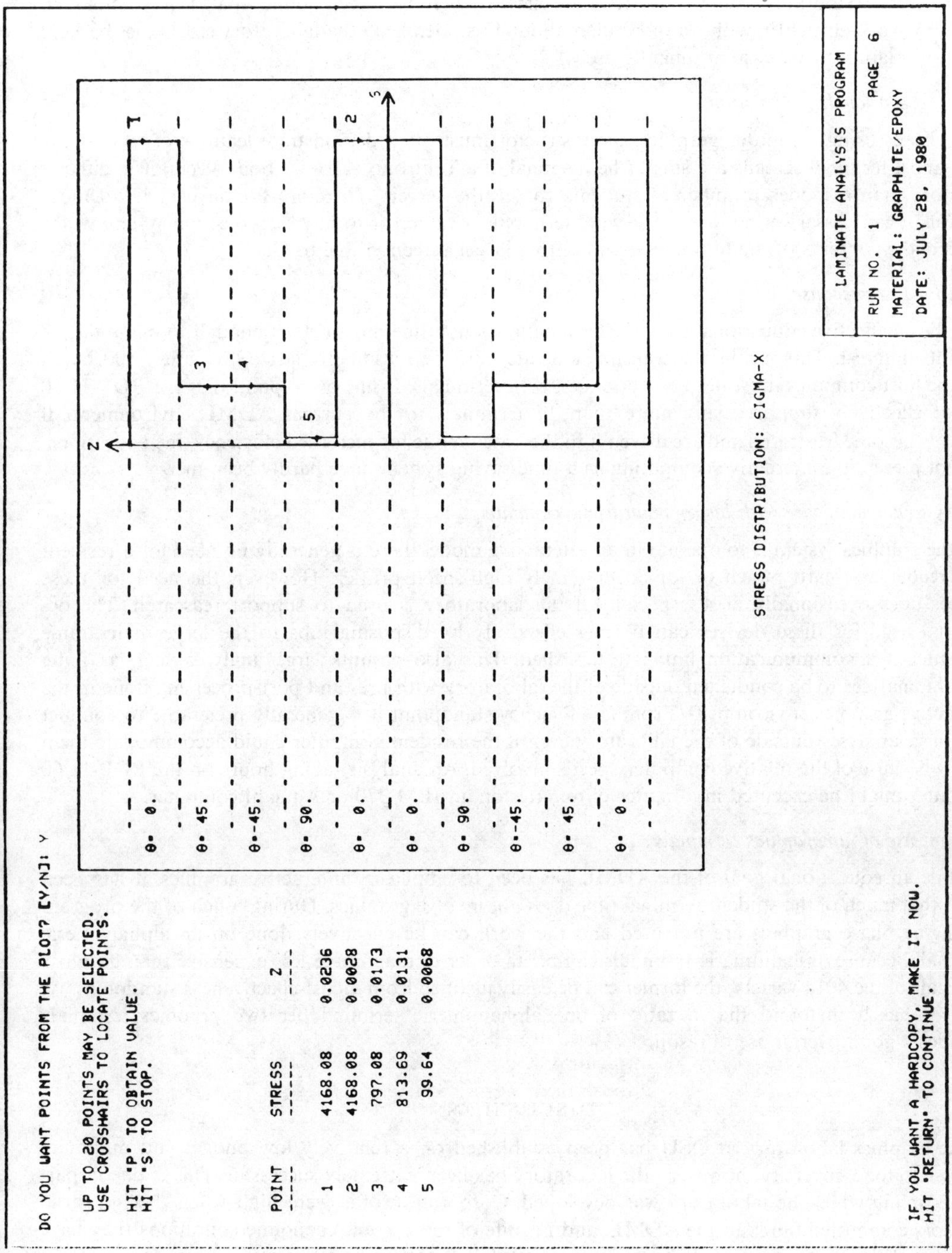

Fig. 7. Frame from laminate stress analysis program used in composites course.

be too small because a single student tends to become easily frustrated and it is generally less enjoyable for the students to work alone. Currently at OSU an effort is being made to structure the laboratories with 2 students per terminal.

Instructor–student ratios

In the beginning classes, it is necessary for the students to have their questions answered fairly quickly if the laboratory time is to be used effectively. It has been found that 1 instructor can generally work efficiently with no more than about 12 students, so the laboratory sizes must be kept small or a laboratory assistant must be used.

Large screen for demonstrations

In classes using computer graphics, the instructor must often demonstrate features of the system. Since most terminal screens are small (the diagonal of a Tektronix 4014 is about 48 cm) it is difficult for more than a modest number of students to see the screen. Therefore for an effective demonstration, it is necessary either to slave several terminals together or to have a projection system which projects the contents of the terminal screen onto a larger screen visible to all.

Need for fast response time

To be an effective educational tool, the terminal response time must be fast enough to maintain the students' interest. This means the transmission rate must be reasonably fast (OSU uses 4800 baud) and the host computer must not be overloaded with terminals. It has been found that the PDP-11/60 cannot effectively support many more than 17 terminals in the current ADML environment. If students become frustrated and are driven into the batch mode for increased efficiency, the educational aims of presenting interactive computing as a time-saving system have hardly been met.

Ability to communicate with larger main frame computer

If the graphics system is to operate in an interactive mode, there is generally no need for a resident card reader and card punch or for an extremely high-speed printer. However, the need for these devices does occasionally arise especially if the laboratory is used to support reasearch. The occasional need for these devices can be met effectively by disposing jobs to the large main frame computer if a communication link is established. This also permits large analyses such as finite element analyses to be conducted outside of the laboratory with pre- and post-processing done in the interactive graphics environment. From an efficiency standpoint it is generally preferable to conduct such large analyses outside of the laboratory even if the resident computer could accommodate them simply because of the relative computer speeds involved. An analysis taking hours on the PDP-11/60 computer might be executed in a matter of minutes on an IBM 370 or Amdahl computer.

Efficient use of nongraphics terminals

While an educational goal of the ADML has been to emphasize interactive graphics, it has been found that much of the student terminal time does not involve graphics. During much of the program debugging phase graphics are not used and the work can be effectively done on an alphanumeric terminal. Because alphanumeric terminals can be an order of magnitude less expensive than graphics terminals of the 4014 variety, the former can be easily justified from a cost-effectiveness standpoint. At OSU, it has been found that a ratio of one alphanumeric terminal per two graphics terminals provides a good overall use of resources.

DISCUSSION

The graphics laboratory at OSU has been established on a relatively low budget and minimum expense to the University; however , the laboratory has been extremely successful. This is due in part to the timing when the laboratory was developed. Corporate profits were high when the industrial sponsors committed funds to the ADML, and in spite of the current economic conditions they have maintained their commitment. It is extremely doubtful that a fund raising drive begun today for a new laboratory would be as successful.

During the last 3 years, the University has attracted seven new faculty members who are interested in CAD and this has provided a high degree of enthusiasm for the integration of graphics into the courses. Current funding does not permit any faculty support so that faculty interest is critical if new programs are to be developed and maintained. Most of the new course development and changes in the old courses to integrate graphics have been done by the new faculty. However, after the changes have been made they have generally been supported by all of the faulty.

CONCLUSIONS

Within 3 years after the equipment was installed at OSU, interactive graphics and computer aided design have been effectively integrated into the design curriculum. This integration has been accomplished on a project and laboratory basis and the emphasis has been on a new way to solve traditional problems. This approach has eliminated the need to make any significant changes in the amount of traditional material taught. This mode of operation has increased the workload of the students; however, this has proven to be one of those rare occasions in academia when the overwhelming majority of the students have welcomed the opportunity to do the extra work because of the educational benefits involved.

INDEX